# Maybe,
## After To-morrow...

# Maybe,
## After To-morrow...

**JK Beukes**

BOOKBABY PUBLISHING
2022

Published by: BookBaby

For reproduction permissions contact: joan@jkbeukes.com

Cover art by: Asep Ariyanto

Proofreaders: BookBaby and Annaliese Perry

Editor: Annaliese Perry

ISBN: 978-1-66785-191-4

Printed in the United States of America on FSC certified paper, which is SFI certified and acid-free.

Author Website: www.jkbeukes.com

*"If wishes were horses, beggars would ride.*
*If turnips were watches, I'd wear one by my side.*
*If "ifs" and "ands" were pots and pans,*
*There'd be no work for tinkers' hands."*

—William Camden

*"In three words I can sum up everything I've learned about life: it goes on."*

—Robert Frost

*For my son-in-law, the late Tedd Perry, aka Swell.*

*Your interest and encouragement spurred me on to complete this novel.*

*Mike, oh, Mike... Who knew how you would change? How hateful you had it in you to be?*

If only I could turn back the clock; blot out the past year. If only my husband would come home! If only he would ring! If only I could be sure he had not gone on a bender! Past experiences notwithstanding.

*If only...* two of the most useless words of all time. I remember reading that somewhere.

The change in Mike had been gradual but escalated over the past year, to the point where I could no longer turn a blind eye. After fifteen happy years of marriage, I could not account for it.

His steady routine had changed; coming home late from work has become the norm—just breezes in with no explanation—invariably, with the smell of liquor on his breath. So unlike Mike! Added to that, he now spends most Saturdays away from home, with his drinking buddies.

Formerly, Saturdays had been reserved for family outings and activities with my best friend Grace, her husband Claud, and their two children.

Under the influence, Mike is abusive to the point that I dread his return, fear for my safety at times. I likened this new Mike to Jekyll and Hyde.

Determined to seek help, I had contacted the Al-Anon group a couple of weeks ago. It seemed a good fit. As luck would have it, they met on Saturday afternoons, at a nearby school. Knowing Mike would not approve, I decided to confide in his mother. Enlist her help before going to that first meeting.

On this sunny Saturday afternoon, I was at my wits' end! As usual, Mike had left home soon after breakfast. George and Benjy, our twin sons, had gone to visit friends and would be home in time for supper.

I took the plunge, went to see Mike's mother, and told her about his drinking, his abusive behaviour, and my intention to attend the Al-Anon meetings.

She was outraged! Never one to admit Mike's faults, with arms akimbo she lashed out at me. "Oh, nonsense! My son is not an alcoholic…you must be doing something to provoke him!"

*This* had been her response to my cry for help. Looking to her for advice and support was an exercise in futility. I should have known better because, whenever there was blame going begging, she found a way to lay it at my door. Ergo, I deserved Mike's abuse.

I stood my ground. Pressed on. Implored her.

"If only you would see my side, Ma. Put yourself in my shoes. Anyway, if I end up going to the meetings, it will be solely to help my family, *not* humiliate my husband."

Her anger was red-hot by this time, and her voice became strident as she continued to upbraid me and vehemently oppose my plan to attend Al-Anon meetings.

"I'm warning you, Eve," she said, stabbing her finger in my direction while glaring at me. "Mike will be humiliated…if you persist in going, it would be like airing your dirty linen in public. Don't you have any pride?"

Her reaction reminded me of the proverbial ostrich. For a few deluded moments, I honestly thought I could reach her. Woman to woman. Her refusal to acknowledge her son's reprehensible behaviour and her cold-heartedness shocked me to the core. Before I left, I appealed to her better nature, asked her not to tell Mike about Al-Anon until I had spoken to him.

"Well, I won't tell Mike about this for now, but you better think twice about going to these meetings, young woman!" Fat lot of help she turned out to be. She was not about to become my ally and made it as clear as running waters.

After my mother-in-law's dismal lack of sympathy and support, I desperately needed a shoulder to lean on. I longed to confide in Grace. *She* would support me. Even encourage me to attend the Al-Anon meetings. I *know* she would, but I am reluctant and too embarrassed to lay bare Mike's weakness and expose the flaws in my marriage to her.

Keeping secrets from Mike went against the grain. It was anathema to me.

*A*nother weekend was upon us. George and Benjy had gone to a birthday party and would be sleeping over. Mike and I would have the house to ourselves tonight. As luck would have it, he was sober when he came home from work—a rare occasion on a Friday night, so the evening was off to a good start…After supper, with lights turned low and soft music playing in the background, I decided to speak to Mike about his drinking problem, tell him for the umpteenth time how it was affecting our marriage and his relationship with our sons.

Sadly, my approach, intended to be tactful and sensitive, failed to hit the mark.

Mike was still in denial but, to my relief, refrained from reacting violently.

"For God's sake, Eve! We've had this conversation before. Just because I enjoy a few drinks with my pals doesn't mean I am an alcoholic! I've had enough, so just stop nagging me about my drinking, will you!"

He hurled these words at me before abruptly ejecting himself from the couch where we had earlier been sitting in a close embrace, stalked out of the room and, with a withering backward glance, headed for our bedroom and slammed the door. Hard!

We have shared the same bed since the first night of our marriage. Tonight, however, the distance between us might as well have been a chasm, and the silence a wall. When I leaned over to caress his face, he gave me the cold shoulder; brushed off my hand as though he were repulsed by my touch.

Mike left the house before cockcrow this morning. Not a word had passed his lips since he'd lashed out at me last night. When midday had come and gone without any word from him, my stomach started a slow and ever-increasing churning. I hoped against hope he had not gone on a drinking spree, using whatever I'd said last night as an excuse. There's no telling what time he will be back. Were I to hazard a guess, I'd be spending the evening without him—who knows, maybe even the better part of to-morrow.

What a way to spend the weekend.

George phoned shortly before lunch. "Mum, everyone is going to the movies this afternoon. Can Benjy and I go along and then sleep over another night? Brian's mom says it's okay. They will pay for our tickets...please, Mum?"

Relieved to have them out of the house while things were so unsettled, I consented. I made myself a pot of Rooibos tea and something light to eat but could not bring myself to swallow the food I had prepared. The warm tea, so comforting, as it trickled down my throat.

The clock on the kitchen wall showed two o'clock. My now frayed nerve endings jangled incessantly as the hour wore on. It felt like the resulting tension was tying knot upon knot in my stomach, and I became keenly aware of a rhythmic pounding in my temples.

With my equilibrium speedily in danger of becoming a thing of the past, I found myself pacing the rooms. Endlessly. Like a caged animal. Hour after weary hour.

Weather-wise, today has been mostly warm and sunny—not all that unusual, even with winter on its last legs, here, in the Western Cape. Still, I feel chilled.

Drawing the Pashmina tighter around me is purely a reflex action. Its softness and warmth barely making a dent on my consciousness as I keep a solitary vigil; keeping an eye out for Mike's return by my living room window—the one which looks out onto the street where we live—barely taking in the outside scene.

As the bright, still warm rays of the sun journeyed across a cloudless, blue sky the afternoon light filtered through the window. Golden dust motes almost mesmerised me as they danced about the room. The sun's rays stroked my upturned face briefly, caressed my being, but failed to warm me. Neither did they help to dispel the gloom that immobilized me.

In stark contrast to the sun-filled scene outside my window, a numbing coldness has been steadily trickling into my body. It permeates almost every part of my being as an overriding premonition of something dreadful afoot adds to my distress.

*F*our o'clock had long come and gone, and I was still standing by the window. My imagination had run the gamut of every possible scenario as I waited. Waited, hour after seemingly endless hour, for my husband to return. Hoping against hope that he would be sober. Praying that things would somehow work out for us. I've been standing motionless by this window now for goodness knows how long, in danger of becoming rooted to the spot. The mental picture this conjured up forced me to smile, despite myself.

My mind, on autopilot, having shut out all things real, conjured up only dark and dreadful images now, and, try as I might to rid myself of them, they persisted.

A raging headache only added to my misery.

I feared repercussions. I feared for Mike's physical safety—his mental stability if inebriated. The longer I waited for Mike to come home, the more I became convinced all hell would break loose, if, and when he did come home! I could not shake this feeling, not for love or money.

Salty tears which had been threatening since morning, those, I'd been holding at bay, stung my eyes, made their way down my cheeks, and spilled warm, onto my icy cold hands. I let them fall unchecked because they provided some relief for my pent-up emotions; those which I had been battling since last night.

*Oh, Mike, I wish with all my heart that you had not left home in such a foul mood…*

*T*he tears had dried on my cheeks. From my window, dead ahead, in the distance, I can see the mountain. *Table Mountain.* Immovable! Strong, and seemingly supporting the sky. I have an affinity for all mountains. Always have. This mountain, however, has such a presence; appears to me to own a benign aura. I call it 'my mountain' because, whenever I stand still to look at it, I come away with the feeling that God, who had created it and me, is ever on my side.

When in conversation with my God, I invariably turn my face toward the mountain, *my* mountain. With its air of timelessness, it had always been my link to the Creator; my lodestar in times past. I strongly believed that Divine justice would somehow, someday, lend my cloud a silver lining.

Looking through the window into the distance, the strangest thing happened then—a smiling face appeared as if etched, deep, in the mountainside. I couldn't move, just set my sights intently on this phenomenon until, at last, it slowly faded away.

*What can this mean? Was it meant to convey a message of hope?*

I wiped away the wetness from my face as I turned my back to the window. My gaze wandered across the room and settled on a grouping of silver-framed photos on the mantelpiece—a mixed bag—two of me as a child, several others showing our twins in varying stages of growing up. One other showed Mike and me during our courting days.

Like one plagued with palsy, I made my way over there. Each photo, in turn, recaptured oh, so many memories. The one of Mike and me portrayed a laughing couple. I picked it up, held it close, as though it were a talisman with the power to transport me to that happier time. Elysian days when we first became a 'couple'.

With the photograph in my now trembling hands, I sat down in my favourite chair, giving rein to the memories which the picture evoked. Memories of our first meeting, almost seventeen years ago, our first kiss, the first time he whispered those magical 'three little words'. In my head, I heard Doris Day's lilting voice as she sang that song. Our song.

When I reached for the photo of me, at age six, alongside my mother, it conjured up memories of my childhood and others that led up to this moment.

The sunset flared, the sun dipped and was gone, and the evening stretched before me like a road.

# Childhood Re-Visited

*M*y father was named Benjamin. A family name. My mother was named Mae. I was Eve, their only child. To the best of my knowledge, it had been my father who named me. Could it be because my biblical namesake had been created by God and I, to my earthly father's way of thinking, was his creation?

Coincidence? I wonder!

He was my *Dadda*. This, I was told, was how my first intelligible prattling came across. I was his *Beckie*—*bekkie* being the diminutive form of the Afrikaans word *bek*, which means mouth. So named because when he first laid eyes on me as a newborn, he declared I had the tiniest mouth he had ever seen. That's how the story goes.

My family is Cape Coloured. I did most of my growing up in various Coloured suburbs in and around Cape Town and the Cape Flats. I started school when I was five years old—precocious, but with a limited understanding of how life outside my immediate family circle worked.

It dawned on me, already, during that first school year, that my life was different. Quite different, when compared to my peers in the various neighbourhoods in which I grew up. Throughout most of my childhood and teenage years this 'being different' was the one constant; the bane of my life, and not always easily put into words. Simply put, I was odd man out. Often.

Children want to blend in.

Bear with me, Dear Reader.

I'll start by saying we seldom conformed to the pattern set by other families in our community. Together, those parents—mother, father, sometimes even live-in grandparents—cared for the children in a stable home environment. Aunts and uncles also were on stand-by.

As for us, there were just three in our family unit. Mother, father, and me, the female child. *My childhood was nomadic*; it lacked a firm foundation. Quite unstable because we sometimes lived quite apart. Each at a different address. A fragmented family. This meant our family connections were fragile, like wisps of smoke. An on-again, off-again affair.

I grew up in a time when a woman's place was said to be in the home. *My* mother did not conform; she was not your run-of-the-mill housewife. In loose terms, I think she must have been something of a 'free spirit'. Her line of work (keeping house for wealthy White families) required that she all but live on the premises.

My mom spent her days off, weekends, and holidays with us. Then, there was the odd time she would be between jobs ('resting' in the actors' vernacular). She would join us and then, for the duration, I would have both my parents caring for me. For now, our family unit was complete, and I lived a normal life. Just like my peers.

These times, overall, were short-lived. My mom invariably found another job, or her holiday would have come to an end.

When my mom had time off, she cooked for us, cleaned our home, and sometimes sewed pretty dresses for me. She loved to make ringlets in my hair after she had washed it. Still, I missed out on the day-to-day nurturing which should have been my birthright.

My father went back and forth during the first twelve years of my life. After that, there was neither sight nor sound of him for the next twenty years. I'd heard him referred to as a 'rolling stone' by a family member. Sadly, there was a wealth of truth in that remark; borne out by his sudden disappearances and reappearances. They were legion.

A cobbler by trade. An entrepreneur—Dadda did not believe in working for a boss. For the most part, *he* was my sole caregiver, but he periodically shut up shop and abandoned our current dwelling. Me along with it. He would leave for parts unknown, with no promise that he would return. It

14

follows then, that he also relinquished his paternal responsibilities in the process.

Despite his frequent absences throughout my childhood, however, he spent more meaningful time with me than had my mother. It may sound like a contradiction, but, looking at the big picture, his presence, even though sporadic, was significant. My dad taught me many things. Left the greater mark on my life. His, a presence to be reckoned with in my day-to-day living. More so than my mother's.

I fretted during his absences; missed him like a piece of bread. Each time he went AWOL, it seemed as if my world were wrong side up; threw me off balance. The reason for his erratic behaviour? *The Wanderlust*. His Nemesis. He succumbed. It was not easy to resign myself to being left behind. Abandoned. Yet again.

With my father out of the picture, so to speak, I would be taken from the place I'd been sharing with him. That place, the one that I had begun to think of as home, would be my home no longer. I'd be uprooted from surroundings and a lifestyle that had become familiar; packed off to live with some family member, a friend, or a friend of a friend, or with total strangers, in a foster home. I felt fragile; displaced. My sense of belonging, shattered!

My mother or some other grown-up would have the task of taking me, along with my few worldly possessions, to my new home, to live in a town or suburb of the Cape previously unknown to me. In the ensuing confusion, a favourite toy, book, or other familiar item that I treasured, would all too often be left behind or lost in transit.

I was a timid child. I quaked each time I was sent to live in yet another unfamiliar place. Being without either one of my parents *and* without my few, favourite, familiar possessions around me was bewildering. Traumatic. Ever-present, the feeling of having been unwanted. Alone. Lonely. It would seem I had no day-to-day claim on either of my parents.

Living in someone else's house was always extremely unnerving at first. Those strangers who sometimes took care of me were always kindly people, but my stay with them was typically short-lived, and, as a result, l felt as though I lived on the fringes of their lives, *not* part of their inner circle. An outsider. Being on the outside, looking in, made me miserable beyond words. Even envious. They treated me well enough, but I did not feel quite at home. *I did not feel loved.*

New surroundings meant adjusting to the different grown-ups who were my caregivers, their offspring, various relatives and friends who came to visit, different kitchens, bathrooms, bedrooms, beds, bedding, food, crockery, cutlery, backyards, and gardens. Different rules and routines each time.

Also, different streets, shops, neighbours, churches, and ministers. Different schools, principals, textbooks, desks, classrooms, classmates, teachers, playgrounds, and routes to and from school. Let's not forget the strange, and sometimes unfriendly, barking dogs I met on the streets. You name it! The list goes on. Ad infinitum.

Anxiety reigned to the point where I would routinely 'lose my breakfast' on the way to school for the first few days. I felt powerless and fearful of all the unknowns lying in wait for me.

I feared my new 'family' would not like me. I feared that this separation from my parents would become my way of life. I feared my rightful place in this world would elude me; prevent me from taking root there.

At each new school, I feared I would be overlooked and not be asked to participate in the school play, or sing in the Eisteddfod, or be chosen to play a part in the Christmas pageants or be part of the school sports team. I was often lonely because I was too shy to ask to be included in the games they played on the street where I now lived. I feared 'they' would refuse or make fun of me behind my back.

Dear Reader, because of the ever-changing parade of people and places, my life was in a constant state of flux, fraught with unfamiliar situations for which I was ill-equipped. Confusing? You can lay money on that! The emotional scars of being so often abandoned by my mother and father ran deep. At times I felt like 'left luggage'. On hold, until its owner comes to claim it. Tears came often, unbidden, without warning when I was young.

Neither parent ever consulted me about these changes. I did not ask for explanations. Back then, children were seen and not heard.

All things being equal, childhood should be a special time. A time of nurturing by one's parents, a carefree time, when life is enjoyed on its simplest level. A time to put down roots! Tender, young plants must be given time to root, to grow firm and strong so that they can withstand the elements. By the same token, every child deserves a secure, loving home where *it* can take root.

*My* roots were delicate and barely had the chance to take hold, before being yanked out again and transplanted in a new location. So unsettling!

*H*ome... *The most beautiful word in any language.* I'd read that somewhere. It was always my dream to have just one home, live there with both my parents, take root there, be part of a happy, normal family and know, without a shadow of a doubt, that I belonged—that I'd be sheltered there, be the girl next door and someone's best friend forever. I couldn't help myself. Who could, were they in my shoes?

Pipe dreams? I continued to dream my dreams, anyway.

Shouldn't parents be the ones to provide this safe harbour? Make the monsters go away? Be the dispensers of cuddles? Is this not every child's birthright? If so, then for the most part I must conclude that I was short-changed!

You only get one childhood—you do not get a second chance at doing it over!

Sad to say, my parents' concern for my physical protection and emotional stability appeared to have been a hit-or-miss affair.

Like a game of peek-a-boo.

At the end of the day, one could opine that mine was not an ideal or even average childhood. This, in an era when life was so much simpler. An era when children were carefree, did childish things like flying kites on a windy day, playing games with abandon—games like hide-and-seek and marbles, spinning the top and blind man's buff, hopscotch and cricket, skipping rope, and playing rounders on a nearby field—and when the term 'dysfunctional family' had probably not yet become a household word.

Try as I might, I just could not come to terms with the fact that my life was so unstable! So unanchored! It did seem as if I were the only child in the whole wide world living this way. I wished, at times, with all my heart, to be someone other than myself. I loathed the circumstances which set me apart.

Oh, to have a life like my peers; the longing was ever-present.

From the outside looking in, it all seemed so simple, so attainable. After all, other children I knew were living this life. Why not me? I longed to be like them, envied them. Some of 'them' were born and raised in the same house as their mom or dad had been. They had grandparents, aunts, and uncles living close by whom they could visit after school, over the weekend, or during holidays.

They read the books and played with the toys which might even have been handed down in their families. They lived lives that were normal, secure, and uninterrupted.

*Their* roots were entrenched, and, in all likelihood, they would inherit the homes in which they were raised. *Their* family ties were strong. *Their* families were 'whole'. 'Whole' families grew together, stayed together, owned a different language, a special dialect if you will. This is how it struck me—forcibly, I might add—when I lived for a while in their homes. I envied them. More than words can say.

I could not decipher their language. It eluded me and made me self-conscious around them; left me feeling excluded. Awkward. Apart. Sometimes, as I passed the houses on the street of my new neighbourhood, I looked in their windows. When I saw the contentment on the faces of the children living there, those same feelings of being excluded and apart, threatened to overpower me.

Sadly, trusting people, especially the adults in my life, became a Herculean task. I often did not know to whom I could turn for help. At each new address, there would be things that perplexed me or made me anxious. Rather than run the risk of being rebuffed, I shied away from asking the grown-ups for help, tried to figure things out for myself; agonizing to the point where I'd do without, rather than expose my neediness.

Because of my inexperience and ignorance, I did not always come up with the best solution, but I owned a fierce, if misplaced, independence. Accepting assistance from others did not sit well with me. Neither then, nor in later life.

It is safe to say, self-confidence became the lesser of my strong suits. Became eroded. No words I knew in my earlier childhood could aptly have described my feelings of being unwanted, an encumbrance to both my mother and my father. A fourth leg on a three-legged stool. Confusion and hurt were among the emotions raging in my young breast each time I was left in some other family's care.

Why did my parents not want me in their lives? What had I done? Not done?

When, months later, my father returned from his wanderings—as abruptly as he had left, I might add—from some place unknown to me, and maybe even to my mother, it would be as if he had appeared out of nowhere. He simply reclaimed me from where I'd been deposited in his absence, and, without much ado, move us into our new home—albeit in an entirely new neighbourhood—resume his role of dutiful father and feature prominently in my day-to-day existence; make a 'home' for me, nurture me, teach me Christian values.

Just picked up where he had left off the time before!

This cycle would be repeated over the years. Way too often. When I was much, *much* older, only then did I become resigned to my lot. Only then!

Still, those interludes were special because he made it up to me (if one can describe it thus) each time he returned, by taking time to teach me things: to love and respect nature; to love the written word; fostered a love of music. I could be sure of being taken to a concert organised by the EOAN Group, or a visit to the museum, or some cultural event happening at the time.

Collectively, I likened these times—his comings and goings—to a patchwork. Some patches coloured in a rosy hue, and others in shades of blue. I built a 'love box' to house my fondest memories. Along the way—during all those years that I lived in other people's homes—I relied heavily on those snapshots from my memory. I retrieved them often. They comforted, when things did not go well for me…more times than I care to remember.

After my thirteenth birthday, my father disappeared again, and, for the next twenty years, there would be no contact whatsoever. For all we knew then, he might as well have vanished off the face of the earth. That being said, in those formative years, my dadda featured prominently in my upbringing.

*I*n revisiting my childhood, I'm reminded that my mother was far less involved in my upbringing. It begs the question, where then, was my mother during my father's absence? Why not step in and take care of me.

As I said earlier, my mother kept the homes of her White employers running smoothly, catered their lavish dinner parties. In short, she acted as a stand-in when the lady of the house was out shopping, playing bridge, or tennis, and whatever else rich ladies did to while away their days.

My mother also tended to and nurtured the little darlings who were left in her care. Children named Alexander, James, Peter, Tessa, Heather, Jill, and Judy, amongst others. In their own mothers' absence, when these children came home from school, my mother saw to it that their favourite snacks were always on hand.

Theirs, the tales of woe she sometimes listened to. Theirs, the tears she dried. Theirs, the scraped knees she tended, the bedtime stories she read, and theirs were the birthday parties she organized. Stepping into the breach was part of my mother's job description.

So, being on the job all day and many a night also—sometimes, for weeks on end—it stands to reason there simply was not much time left over for her to 'mother' me. No friends were ever invited to celebrate my childhood birthdays.

That was our way of life—how I grew up.

Emotional disconnect!

My mother gave me several dolls and a little dollhouse when I was a child. One doll stands out in my memory because it had long, curly brown hair—much like mine—and rosy painted cheeks and big brown eyes set in a porcelain face. The eyes shut when I laid it down and it said "Mamma" when I pressed on its tummy. I loved pressing its tummy!

Did the sound of my doll saying "Mamma" so often go down well with those people who were nearby? I can't remember that far back, unfortunately. My mother also made sure I had pretty dresses—some she made herself, and there were always matching hair ribbons. The dresses would eventually be discarded because I would have outgrown them, but the fate of those dolls elude me to this day.

I own two tangible mementos of my childhood. Two studio portraits. A measly two! These two photographs were discovered many years later when I visited the home of a family member in Knysna.

*My* parents saved neither book, nor toy, nor favourite dress, nor even a school report for me to keep track of my yesterdays. No photos of grand-parents and other family members, or special family gatherings were ever put aside in an album for safekeeping and handed down to me like other parents are wont to do. No, Sir!

Taken at face value, my childhood and all it entailed held no special meaning for those who were its custodians. For the most part, I rely on mental snapshots—the ones I saved in my 'love box'.

One faded, somewhat tattered photo, taken at Van Kalker's studio, shows me at age four, or thereabouts, alongside my mother...I wore a pink dress my mother had made for me. A sort of salmon pink, with a round, smocked yoke. Embroidered rosebuds in many colours and tiny, green leaves were scattered on the yoke. The fabric was georgette if memory serves.

When I was much older, I chanced on this photo while visiting my grandmother's house. It transported me back to a time long gone, conjured up vivid images of my mother, sitting by the window which looked out onto the street where we lived. I see her with a thimble on the middle finger of her right hand. See, even now, how the fabric was draped over her left hand, and how it pooled in her lap while she embroidered the different coloured roses and green leaves. Skeins of embroidering floss in various pastel colours were laid out on a table beside her.

A smile of pure satisfaction settled on my mother's face as she completed each little rosebud or leaf. In awe of the way she created the tiniest, most perfect rosebuds and leaves, to this day, I have no idea where or how she acquired this skill. She never taught it to me. I tried, on my own, a few times, but never came close to mastering the technique.

I watched as the dress was being made. From start to finish. Impatient, to try it on.

At last! The hem was sewn and a little pearl button in place. The dress was lovingly pressed, and I was agog while awaiting the final fitting! I remember, to this day, how the fabric seemed to slither, over my head, how it rested lightly on my shoulders, could feel Mommy's cool hands on my skin as she adjusted the little puff sleeves…just so! I still remember how it felt when I was being twirled around ever so firmly so that she could slip the little pearl button through the loop which fastened the dress at the back of my neck.

Whenever I wore that pretty dress or any other that my mother made for me, I felt like a princess. Like those in my storybooks. This, too, I remember. Vividly.

The other photo was taken full length, also at Van Kalker's studio. The occasion? Auntie Lizzie, my mother's younger sister, had married Uncle Owen. My mother, father, and I were grouped with the newlyweds. If memory serves, I was about ten years old at the time.

Again, I was wearing an outfit my mother had made. This time, a pleated tartan wool skirt worn with a bolero of the same fabric, and a long-sleeved, white blouse. A pill-box style hat—of the same fabric—completed this ensemble. My black shoes had been polished to perfection by my dad, and my ankle socks, which had been washed by my mom, were as white as chalk.

Sewing was just one of my mother's many talents; she excelled at everything and anything she put her hand to. She wasn't always around to cook Sunday dinners for my dad and me, but when she did, and a pot-roasted chicken was on the menu, the aroma which wafted through our home was second to none. That chicken would look and taste as good as it smelled. This memory lives on in my taste buds.

Place a bunch of flowers in my mother's hand and she'd create an arrangement that was beautiful, and quite unusual. Using flowers from their garden, a particular arrangement she made at her place of work stands out in my memory. Here, she used shades of pink cosmos and some greenery. The result resembled a peacock's tail. Striking! This, without any formal training.

There were no bread machines back in the day, but my mom did not need one. She kneaded the dough by hand. The texture of her homemade loaves was fine and tender—with substance—a slice of heaven! Even before the loaf came out of the oven, my father and I used to toss a coin to see who would claim the crust. That was done purely in fun because we always shared it anyway. Everything my mother did, was done to perfection.

Unlike my dad, my mother always stayed in touch. When she lived reasonably close to my latest address—times when my dad had gone AWOL, and my 'home' was with some other family—we would meet after school on some of her days off. Other times, when she and I lived too far apart, we kept in touch by mail. I was always impatiently on the lookout for an aerogramme or a postcard.

My mother never came empty-handed on her visits. There was always a parcel for me to unwrap. It might be a new dress that she'd made to replace one I had outgrown, or pretty ribbons for my hair, or a package of treats to take 'home'—not unlike your garden-variety tuck box. For the most part, I remember looking forward to our meetings; remember, also, the excitement which had welled up in anticipation, or, as the case may be, the anxiety in case she did not show up.

For the most part, we would meet outside my school, then we'd head for the city. Once there, a walk to the Grand Parade was always in the cards. Here, I was allowed to have a strawberry milkshake or a glass of root beer and my favourite Attwells' fresh-cream doughnut from one of the vendors. Next, we'd find a bench where we'd sit so that I could enjoy my treats.

My mother always asked to see my schoolbooks while I munched on the doughnut and sipped my drink. We talked about school and other things for a while. Those times always flew by. My mother would accompany me to my new dwelling. Once there, she'd spend some time with my caregivers.

A heaviness settled on me toward the end of her visit. When that moment came, she and I walked together to the front gate. Once we'd said our good-byes, I stood there, watching my mom as she walked away from me towards the street corner.

In the moments it took her to reach the corner, my thoughts went to a happier time when we were together as a family. I smelled again the appetising aroma of her chicken pot roast which had wafted through our little home when she cooked our Sunday dinner—nothing, nothing ever smelled more like home to me—felt the comb on my scalp as she made ringlets in my curly hair; saw the pretty bow she had tied in my curls; saw my reflection in the mirror when I wore the dress with the smocked yoke which she had made for me.

I saw her pause in her stride, just before she turned the corner so that we could wave good-bye to each other. Now, she would be lost to sight. Gone, to live her life.

Unencumbered.

Once my mother had finally rounded the corner, it was as if the physical ties to my family disappeared along with her. Uppermost in my mind, invariably, was the feeling that I was waving good-bye to the love I needed to see me through. Aware, also, of feeling disconnected, adrift, like a balloon let loose into the wide, blue yonder.

The reality that I would once again be without kin of my own surfaced each time we parted. It hurt! I felt forlorn! Bereft! These feelings craved an outlet. I cried. Quietly. By the gate. In the dusk.

My life with my parents lacked continuity, and I had no say in the matter.

When all is said and done, those brief interludes did not do much to create a strong bond between us—my mother and me—more like a temporary sharing of space, waiting it out. Because I had received little mothering in its true sense during those crucial, formative years, I learned to cope without 'mothering' long before I came to terms with my father's many absences. The imprint my mother left behind was transient.

My mother was kind. She was generous. She was outgoing. She was also quite superstitious. She shied away from black cats. Horse racing was one of my mother's passions. Numbers and omens featured prominently in her day-to-day life, and her dreams were the mainstay of her betting system.

In these dreams, the winning numbers were sometimes 'revealed'. Should a given number, or numbers, grab Mommy's attention during her waking hours, she took particular note. These would then feature in her calculations.

Colours, too, played a significant part in her selection. Like when the colours in her dream matched those worn by the jockey mounted on a horse she had picked. She took these phenomena into account and used them in her 'system', hoping against hope they would bring home that elusive pot of gold. Her system worked. Quite often. In a small way.

Sadly, there were also times when all her calculations yielded no joy. I'll say this about my mother, she was a good sport. She took it on the chin when she had a losing streak, then, with a smile, she would say, "Maybe my ship will come in next time."

I became fluent in the racing jargon. When I was old enough, I sometimes accompanied my mother to the racetrack in Kenilworth for big events like The Queen's Plate. Once in a while, when, for some reason, my mother was unable to go herself, she persuaded me to go to the racecourse on a Saturday to place her bets. I always took a friend along.

Being there without my mother was a heady experience; made me feel grown-up. On these occasions, she gave me detailed instructions to follow. I would be made to repeat them until she felt I had it all down pat.

At the racecourse, the air was electric once we passed through the turnstile; the place abuzz with Bookies shouting the odds for an upcoming race and the constant chatter of people excitedly milling around. Placing my bets and waiting impatiently for the commentator to announce, "They're Off!" was a rush like no other!

My heart beat nineteen to the dozen, and the blood pounded in my ears by the time the horses raced down the last lap to the winning post. Oh! The excitement on the days I collected our winnings. Had I backed a loser, well…*that* story would have to wait for another day!

$\mathcal{M}$y father did not let the grass grow under his feet once he was back from his wanderings. No Sirree! In no time flat, he would be setting up shop in someone's vacant garage, or in a store-front, close to our new home.

Tallied in real-time, when compared to how much time my peers spent with *their* dads, one could argue my father's presence during my childhood did not amount to much.

All too true!

In any event, when he *did* return, he took his role as parent seriously. As a rule, he was my main caregiver during those disjointed periods. He then devoted himself to my well-being; took the lead in developing my character. His influence was tangible. Be it ever so humble, my 'family home' was where he happened to be. I still consider those times when he took care of me as being the more stable periods of my childhood.

He was a powerful swimmer. He taught me how to swim and instilled in me a healthy appreciation for the sea and its moods. I remember his telling me, "The sea is magical; it draws one in." Another time, he cautioned me when he thought I was wading in waters too deep for my safety.

"Don't do what I do, do what I tell you!"

For the duration, I felt somewhat secure because my life followed a pattern, it was in sync with the neighbourhood children with whom I played each day. I went to school, ran errands for my dad, listened to my favourite stories on the radio, read whatever books I could lay my hands on. Small chores at home and at his workshop—as well as my homework—were done under his watchful eye.

His penmanship was copperplate perfect, and he was meticulous about mine. When I started writing in cursive, it had to be flowing and the lettering just right, else it would not pass muster. Inevitably, I would have to start over again. My father was exacting. In his opinion, things had to be done right, or not at all. If, at any time, I tried to make an excuse for a job not well done, he would say, "A bad tradesman blames his tools!"

He was soft-spoken and caring, too, but I can't say there was much outward show of affection, nor do I recall sitting on his lap. His embraces were few and far between. I was in awe of my father, and I tried my best to be good, to please him. Ever hopeful he would not leave again.

He gave me pocket money each Friday, some of which I spent on *The School Friend*, a weekly girls' magazine. His usual quip when he handed me my pocket money would be, "When you look after the pennies, the pounds will take care of themselves, so don't spend it all in one place. Save some for a rainy day!"

My parents gave me many presents over the years. When he was around, my father gave me presents for birthdays and at Christmas. On my sixth birthday, he gave me a box of tin soldiers, a toy war tank, a jigsaw puzzle, and a book with pages picturing different dolls. There were also pages of different outfits with matching handbags, hats, and shoes. These outfits were paper cut-outs and interchangeable. You stuck them on the pictures of the dolls. I remember it as though it were yesterday! So much fun!

A motley list, to be sure. How would Sigmund Freud have interpreted this…I wonder?

In all fairness—on another occasion, my dad also gave me a miniature china tea set, complete with a little tray, cups and saucers, a teapot, milk jug, and sugar basin. All, painted with pretty, tiny flowers. The tea set came with tiny teaspoons too. One year he bought me a train set. He helped me hook up the train rails and coaches. We played together for what now seemed like hours at a time. It became a favourite pastime for the months he stayed put.

Books were a sure thing. I well remember the time my dad gave me a book entitled *Gulliver's Travels* by Jonathan Swift. It was beautifully illustrated. Then, on another occasion, a book about birds. On yet another, one about butterflies. Sadly, with the many moves I was subjected to over the years—some, on the spur of the moment, I might add—I lost track along the way of the train set, the many books, and other gifts my parents had given me.

Strict. That could have been my father's middle name! However, his praise was prompt and his reward unstinting when he thought I had done particularly well. So, one could also say he was fair.

My dad was a creature of habit. Each night he placed the contents of his pockets on a shelf in his wardrobe. One time, when I was in my first year of school, I took a fancy to a foreign coin of his. I wanted to show it off at school and removed it from his wardrobe while he was out of the room. When he was about to return those items to his pockets, he immediately noticed the coin was not in place and questioned me.

I was nervous; afraid of being punished. I lied. It would have dire consequences. With a look on his face that told me I had better own up, my father questioned me further. I owned up; handed him the coin.

He prized honesty. He would *not* stand for being lied to. I was about to learn this the hard way.

Taking the coin from me, he asked in a stern voice, "Why did you take my coin?"

"I wanted to show it to my teacher and my friends," I replied tearfully.

"You should have asked me. Do you know that taking something without asking is wrong?"

"Yes, Dadda." At this point, I was choked up, scared, and could barely say the words.

"You did two things wrong. You stole and you lied to cover up, so you should be punished. If I don't punish you now, you'll grow up to be a bad person; one who does not respect other people's property. I do not want you

31

to grow up thinking it's alright to steal and tell lies. Taking things that don't belong to you is a sin! I want you to grow up to be good and honest. Do you understand?"

I nodded with tears streaming down my face. Blinding me. Without further ado, he punished me. A certain part of my anatomy bore the brunt of it.

It was painful! Extremely painful! Traumatic!

A harsh punishment, but, by punishing me in this manner, my father wanted me to know, in no uncertain terms, that actions have consequences. Before now, I had been mostly scolded for disobedience or other childish lapses. Other times, I was made to write lines, or forgo my pocket money, or not allowed to play with my friends. Not *this* time, however!

My father maintained, there is only one truth and, to quote, "Telling lies to cover up something is the coward's way out. When you tell the truth, there is no need to add to it or to take anything away. At any time. It is *that* simple. The truth remains just that—it's unchangeable!"

Along the way, I learned being honest isn't always easy, but the lesson I learned on that occasion fostered in me a healthy aversion to telling lies *and* being lied to, I might add. Along the way, I also learned that telling the truth has its own reward. This would be my credo. God willing, my children would adopt it too.

He smoked a pipe, my dad. He only ever smoked a mixture of rum and maple tobacco. With no trouble at all, in my mind's eye, I see him…how he used his thumb to tamp down the tobacco in the bowl of the pipe. I see him behind his workbench, intent on his work, his pipe clenched between his teeth—the fragrant aroma wafting upward around his head as he puffed away after having put a match to it.

He will always fondly come to mind when the aroma of burning rum and maple pipe tobacco is in the air.

A black leather guard sheathed the index finger of his right hand. I remember asking him why he wore it. He told me the knife had slipped while he was cutting leather for the sole of a shoe. It had made a long gash, almost to the bone, along the outside of that digit.

He went on to say that he had been working on a rush job, so he could not spare the time to go to the clinic to have it stitched. Instead, he bound the finger tightly with his handkerchief, kept the bandage secure with some twine and just kept on working. He continued to dress the wound daily but neglected to have it stitched. It healed after a time but was always tender along the scar. Tender and stiff. That stiff finger, all too obvious when he was loading his pipe with tobacco.

There was a second injury. This time, to his left knee, resulting in a slight limp which gave him a distinctive gait. I don't recall my dadda ever telling me how he came by that one. I often saw him massage the knee when he was seated, however.

Reading was one of my father's loves and it rubbed off on me. With his help, I learned to read before I started school. I would later be an apt pupil. I credited this to my father's early influence and encouragement. Most evenings saw us, each content to sit with nose buried in a book, while we waited for a favourite radio program to air.

My father also loved music; loved to sing. He had a pleasant singing voice, as did my mother. Whenever I hear the songs he sang or hummed in those far off days, I'd say to myself or out loud if there happened to be some-one within hearing, "My father used to love that song."

It follows as day follows night that he would foster this love of music in me. To this end, he initiated piano lessons for me with two kindly, retired spinster ladies who happened to be sisters. They lived in our neighbourhood and taught music—I believe, he bartered his cobbler's expertise in exchange for those lessons.

So, there I was, eight years old at the time, walking proudly to their house, two afternoons each week for my music lessons, my music books under my arm. Of course, my homework and my handwriting exercises would have been duly vetted by my father before I could leave. I was over the moon when I went there to learn about crotchets and semibreves, middle C, and the musical alphabet. It set me apart from my peers.

For once, *being different,* meant I could hold my head up high instead of cringing at the mere thought. We did not own a piano, but my dad, ever resourceful, arranged for me to practice at the home of a fellow 'Lodge' member who happened to live across the road from my father's workshop. Who knows, maybe a bit more bartering came into play?

Weekly tap dance lessons with 'The EOAN Group' was another activity in which my father enrolled me. Unfortunately, both piano and tap lessons were short-lived, because not too many months later, the wanderlust would creep into his soul. Without warning, he would be gone. Yet again! Like the morning mist. A puff of smoke! The wherewithal to pay for these lessons disappearing along with him.

Though not exactly in the cultural category, still, I feel it worth mentioning that my father loved playing cricket. I went with him some Saturdays to watch when he played for his team. Then, there were the times when we'd go to Rondebosch Common on a sunny Sunday afternoon. My dog Monty and I would run around to our hearts' content, whilst my parents sat there, reading the weekend edition of the *Cape Argus* or just dozed on a rug, in the warm sunshine.

My father believed in God. When he was 'home', it was he who made sure I attended Sunday school and took me to church services on Sunday evenings. I remember, too, my mother sometimes being with us. There we were, with me skipping happily between the two of them, my hands in theirs, and, from time to time, they would give me a boost, making a game of swinging me up in the air.

As I recall these early Sunday evenings on the way to *Evensong,* I see that the sun had not quite set; its rays dimming as we made our leisurely way there. Still, we were always among the first to arrive because my father was a stickler for punctuality.

There was always an air of excitement—of anticipation—when my dad was around. Blessed with a bountiful sense of adventure, he took me to whatever cultural event was happening at the time and planned all kinds of excursions for us—with my mother being at work, it was almost always only the two of us. He loved rooting around the various vendors' tables on the Grand Parade in Cape Town and invariably found an item or two which he could put to use. We often did this on a Saturday and even on a Wednesday, during my school holidays.

My dad refused to buy anything there without first haggling and striking a bargain. On these outings, we also strolled down Adderley Street to admire the goods displayed in the pricey department store windows. Window shopping. We did this often. It was almost a ritual.

"Just you wait, my girl, when my ship comes in, this is where we'll be shopping!" My father often spoke about the things we would do—when his ship came in.

Speaking of ships…our walks along Adderley Street sometimes ended up at the Cape Town Harbour, especially when a ship of note or a passenger liner like the QE2 was docked there. We would admire their stately lines from the safety of the wharf, while my dad explained the ins-and-outs concerning these vessels.

Most of the things he told me at the time were way over my head, but I listened raptly to every word, loved the deliberate way in which my dad spoke when he wanted to educate me. I recall, even now, the feeling of contentment just to *be* there with him, my hand securely in his.

Could it be, my father secretly dreamt about sailing the wide seas?

He loved nature and plant life. On a sunny Sunday afternoon, we might stroll along Government Avenue, where the branches of the stately old oaks stood proud and came together overhead as though they were embracing. On these leisurely walks through the Cape Town Gardens, from time-to-time we'd pause to admire the different fauna and the abundance of beautiful flora.

On one of these outings, my dadda pointed out a stand of strikingly, beautiful, blue delphinium. Picturesque! A sight for sore eyes. One, I would long remember.

A visit to the art gallery and the museum would then follow. Those mummified figures of the pre-historic animals and earlier peoples were somewhat scary when I was younger. Extremely life-like. So much so, that I half expected to see them step out of their huge glass cages.

After our tour, we wended our way along the avenue in the direction of the train station, stopping at intervals to feed peanuts to the squirrels. No trip to the city, however, would be complete until we'd had a refreshing cool drink or ice cream from one of the vendors on the Parade.

When we reached Cape Town railway station, I'd be given a penny with which to weigh myself on one of the scales on the platform. Another ritual— just one of the highlights of our outing!

We often travelled on the suburban line to Kalk Bay Harbour on a Saturday, also on a weekday during my school holidays. Here, we watched the fisherman unload their catch, fresh from the sea. In hindsight, organised chaos is how I would describe the atmosphere. Invigorating, too. Abuzz with people clamouring for attention above the noisily squawking seagulls, who were diving for the entrails which the fishermen had tossed overboard. Those people wanted to buy their fish almost before the catch was hauled from the boats. My dad included.

The smell of the ocean, mixed with the oily fumes from the trawlers, *and* the sound of the waves lapping against the walls of the harbour, *and* the fishing boats which were anchored alongside, *and* the feel of the sun—warm on our faces—*and* a stiff breeze ruffling our hair, *and* the cobblestones under-foot, *and* the salty taste of sea-spray on our lips was part and parcel of our outing. Par for the course! We imbibed it all while strolling back and forth along the quay. My dad was a mine of information when it came to naming the fish and the best way to cook them.

On a sunny day, during my school holidays when work was slow—and on other weekends—my father packed a few sandwiches in a brown paper bag. These and a couple of bottles of cool drink were packed for an impromptu picnic at the beach. We'd head out by bus and train in the early morning, sometimes, for Clovelly. Once there, I'd make a beeline for the water, splashing about to my heart's content. Playing in the shallow, warm, brown waters of the creek was idyllic! I played there with abandon. Meanwhile, my dad reclined on a blanket which he'd spread out on the sand, his reading matter and the provisions he had brought within easy reach. I felt safe, knowing he would be casting a watchful eye over me from time to time.

Later, with the sun riding high in the sky, my dad and I ate the sandwiches and shared a bottle of 'Coo-ee'. In my opinion, nothing could surpass the taste of those fish paste sandwiches my dad had made or the lukewarm Iron Brew that washed them down.

Simonstown was another favourite destination on the Suburban train line. My father sat on the sand and watched the ebb and flow of the waves before taking a plunge. I collected seashells, but before too long, the gently lapping waves and shallow waters would beckon me. When I'd had my fill of the sea, I'd join my dad, entranced by the seagulls swooping effortlessly in the sky and simply let the sun's warm rays dry my body. We built sandcastles together, and it was here that my dad gave me my first swimming lesson.

My dad made friends with strangers in record time. He had a mountain of small talk on which to draw. I had great difficulty emulating him. When a family settled near us on the beach, he would have no trouble striking up a conversation with them. As a result, I'd end up playing with those children instead of being on my own.

However, all good things come to an end! At day's end, we would pack up and retrace our steps. Before heading for the train station, though, we'd stop at a nearby fish shop to buy a 'parcel' of fish and chips for our supper. Then, while waiting for the train to take us on our return journey, we'd look for an unoccupied bench on the station platform and seat ourselves there while we enjoyed our 'supper'. Sometimes, with a pickled onion or two thrown in for good measure.

The 'parcel' was always wrapped in newspaper and invariably reeked of vinegar. Oh! the smell! It sent my gastric juices haywire! Without fail! Like you wouldn't believe!

With the 'parcel' between us on the bench, we ate with our fingers. Cutlery not required! Each time we had a fish and chips 'parcel' my father would laughingly say, "Fingers were made before knives and forks, Beckie." He made sure we would have ample time to enjoy our 'supper' before the train pulled into the station. A fiery, setting sun, our backdrop.

*I* believe I was quite young when my father introduced me to the bioscope. Shirley Temple, famous child star, took part in the first film he took me to see. She was all the rage at the time. Being a novice to the movie theater, I expected her to step out from behind the screen and appear in person on the stage when the film ended. I remember being distinctly disappointed and puzzled when she did not.

My father patiently set me straight.

The city of Cape Town hosted an International Trade Exhibition on the Foreshore around the time I was about ten years old. It was there my dad introduced me to the unique treat of candy floss… Oh! The smell of it! The taste!

How to do justice to the sensation as it dissolved and disappeared in my mouth? Indescribably amazing! In a word, unforgettable!

Decades later, whenever I'm at a fair and get my first whiff of that sugary confection, my mind freely conjures up that perfect yesteryear day.

Boswell's Circus was an annual event on the Cape Town Foreshore. If my father happened to be around at the time, a visit to the circus was a sure thing! Back then, as far as I was concerned, the act of contorting should have been listed as one of the seven wonders of the world. My jaw dropped and my eyes popped, as I watched those artistes bending and twisting their bodies as though they had no bones. I was always nervous when the acrobats did their thrilling, high-wire stunts. During these acts, I'd shut my eyes tight, and open them only after my dad told me the acrobats had their feet placed safely back on solid ground again.

I recall those times and the activities he and I shared back then with nostalgia. Those memories are housed safely in my 'love box' and will rub elbows with the ones I have yet to make.

It pleased him no end when I came first in my class at school. However, when my marks put me in second or third place, those results did *not* meet his standards. He made that clear. Most emphatically! Then he'd push me to strive for more. Aim higher. Be it at school, or even a chore for which I was responsible at home.

My dad loved to show me off, and, at the drop of a hat, paraded my budding talents to all and sundry. He was genuinely proud of me. When I'd excelled at one thing or another, his favourite comment would invariably be, "You, are a chip off the old block!" High praise indeed, coming from him. Content, then, by all appearances, to be present as my dad.

Spurred on by him, I did my tap-dance routine, recited a poem, or sang a song at my school's Friday afternoon penny-concerts in my primary school days. He searched out the sheet music for the songs he thought would be appropriate and enlisted the help of my friend who played the piano. I had to practice daily after school once my homework was done. These practices lasted until Dadda felt I was ready to perform on stage. When his work was slow, he would sit in on these practice sessions.

Sir Thomas Beecham and Arturo Toscanini have nothing on my dad when it comes to perfection!

Images of my father standing behind his workbench with his awls, knives, rasps, tacks, and pricking wheel close at hand, come easily to mind. So, too, images of his shoe lasts and hammers, different needles and threads, nails, and the glue that held the parts together. These were some of the tools of his trade. He treated them well.

The following two signs, written in his beautiful copperplate, always graced one of the walls in his workshop: "If You Don't Ask for Tick, We Won't Be offended!" Also, "Our Soles For Yours!"

Those signs often raised a laugh, and customers rarely failed to comment.

A perfectionist! A master at his craft! That is how I would describe my dad! His hands, rough and scarred from cutting the leather he worked with all day long; skin darkened from the residual stain and shoe polish. When at work, he always wore a leather apron. Well-worn, shiny, and lightly scored in countless places—evidence of much use; darkened also in places by smudges of glue, and shoe polish, and stain. From time to time, he ran his knife across it as though it were a strop. Almost an involuntary motion; more than likely, mere force of habit.

I was fascinated by his expertise, the easy and practiced way in which he handled the leather and the shoe he was mending. I loved to watch him when he had his lathe running; first, it sanded and smoothed the rough, leather edges of the heels and soles, then polished and buffed the uppers to a high shine.

The smell, unique to singed hide, lingered long. I see him as he turned a shoe in his hands, this way and that, inspecting it with a keen eye. I see him, then, smiling in satisfaction at his handiwork, the left side of his mouth turned up slightly, giving him a roguish look. Were I to put my mind to it, I think I could summon up the sounds and smells peculiar to each phase of the job at hand.

As for the melodious sound of his voice as he quietly hummed along to a catchy song on the radio or whistled a tune through his teeth while he worked, I have no trouble recalling those either!

He attended the Freemasons Lodge meetings on a Sunday evening after we'd been to church and cut quite the dapper figure—hair sleeked back with Brilliantine, shoes shining, the crease in his trouser legs sharp as a knife-edge!

The Annual Freemasons Dance was *the* event for my parents. If he happened to be around at the time, my father escorted my mother to the dance, and it was a treat for me to watch them while they were getting dressed. Excitement pervaded the air!

Dressed to the nines, they made a striking couple. My dad, clean-shaven, freshly barbered, wearing a well-pressed, black suit with snowy-white shirt and black bowtie. His pocket handkerchief in place. My mother loved florals and soft, flowing fabrics. Her gown would be in the current fashion; one she had made herself. Especially for this occasion. She had the figure to do justice to her creation.

My mother wore Tangee lipstick. Always! Nothing but! Whenever she applied it, I watched in fascination. First, she applied it to her top lip and then she brought both lips together a couple of times, making a smacking sound while transferring some colour to her bottom lip. That done, she would run the third finger of her right hand firmly across both bottom and top lip to even out the colour. Even though I don't remember the exact shade of her lipstick, I *do* remember it was a vivid red. Its fragrance enveloped her and lingered in her wake.

However, the aforementioned events were interspersed with periods when my father and mother were not on hand to take care of me, but these happy memories, too, found their way into my 'love box'.

*Q* was eleven when my father decided that the three of us should visit his family in Riversdale to spend my three-week-long school holidays with Auntie Leah and Uncle Tom, my dad's paternal uncle. They had several children and grandchildren. This was when I first became acquainted with them. To this day, I have fond memories of a motherly Auntie Leah and tall, kindly Uncle Tom and their generous hospitality. Also, their many, warm-hearted offspring who adored my dog, Monty.

A German sausage breed with a sleek, tan coat, he was my friend. He was supposed to protect me, that's why my father named him after Field Marshal Montgomery.

Well, wouldn't you know, at the end of those three weeks, my dad decided we would extend our stay so that he could assist Uncle Tom in his shoe repair shop. My mother went back to work in Cape Town, and I was promptly enrolled in the local school for the balance of the year. It would now be the second time I had been obliged to attend two different schools in the same school year. So disruptive!

My new school was set way, way, at the top of a hill. Climbing that hill in the early morning and inhaling the fragrant *Fynbos* which grew there in profusion was intoxicating, unforgettable. Being part of a happy band of cousins and new-found friends made it the most memorable part of my day. A sharp contrast to my previous experiences.

Before, when I was transferred to a new school—*yet again, the new kid on the block*—I felt displaced, and, in those new surroundings, it was not unreasonable to find that my classmates, or the children on the street where I lived, already had a 'best friend'. They had grown up together; known each other since they were knee-high to the proverbial grasshopper. I was the odd one out! Being the odd one out was a handicap. I yearned, then, to live the life of the girl next door. I made no real, life-long friends because I did not stay in the same place long enough, and invariably lost touch when I moved on again.

Oh, to be someone's soulmate. If only for the duration of my stay.

Real friendships, real connections, however, meant sharing, confiding. I was reluctant to share. Already, from an early age, I was embarrassed about my family situation—the truth about having so often been abandoned by my parents was too painful to lay bare. It made me turn inward. I built a wall around myself; used it to shut out the hurt, to hide my fear of rejection and mask my earnest longing for acceptance.

Although owning the wall meant I could feign indifference when things did not go well, disadvantages came with the territory—as I was to discover, to my detriment—akin to a two-edged sword. Things had a way of not going well quite often, so this wall had to be reinforced many, many times during my childhood and beyond.

Some of my peers wrongfully assumed I was 'stuck-up', so they shut me out. It followed, then, that I would not always be on the receiving end of some hot topic, or privy to the secrets which the girls shared only with true and trusted friends, or be invited to their birthday parties.

In Riversdale—wonder of wonders—there was no need for the 'wall' because I was accepted and protected by family members who were well-established in the community. The cousins had taken me under their wing. This was a welcome change; it made for an easy, almost seamless inclusion.

*M*y father was an avid reader. It rubbed off on me. Reading became my first love. My passion! From an early age, I read bedtime stories to myself. At school, I devoured my first readers.

Books were magical. Books were peopled with fairy princesses, fearless heroes, and happy endings. They provided me with an escape route, a refuge when I was unhappy. All through my childhood and even beyond my teens, I took this route when I needed to turn a blind eye to reality and sad times; times when the lack of connection to my parents threatened to overwhelm me.

Life became friendlier between those pages, and, along the way, certain characters became my imaginary friends. Friends who would always be on my side. No questions asked!

At times, these 'friends' became surrogate parents, waiting for me at the end of the day, providing the love and comfort so often and so sorely lacking in my life. I could take them along wherever I went. *They* did not let me down! Having slid between the covers of a book, I could become any one of the characters depicted.

I was a sensitive child. Impressionable. One, blessed with a vivid imagination, so it's not outside the realm of possibility that the fairy tales I read over the years fuelled my imagination. Being powerless to change my situation, it is true to say I lived inside my head a lot during those childhood and early adolescent years.

It became the easiest thing in the world for me to cast myself as the heroine of the story I was reading at the time. More so when the heroine prevailed and said story had a happy ending. Sometimes, though, fairy tales, the ones told by the Brothers Grimm and their ilk, had sad endings.

I dried my tears then and coped—albeit with some trepidation—with the ghosties and ghoulies who had snuck under my bed, or into the wardrobe, or the ones who hid behind the curtains before I came into the bedroom at night.

It was no hardship for me to imagine that the space I was living in at the time was but a temporary one; that I was there only until my real life fell into place. Part of me clinging to the fantasy that the beginning of my *normal life* was just around the corner.

There were times when, to make life bearable, my fertile imagination found another escape route. I simply convinced myself the life I was living was not mine; *the horrible stuff happening to me were figments of my imagination.* Yet another time, I'd create some fantasy about the hospital having mistakenly given me to the wrong parents.

Sadly, I was obliged to come back to earth, where happy endings resembled rainbows. Visible. Yet, always just outside my reach.

Picture me, Dear Reader, living a life of wishful thinking, giving in to flights of fantasy. Pure coping mechanisms…all too temporary, and to no avail, because my flights of fantasy invariably led me to the same dead-end street, with nary a corner in sight!

When my parents were together, there were no raised voices that I can recall, nor did I ever hear them say harsh things to each other, but they lived apart a lot; separate from each other. Without me. Why?

People whispered. I heard. *Abandoned*. This word, not yet part of my vocabulary in those innocent, green years. *That* was not the only word...

*Shunted from pillar to post* came to mind.

As I grew older, however, I understood what those people had been saying; suspected that looking after me might have been a handicap to the lifestyle my parents had wanted to lead.

By this time, I had learned the words that could aptly describe how I had felt back then. Words that would have framed my thoughts and emotions to a T. Words like frustrated, bereft, neglected, unwanted, insecure, unloved.

Harsh words, but not inappropriate to my way of thinking. They all fit the bill, and none of those words implied that nurturing or my peace of mind was always a priority for my parents. They had given me life, then, quite often tossed me aside. I was confused; crushed by the lack of ongoing parenting. On occasion, a deep resentment towards them made itself felt.

In later years, it became as clear as an unmuddied lake, ours had been a non-cohesive lifestyle. Looking at the big picture, I ask myself, *Could the insecurities and lack of self-confidence which did, and still does, plague me stem from this neglect and lack of your garden variety parental connection?* Granted, I am no psychologist, but my inherent common sense strongly leans toward this conclusion!

Some might disagree and say, "Get over yourself!"

To them, with due respect, I say, "Walk a mile in *my* shoes!"

*Get over yourself?!*

What chance does a house built on a shaky foundation have when faced with the storms of life?

*Get over yourself?!*

Take it from one who knows, Dear Reader, *that* is more easily said than done.

Still, mixed in with my unhappy memories, I do have happier ones of the times when the three of us were together. I often called them to mind, found comfort, plodded on. *After all, it's not up to my parents to fix how I feel about myself. It's up to me.* This, too, was something I'd read somewhere… and also easier said than done.

*I*t was mid-December. I was twelve years old and would be turning thirteen in less than a month. It would be a red-letter day because my dad had promised I could wear nylons when I turned thirteen.

School, throughout the Cape, was over for the year. Summer holidays had just begun. My school report, which did me no end of credit, Dear Reader, had been duly scrutinised by my dad. With a smile lurking behind his brown eyes, he looked at me for what seemed an eternity, then said, "There's always room for improvement, you know!" He knew I had worked hard and was pleased with my marks. I could tell.

Now that the school year had ended, the promised visit to my maternal grandmother—'Gramma', to me, ever since I started talking—in Knysna was in the bag. We would be leaving at the end of the week, that's what my dad told me. There, I had it! Straight from the horse's mouth! The three of us would be in Knysna in time to celebrate a special event. My grandmother would be turning seventy-five on December twentieth.

To celebrate this milestone, all the aunts, uncles, and their respective offspring would be visiting. Family friends too, old and young. Our visit would extend to Christmas and well into the New Year.

My maternal grandfather died when I was a baby, so I have no recollection of him. Gramma, their five daughters, and two sons survived him. All but two of those children had long since married and had children of their own. Gramma's two youngest children, Reuben and Dorothy, still attending school, were the only ones still living at home. Dorothy and I were born less than one year apart. She was the older, and rarely let me forget it.

Gramma's oldest son, one other daughter, and my mother had moved away and lived in various parts of the Cape. Gramma's other two daughters lived nearby with their own families.

Holidays in Knysna were always a happy time for me, because I had cousins galore with whom to romp around, and renewing old friendships was a distinct possibility.

Before we were to leave for Knysna, my dad surprised me with a pair of white shoes which he had bought for me. 'Dutch' heels were the 'in' thing at the time. Having those shoes made this young girl feel grown-up because the heels were a little higher than those typically worn by her peers. My dad decided I was old enough to do my 'Christmas shopping' unsupervised. He gave me the money to buy myself a hat, a handbag, and gloves to match the dress my mother had made for me. I am happy to say, my purchases all passed muster.

*All things come to those who wait!* That's how the saying goes. However, the days leading up to our departure passed slowly, much like pouring *Lyle's Golden Syrup* from its tin on a cold day. To me, it seemed like time had stood still.

Finally, "D-Day!" We were packed and ready to depart. Our journey would take us from Cape Town to Knysna, via passenger train along the spectacular Garden Route. It being summer, the wildflowers growing on the slopes along the train tracks would be in abundance.

My parents and I had made the journey to Knysna at various times, ever since I can remember. Dadda had reserved a compartment for the three of us because it would be an overnight journey. It went without saying, I would be claiming the top bunk. Always fun! It meant I could watch the changing landscape unfold, and, when darkness finally fell, I could look out into the velvety night; could look up and see the stars and watch the moon as it travelled leisurely on its journey across the Milky Way.

Sounds of barking dogs, way off, in the distance, becoming fainter and fainter now. The wheels of the train going clackety-clack as they rode the rails to our destination. While I lay in my bunk, waiting for sleep to overtake me,

I listened to the sounds I had come to love, as the train travelled on into the night.

The soothing, rocking motion of the train conjured up an image of a mother rocking her child into the land of dreams; lulling it to sleep. Cosy and content, I drifted off. I was half-awakened several times during the night by the mournful sound of the train's warning siren as it approached the countless level crossings before we reached our journey's end. My land of dreams claimed me each time before the last echo had registered on my consciousness.

To this day, the sounds associated with those train journeys from Cape Town to Knysna along the Garden Route live on in my memory. I can recall them easily—at the drop of a hat!

It would be late afternoon of the following day before we eventually reached Knysna. For the last leg of our journey, we would take a bus from the train station to where my grandmother lived. Back then, it was almost always the same bus driver. He was familiar with the regulars who travelled to-and-fro; had known their families since day one.

Once told of someone's destination, he could connect the various family ties and strike up a conversation about the people who lived in that neighbourhood. Call them by name. Pass on tidbits of information about the locals. He greeted us like old friends because he remembered us from previous visits to my grandmother, and there was no need to tell him where we were going. Then, when we reached our stop, he could be relied on to send greetings to the families we would be visiting.

Our bus journey ended some hundred yards from my grandmother's home. A few family members would already be gathered, excitedly awaiting our arrival and eager to lend a hand with our luggage.

Their welcome was warm and enthusiastic. Everyone had something to say and questions which they simply could not wait to ask, as they led us to where Gramma would be waiting for us.

The family home was almost off the beaten path, in a tiny hamlet called Begai, about four miles outside the town proper. A railway line ran between the National Road and Gramma's property. Fortunately, the only trains which ran along these tracks were the 'goods' trains that carried the lumber to and from Thesen's lumber yard some miles away. They rode the rails a couple of times each week and gave warning—long and loud—of their impending approach.

Once over these tracks, a rustic, weather-beaten, wooden gate already sagging on its hinges opened onto the property. The pathway leading to the house took no turns, just went in a straight line from there to the stable-type doors which opened onto Gramma's spacious front room. Lining this pathway were the fruit trees my grandfather had planted after the birth of each of their five children.

Those trees, so lovingly planted by my grandfather, still bore a bountiful harvest in the summers I spent there. I remember the air would be redolent with ripe fruit; quite heady when one walked down this pathway on a hot summer's day. Peaches, figs, plums, apples—calling out to be picked and eaten on the spot—as they so often were. We children simply gave them a quick rub on a sleeve or the hem of a garment. No pesticides were ever used; only good, smelly manure.

The dwelling stood on an enormous piece of land, set deep off the national road. Built along simple lines, it was white-washed, single-storied, with an attic. My grandfather had built it with the help of my grandmother in the early years of their marriage. It boasted a thatched roof, as did almost all the neighbourhood dwellings. The doors, window frames, and trim were always painted a pretty blue.

Not grand—not by any stretch of the imagination—just warm, welcoming, homely. Both the owner and her home. To me, back then, there was no lovelier or friendlier place on earth!

Two aged, unpainted wooden benches stood in place, one on either side of those stable doors, the top half of which was invitingly open. If memory serves, those benches had always been there. Their seats and backrests, worn satin-smooth from frequent use, an invitation to all and sundry to take the load off one's feet. Even if only for a wee while.

My grandmother, a doughty, if diminutive, lady, proved herself more than handy with a paintbrush over the years. On my last visit, many, many moons later, though, the paint showed signs of having faded somewhat. My grandmother was somewhat faded too by that time but still pretty, with nature-made, pink spots on her cheekbones. Like little luscious, ripe apples. Her hair by now a silvery-white, twisted into a bun, high on the back of her head—worn this way since time immemorial.

We met Gramma halfway down the path. Impatient for our arrival, she had come to meet us. Her embrace was warm and welcoming. No one ever hugged me like Gramma! The moment we set foot inside the house, fragrant coffee for the grown-ups, cool drinks for the children, together with sandwiches and my gramma's light-as-a-feather scones, were the order of the day. Children were promptly dispatched out of doors, to enjoy theirs under a shady tree, thereby giving the grown-ups a chance to catch up and discuss such details as were not meant for *little pitchers with big ears*.

*G*ramma's attic held all kinds of interesting stuff. A treasure trove. Rooting around up there became a favourite pastime during the school holidays. There were books and board games, and back copies of magazines that told intriguing stories about life and romance on the ranches and the rodeos in the United States of America. They caught my fancy and, on flight of fancy, I winged my way there. Time, after time, after time!

There, in her attic, at the tender age of twelve, going on thirteen, is when I discovered the likes of *Gone with the Wind* and fell in love with its heroine, the spoiled and willful Scarlett O'Hara. *Forever Amber* and *Pride and Prejudice* also became lasting favourites. Other, more juvenile reading, treasures such as *Rebecca of Sunnybrook Farm, Anne of Green Gables,* and *The Hardy Boys*, to mention but a few, were amongst those I had chanced upon during my earlier forages in her attic.

My taste in reading matter is catholic, always has been. With one of these 'finds' in hand, I'd settle down somewhere to read and brook no interruption. My nose would be buried deep in its pages. For hours on end, I'd be oblivious to what was happening around me. The family knew better than to think of prying my latest discovery out of my hands. Mealtimes excepted. Naturally! The house rule was clear: 'no reading at the table during mealtimes'. I'd be loath to put my book aside then, but a growing girl does need sustenance.

My grandmother was a stickler for good table manners. No ifs, ands, or buts!

Various shade trees dotted the property at intervals. I climbed every single one of them in my salad days. Up, way up, in the leafy bower of an old oak tree, I'd be secreted with my latest find in which to bury my nose. With some fruit plucked from a nearby tree in my pockets, warm and still fragrant from the sun's hot rays, I would be in my element back then!

Sometimes I'd lie on my back on the grass, secreted under the drooping fronds of a giant weeping willow. I'd listen dreamily, with half an ear to the birds chittering overhead and the sounds of nature drifting lazily on the warm breeze. All the while, watching the scudding clouds and letting my imagination run riot while I studied their shapes.

Were I to lie there long enough, among other things, I would discern a plethora of shapes, from prancing puppies to lounging lizards, to fluffy cottonwool balls, to marshmallows piled high on a plate. Also faces with large, beaked noses! After a while, the clouds dissipated and there would be just a huge patch of brilliant blue overhead. In those carefree days, for me, this was a pastime second only to having an unread book to devour or enjoying a slice of Gramma's mouth-watering chocolate cake.

When our holidays came to an end, I left the books safely tucked away in the attic, because I wanted them to be on hand for my enjoyment the next time I visited.

In later years, I bought my own copies. Read and re-read them, and when, for the umpteenth time, I held any one of these treasured tomes in my hands, lost again in its pages, I had no trouble reliving the time spent in the Begai of my far-off, green years.

It was no free ride for me while we were there. Oh, no! I was given chores to do. I felt important when I was sent to 'fetch' some potatoes or onions or green beans from Gramma's garden. I loved helping my grandmother when she did the weekly wash for the rich people who spent their summers at The Heads, but by the time the washing was hanging on the line, I was usually drenched.

Gramma once told me, "A woman who wets herself on wash day like you just did, can expect to marry a poor man."

After much cajoling on my part, Gramma taught me how to iron the handkerchiefs she had washed. She was meticulous about how she wanted things done. When I had done ironing those handkerchiefs, they came in for much scrutiny. Believe you me, their corners and straight edges had to be lined up. Just so!

Looking back, I can see Gramma's teaching set the bar for me in how these things ought to be done.

*G*ramma's neighbours and family members lived fair distances apart, and one walked over hill and dale to the nearest farm for fresh milk, or even the meat of some unfortunate, fat, pink pig that had been freshly slaughtered.

Most men in my grandmother's family, and just about all the men in her neighbourhood, owned a musical instrument of some kind. It was not unusual for a few to stop by after supper, toting their chosen instrument. They came with wives or girlfriends in tow and gathered outside on these balmy, summer evenings. There, they played, for hours under the stars.

The plaintive note of a violin, the lively notes of harmonica, banjo, concertina, or the thrum of the guitar floating through the open windows and doors, could be heard in each part of the house. Their music set one's toes a-tapping to its lively rhythm. Friendly banter and laughter were part and parcel of these impromptu get-togethers.

These musical evenings made for a convivial atmosphere at the end of the day, and they invariably ended with a lusty sing-along that lulled me to sleep.

Both my parents had pleasant singing voices, and they joined in singing the well-known songs which had stood the test of time. Each time I heard them singing along, heard the way their voices blended I felt cocooned, somehow. The phrase "God's in His heaven—All's right with the world!" came freely to mind. Mr. Robert Browning certainly knew what he was talking about!

One such night at my grandmother's home stands out vividly in my memory; a scene, set in a time and place during my childhood, that was special to me in more ways than one. This night, though, would not end in a mere sing-along! Oh, No! On this night, we were going to have a party to celebrate my grandmother's birthday.

There would be music. Naturally. Dancing too! Did I but know, Dear Reader, this was to be the night I'd have my first dancing lesson!

It was twilight. The sun had been slowly setting in a blaze of red and orange hues. The house had been a hive of activity the livelong day. Gramma and her daughters had been hard at it—cooking, and baking, and cleaning— starting soon after the first cock crowed. Now, the evidence of their labours already on display, put my salivary glands to work.

Windows and doors were open, letting in the intense, sweet fragrance of the honeysuckle vine which grew on a trellis just outside the front door. Everything was done, and done to my grandmother's liking, in readiness for the expected company.

All of us, decked out in our Sunday go-to-meeting finery, were waiting with my grandmother to greet her guests. Other family members and friends were arriving in a steady trickle, willing and eager to be part of the feasting and merrymaking which would follow.

As is their wont, the women came bearing time-honoured, favoured dishes…could be some *boerewors* fresh off the *braai,* or *sosaties,* or a chicken, which had been slaughtered earlier in a neighbour's backyard and roasted to perfection.

Two trestle tables, set aside to hold their delectable offerings, now lined one wall of the spacious 'front' room. Tables, bedecked in my grandmother's pristine tablecloths; starched and ironed with not a crease in sight.

Heaped bowls of sundry potato favourites and other vegetables, freshly harvested from their gardens, were placed on the waiting tables. An aromatic *bobotie,* a bowl of yellow rice—with raisins, naturally (to be served with the *bobotie)*—nestled cheek by jowl against a platter of succulent ham. That pig, I'll have you know, Dear Reader, had lived a good life before it was slaughtered!

I spied two big bowls of jelly—one greengage and one strawberry—and a huge jug of custard at the ready. No party, to my way of thinking, would be worth its salt without a bowl of jelly and custard. A trifle and a scrumptious, mouth-watering, three-layered chocolate cake with butter icing had been placed front and center. The latter, my grandmother's favourite. Mine too, by the way.

Generous neighbours had contributed heaped plates of pumpkin fritters smothered in cinnamon sugar, and *gemmerkoekies,* and *soetkoekies,* and *melktert,* and *hertzoggies.* Also, a couple of loaves of banana bread, sliced thick and well buttered.

Mounds of fudge and pink coconut ice also graced the table and being summer, there were slices of juicy, bright pink watermelon, lovingly tended and hand-picked by my grandmother from her garden.

Typical, wholesome, comforting country fare. All-time favourites. Catching a whiff of each mouth-watering dish as it was brought into the house was driving me to distraction.

Oh, boy! Were those tables ever loaded to the hilt? You can bet your little cotton socks!

Gramma had brewed a huge batch of homemade *gemmerbier*[1] (ginger beer) two days before, and I'd helped her pour the fragrant, bubbly liquid through a funnel into sterilized bottles—the gingery perfume tickling my nose all the while. Those bottles, with their now fully fermented brew and raisins floating to the top, were lined up like so many soldiers at the end of one table. Drinking glasses of all sizes and shapes at the ready, close by.

I cast my eyes over the spread and made a mental note of all those mouth-watering treats. My gaze lingered on the *gemmerbier,* and some yummy-looking jellies, a wedge of *melktert,* and a slice of chocolate cake were destined to grace my plate. I'll have a slice of watermelon afterwards, thank you. Make it the 'crown' part, if you please. I made a mental note to put some fudge in my pocket for later, plus a piece of coconut ice for good measure.

---

1    Gemmerbier Recipe on Page 297

For starters, though, I planned to sink my teeth into a tempting slice of the steak and kidney pie that my mother had made.

Wafting through the open windows and doors from outside came the mingled sounds of dogs barking nearby, cows lowing in the distance, chirping sounds that crickets make, and the heady fragrance oleanders exude on a hot summer's night. A unique and memorable combination; typical of nights in the countryside where my grandmother lived. It forever set the scene, in a time and place where I felt I belonged.

Boisterous younger children were running around, getting underfoot, their laughter carefree and excited. Shrill! Young and old were infected with the spirit of fun pervading my grandmother's home that night. The music-makers were in full swing. Altogether, an intoxicating atmosphere.

The moment had arrived. None too soon! That's how I interpreted the gurgling noises emanating from my stomach. It was time to bless the food and give thanks for the many blessings in my grandmother's life. Her minister was already on hand—one of the first arrivals—waiting to do the honours.

Everyone had gathered in my grandmother's 'front room'. With eyes closed and hands folded, we listened to Reverend Tembe's prayer. After what seemed like an eternity to me, and others, I'm sure, we heard him say the 'Amen'. It echoed around the room; one voice after another repeating it in various stages of relief—more so the younger ones. *Their* patience had been sorely tried.

It was time for us to tuck into our favourite foods piled on our plates. I joined my young cousins and others outside to sit on makeshift benches and dig in. It wasn't too much later when not a morsel of the delicious spread remained to tell the tale. Like all who had gathered, I was finally replete.

Before one could say, 'Jack Robinson', the tables were cleared and dismantled to make room for the dancers. Any leftover foods had been set out in the kitchen for snacking as the evening wore on.

*S*tanding on the sidelines, I watched some of the grown-ups, my parents included, as they made their way to the center of the room. Swaying to the music of guitar, violin, banjo, concertina, and harmonica.

In my eyes, my parents outshone all others in the room. My father, dark-eyed, with almost black, wavy hair; swarthy complexioned and a fetching, lop-sided smile. A handsome man, trim, ever-so-slightly taller than my mother. He was the perfect foil for my mother who was fairer, with huge, chocolate-brown eyes. A slender, wide-eyed beauty with her hair done in the current 'Victory Roll'. My mother's hair always shone like polished chestnuts.

They seemed to be enjoying each other's company at this large gathering of family and friends. As I watched them dance, my father caught my eye. When the music stopped, he hurried across the room towards me. Holding out his arms, he asked, "How about this dance, young lady?"

This was the first time I'd been asked to dance and shyly told him so. His reply was spontaneous, his tone was inviting as he said, "Well then, isn't it high time I taught you?" I nodded wordlessly in reply.

Ecstatic, although shy and extremely self-conscious, I willingly followed my dad onto the makeshift dance floor as the home-grown band signalled the start of the next dance. Feeling ever so important, I looked around the room to make sure all my young cousins and friends were aware of this weighty occasion. I was, after all, the only one of my peers who had been singled out in this way.

As if on cue, the other grown-ups had left the floor and stood on the sidelines, cheering us on, setting the stage for my dancing debut. My father was an excellent dancer, and I was to learn, in this, too, he was an excellent teacher. When he took my hands in his own, he gave them a gentle squeeze, as if to say, "We're in this together, you and I. Let's give them all something to talk about!"

My father led me onto the floor and, in soft tones, he whispered encouragingly, "Don't be nervous, Beckie, we'll be dancing the Waltz. It's easy. I'll lead you and we'll repeat the steps together. Like this: 'One-two, step together. One-two, step together. One-two, step together...' You'll soon get the hang of it. Just keep repeating the steps in your head as we dance around the room. Think you can do it?"

I nodded my head, and at the same time tried not to lose count.

"Alright then. We'll dance until the music ends. Okay?"

I remember looking down at my feet several times. My dad saw this and remarked on it, "Don't look down at your feet, Beckie. Concentrate on my lead. Always listen to the music and move to the rhythm."

It seemed a lot for a twelve-going-on-thirteen-year-old to remember, but I was game, even though my heart was pounding, threatening to pump itself right out of my body, and, in doing so, stop me dead in my tracks. Right there and then!

Still, I gave it my all, wanting desperately to do well—to please him. I must have succeeded to some extent, for his smile was reassuring all the while as if rewarding me for my effort. Everyone clapped in time to the music, still cheering us on.

As was to be expected, I made a few false starts at the beginning but with each new step and each turn around the room, my confidence seemed to grow. He was patient and seemed to be enjoying the experience. I could tell by the smile in his eyes. When the music stopped and the dance ended, I was elated because my father had taken the time to dance with me.

Amidst a background of clapping and calls of "Encore"! I heard the satisfaction in my father's voice when he complimented me.

"Thank you, young lady, I enjoyed this dance. You're a natural, Beckie. I'm proud of you. Keep this up, and we'll have a South African Ballroom

Champion on our hands!" A broad smile settled on his face as he affectionately stroked my cheek and steered me to a group of my peers who had been watching us from start to finish.

At a loss for words, somewhat shy, overwhelmed by the attention and the occasion, I let myself fade into the background.

This was the first time I had been singled out as a dancing partner by any member of the opposite sex. My dad was pleased with me and had told me so. In no uncertain terms. Over the moon, knowing I'd earned his praise, I savoured the moment. *Surely, my heart is not big enough to hold all this happiness and pride.*

I embrace the memories of that night. The sounds and smells it evoked would long hold a special magic for me. Also, memories of the happy and uncomplicated time spent with both my mom and dad in Knysna, the place where I was born—hold them tight, for they rank as some of the happier ones of my childhood. In later years, whenever I felt lonely or blue, I turned the pages in my 'love box', flooded my mind with those images.

Relived, they were akin to being served a meal of 'comfort food'.

A talisman, so to speak, against leaner times.

Had I but known...sadly, there would be no repeat performance. My father did not dance with me again.

Not even at my wedding!

My parents and I headed home to Cape Town after the New Year celebrations in Knysna. Just in time to celebrate my thirteenth birthday. My father gave me the nylons as promised and a pair of leather sandals he had made for me. A perfect fit. The dress my mother had been sewing for me was also finished in time for my birthday. To top it all, she cooked a finger-licking roast chicken with all the trimmings for our supper.

One week later, my father disappeared...like morning mist. To carry on his life elsewhere. Severed his connections. Shucked off his responsibilities, and, it would seem, quit being my father. Yet again! The home I had shared with him for most of the previous year would be my home no longer. Would he miss me? Feel remorse? Feel guilt-ridden? Ever?

Who knows! I lost sight and sound of him for many years after our holiday in Knysna.

My mother would soon be going back to work, so the pattern of being separated from both my parents would be repeated. Once again, sending me on a rollercoaster of emotions.

This time I was sent, pell-mell, to live with family in Uitenhage. Auntie Lizzie and Uncle Owen were not strangers. They had also been part of Gramma's celebrations in Knysna, and I had often played with Leonard and Dorothy, their four-year-old twins, when we were all together at Gramma's house. I liked those two. They were bundles of energy and quite adorable.

My aunt had kindly offered me a home until my father returned, or my schooling was complete. She and her husband would see to all the formalities of enrolling me in a nearby college.

*This* train journey would be an even longer ride than the one to Knysna.

*F*eeling displaced and forlorn, I did not enjoy the train journey to Uitenhage and arrived mere days before the start of the new school year. Auntie Lizzie and Uncle Owen invited neighbouring families for a *braai* the next day.

I was introduced to three girls and four boys who were about my age, give or take a year or two. Everyone was welcoming and friendly. The young people offered to show me around. The whole gang walked me to school on my first day and pretty much included me in their everyday activities.

I was part of a group. I had an 'in'! The move to Uitenhage looked promising.

Sometimes, after school, when my aunt was needed at the little grocery shop which they owned, or when she and Uncle Owen went to church on Sunday evenings, she asked me to look after the twins. I read them their favourite stories. More often than not, they were the same ones I'd read to myself—not that many years ago.

I liked playing with them. They were the siblings I'd never had.

Auntie Lizzie cared for me as though I were her daughter. She spared no effort to make me feel at home. Much like my father, my uncle took a lively interest in my progress at school, and I felt free to call on him when I needed a problem solved.

In times past, when I was depressed, my interest in school became lackluster and my performance less than my best. All in all, things went well for me while I lived with my aunt and her family. I followed a happy routine during the school year. I studied under the watchful eye of my uncle and sometimes in the company of my newfound friends. Exams, like death and taxes, were a sure thing but they posed no problems now. School holidays were carefree and lots of fun.

There were letters and the odd parcel from my mother. I still missed the life I had with my dad, though—wondered when, or whether, he would contact me—still longed for a permanent place where I lived with *my* parents. *A place I could call home.*

My nomadic way of life was a persistent, sore spot; a wound which is scarred over—not quite healed, and, as the years went by, I had become somewhat inured to the neglect I had endured from my parents. Living in this loving family environment, however, made being away from both my parents somewhat bearable. Besides, I was older now, my horizons broader.

I was invited to share in most of my new friends' activities. The girls and I exchanged knitting and crochet patterns and tried out new hairstyles when the boys were otherwise occupied. We cheered them on when they played against visiting rugby and cricket teams, went as a group to the movies on Saturdays and church on Sundays.

When there was a birthday or other special occasion for which to prepare, the girls helped with the baking. They taught me the secret of baking scones which are light and fluffy.

All too soon, that school year came to an end, and with it, some disturbing news. My sojourn in Uitenhage was destined to come to an untimely end because the company my uncle worked for was transferring him to Johannesburg. My aunt and their children would be moving with him early in the following year.

Their home had been my haven for a little while. One I would be loath to leave. I had made friends, had settled down in this place, and had expected to have much more time with this family.

When my mother was told about the new developments, she promptly enrolled me at a boarding school in Cape Town. This, with some influence from her employer. She had also arranged for me to leave Uitenhage before

Christmas. Auntie Lizzie, seeing my distress at this unexpected development, suggested I leave after my birthday.

Thus, it came about that I celebrated my fourteenth birthday in Uitenhage with family and the friends I'd made there. My feelings were mixed. On the plus side, a birthday party in my honour was not something which happened as a matter of course. On the other hand, it meant my time with these caring people would be drawing to a close. That hurt!

To further add to my distress, my birthday came and went with no word from my father. My mother's letter, however, along with a parcel of clothing and treats, arrived on time. Also enclosed, was some pocket money and the train fare to Cape Town.

Time to say good-bye—all too soon! There were many tearful partings and promises to keep in touch with my friends, neighbours, and Auntie Lizzie's family. The twins and I had bonded like siblings. Saying good-bye to them tore at my heartstrings. Who knew whether our paths would ever cross again?

Those young people, who had become my firm friends, almost from the time I first laid eyes on them, would walk me to the train station. My luggage consisted of one suitcase and a little hamper of eats, lovingly provided by my friends and my aunt. The boys—Ivanhoe, Wesley, Humphrey, and Henry—would take turns carrying my luggage. They insisted!

The girls—Mona, Sally, and May—stayed close to me. We walked arm-in-arm behind the boys. The gang stayed with me until my train pulled out of the station, waving frantically until the train rounded a bend. When they were finally out of sight, I leaned back against the seat, staring out the window—at nothing.

It ached somewhere inside me, in a place where it had not hurt before. I felt a tightening of my throat and felt the wet, hot tears pooling in my eyes, but I blinked them back; refused to let them fall.

Were I to give vent to my feelings, I feared the floodgates would uncork copious tears! I would be crying for the many friendships, the loving family connection, as well as the safe place left behind. Plus, I had no idea what adjustments I would have to make once I set foot in Cape Town. At this point, it seemed highly unlikely that my dream of having a home with both my parents would ever come true. Being a 'whole' family did not seem to be in the cards—not for the foreseeable future, anyway.

Fair enough, between the two of them, my parents ensured my physical well-being in their absence. What about my emotional survival? This is where they came up short; there were no two ways about it!

My childhood was slipping away. The excuses and allowances I had previously made for my parents' continued absences had become shopworn! They had repeatedly sloughed off the responsibility of my upbringing like a snake shedding its skin…without a backward glance?

The hurt I felt with each separation from my parents had accumulated over the years; the weight of it was sometimes more than I could bear. Did it not occur to them that I might be feeling miserable, insecure, frustrated, because they palmed me off, time and again—onto others who were kind enough to take care of me?

There were times when these feelings came at me as though they were waves, threatening to wash over me, overwhelmed me, left me floundering, out of my element, like a beached whale. When I was much younger, I cried bitterly each time I was abandoned by my parents. As the years went by, I became increasingly hardened and resigned to my fate. I cried fewer tears now, and I promised myself, if I were lucky enough to have a family, I'd do whatever it took to protect them, provide a secure home for them. Keep them safe!

A whole year had gone by since my dad had gone AWOL. Until now, he had never been gone this long. To all appearances, he had quit being a dad and, for all we knew, he might well have fallen off the face of the earth. It was beginning to feel as though he were a figment of my imagination.

Had he kept in touch with my mother during the time that he had abandoned me? I don't know. I only know I still lived in the hope that my dad and I would someday be reunited, even though my hopes had been dashed and broken before. Times without number.

A mystery surrounded my father's persona and current whereabouts. *Did* I question my mother? I doubt it, quite frankly. Children did not ask questions, back then.

We were told, "Ask no questions and you'll hear no lies!" We were to be seen and not heard. Remember? I had question upon question in the meantime.

Why was he no longer part of my life?

Was he travelling the world?

Did he feel guilty for having abandoned me?

Did he miss me at all? Did he not care that we were all missing out?

Did he wonder what my life was like, whether I was happy? Or not?

Did he wonder whether I would pursue nursing like he had wanted me to?

Did he even give a second thought to the fact that I had had the *right* to his wisdom and protection; that I would have benefitted from it?

Had he lost his memory?

Did he have another family? Could this be the reason he stayed away?

Would he ever show up again? Had he quit being my dadda? Was he dead?

I knew him to be an intelligent man, but he did not always make intelligent choices. Or so it would seem. He was fallible, after all. I'll grant him that. Had I been born a boy, one who would have carried on the family name, learned Dadda's trade, would he have cared more? Shared a permanent home with me? Encouraged and inspired me to higher learning?

In those far-off days of my childhood, my father had said, "I want you to be 'someone'...a credit to the community and our family when you grow up." He believed nursing was a noble profession. It was his wish that I become a nurse and follow in the tradition of his mother, his aunts, and his female cousins. He conveyed this to me often.

For his wish to become a reality, I would need his support. This salient fact must have escaped his notice, however, because he did not stay put nearly long enough in the ensuing years. I never did make nursing my career. In my teens, when I was old enough to figure out how best to get on with the business of living, gratifying my absentee father's wishes was not a consideration.

Disappointment and anger reigned, instead, for the way he had abandoned me.

Did it not dawn on him how his absence impacted my psyche, made me lose sight of my self-worth and the goals he and I had set for my future? To my way of thinking, leaving me to fend for myself was an unforgivable lack of insight and negligence on his part! Cold! Uncaring!

Where *did* that leave me?

Sorely in need of a father's perspective and guidance when faced with some inevitable, weighty decisions, I'll have you know. Decisions which, at such a tender age, I was ill-equipped to make without his input. I had been obliged to carry on without his and, all too often, my mother's guidance, supervision, and support. Poor judgement at times proved my undoing; lack of confidence had become a distinct liability—potentially prime ingredients for a troubled adolescence.

I lived in hope, daily, during my green years. Even now, overriding all my sadness and confusion, I continue in the hope that someday my parents would make a permanent home for us. A normal home. Ever hopeful that my dad would stick around. Even now, a little voice, unbidden, in wistful tones was wont to whisper, *maybe, after to-morrow…*

*R*etrieving memories from a distant past can be tricky, and, as time passed, my musings on my childhood could have become somewhat flawed. So, my father may not have been exactly who I thought he was, rather, who I needed him to be at the time. This, I *will* allow.

*This,* I know, for sure! My life would have been different, could have been worse—all the more barren had my dad not demonstrated, albeit sporadically, that he cared. Cared enough to sometimes put me first, to be my mentor when the spirit so moved him.

Doubtless, my life would have been more rounded. I would have made fewer mistakes had I been the beneficiary of his wisdom and experience; happier, by far, if only he had kept in touch, made himself accessible when I was growing up. Whether I was in crisis or not.

Had I but known…many waters would perforce flow under the bridge before we would meet again.

During the years he was absent, my wedding day would be just one more milestone in my life without him. His absence on the day I became a bride would forever give the lie to one of my childhood dreams: the one where my father would tell me how proud he was of me; give me his blessing for a long and happy married life; tell me how beautiful I looked…like a princess!

Part and parcel of the same dream was a vision of myself, walking down the aisle on his arm, to the strains of *Jesu, Joy of Man's Desiring.*

The hope, that he would someday be part of my life again, lived on, though. Hope springs eternal. It bears repeating.

My father _did_ contact me. Twenty years after my thirteenth birthday. Out of the blue! As was his wont in years past. He offered no explanation for his long absence, or why he chose this time in his life to reach out to me. I didn't ask. Our connection had frayed, and we had become strangers in the intervening years.

Were I to hazard a guess, I'd say it must have been an extremely sensitive area for him! Maybe, in his opinion, it was a case of _least said, soonest mended_. As for me, I was too proud. Too inhibited. Too afraid of going _where angels fear to tread_.

He visited often and happily acquainted himself with Mike and our twin boys. Our relationship, his and mine, was on the road to recovery. At snail's pace.

Had I but known. Two years would be all the time he had left.

I had no inkling that he was not well. Had he, himself, known? If so, I daresay, he must have had his reasons for not taking me into his confidence. I, being unfamiliar with the person he had become, did not recognize the signs which would have been a dead giveaway.

No pun intended.

In retrospect, I imagine he needed to reconnect after all those years. Reconcile. Who could know the regrets with which he had been living all those years we'd been estranged? I daresay, we both lived, each with our own secret desires and regrets. Both had questions we longed to ask. Could have asked. Should have asked.

Then he died.

Suddenly!

Too late, then, for explanations and answers. My time had run out for the questions that were burned on my brain and had died on my lips. Who knew which questions he might have wanted answered?

My dad was dead. Time had come to attend his funeral. The leaves on nearby trees fluttered in a stiff breeze. The sky was gray. The clouds chased each other across a leaden sky.

Leaden. A reflection of my spirit.

Woebegone. A feeling with which I was all too familiar. Today, however, it was not the sadness of old; the distress of not knowing when, or whether, my dad would return to make a home for me. My distress, now borne of regret, because our connection had been irrevocably severed.

An 'absentee' father. Without question. To the onlooker who saw only part, not the 'big picture', he might not resemble their idea of a good parent. I knew this all too well. To me, when all is said and done, he had had redeeming qualities. The onlooker—my mother included—when all is said and done, was not privy to my many memories.

There were many more facets to my father. Sadly, they will forever remain hidden from me.

I cried inwardly at his graveside. I let the tears roll down my face when I was alone. Tears of regret, mingled with tears of thankfulness for the time he had spent with me—fostering an appreciation of the arts, teaching me the waltz, instilling in me the importance of being truthful, to strive after perfection, to be kind to animals, to love nature, to be God-fearing. Among other things.

He had taken prodigious pleasure in educating me when he was my caregiver; made the lessons memorable. Had we spent more time together during my adolescence, in my teens and later years, his guidance, then sorely needed, would have been invaluable.

Lastly, I cried for my 'love box' of memories—not quite full because there would be pages that could not be written. Now and forever, I would lament time lost; precious moments my family and I would never again share with my dadda. Moments in time that might have been and will not come to light now. Our time had been cut short.

It eased my pain to picture him, his face a study in animation, as he remarked on the talent and grace of the once-famous ice skater, Sonja Henie. I hear his voice as he spoke to me about myriad subjects…the reason the tide ebbed and flowed; waxing at length on the paintings of the old masters; enthusing over the delicate, diaphanous wings of a butterfly, and explaining, in detail, the fascinating life cycle of these amazing creatures—from egg to caterpillar, to chrysalis, and, finally, its emergence as a spectacular butterfly; the miracle alive in flowers and all plant life.

I knew he attributed these miracles to his Creator.

His words, painting pictures so vivid, I could almost see and smell whatever it was he was describing at the time. In retrospect, I appreciate to the nth degree my father for sharing time with his young, impressionable daughter. Interludes, sandwiched between his many, long absences.

A 'rolling stone' to the end and, true to the adage, he 'gathered no moss'. That is so true of my dadda. It came as no surprise that he left me no worldly inheritance; nothing I could take to the bank, nor hang on a wall, nor recline in, nor any silverware I could fondly polish from time to time and display nostalgically when company came.

To his credit, as I see it, he left me a legacy of greater value. I own many priceless memories which have no place in a bank vault. I can, however, unfurl and savour them; connect myself to him. Any time I choose. With no trouble at all.

While I walk this earth, I believe I will be able to conjure up the sound of his voice when he was pleased, or not. Play it over and over in my head and be reminded how l felt when he was close by.

At will, I can mentally retrace our steps when we went for Sunday afternoon walks on the Rondebosch Common; connect the smell of him to the earthy smells which abounded there; feel his strong arms as he kept me afloat in the sea, whilst teaching me to swim; hear his voice, urging me to be watchful, because the sea could be treacherous.

I can connect with him as I continue to love and respect Mother Nature; make her my friend and, by the same token, befriend her. In my turn, in some ways, hopefully, pass this on to my children. They, then, to theirs. All things being equal, a legacy that will keep on giving.

The glow that had washed over me when my dad smiled at me and praised me for a task well done and when we danced the waltz has not yet faded. Neither has the sound of his voice when he sang along with the radio to a popular tune, or how the fragrance of 'Bay Rum'—the only aftershave lotion he ever used—lingered in the bathroom each morning.

These mental snapshots together with others in my 'love box' enable me to relive special times of bonding, sharing, learning; strong reminders of the all too brief times when I was part of a 'whole' family. Some had long been suppressed, had perforce, lain dormant, jumbled in a pile in my memory bank; waiting to be sorted through.

In time, I did. Painstakingly. Trying to make sense of my life and why my parents had trusted my upbringing to anyone available to make room in their life for me. I can only conclude both my mother and father did what was expedient at the time.

Did my dadda regret those things he never experienced with me? Like being on hand to read my school reports, like seeing me off on my first date, like being around to hand me 'the key' on my all-important twenty-first birthday, like meeting his future son-in-law, like giving me away on my wedding day or holding his newborn grandchildren in his arms? I had wanted him to be part of those momentous occasions. More than words could say!

My father never said he loved me, but, after having revisited my childhood memories for the umpteenth time, his actions during our times together— in my humble opinion—spoke volumes. Brief, though they often were.

For that little while at least, I could claim to have been 'Daddy's Girl'.

Without question!

# And So, Life Goes...

"To everything there is a season,
and a time for every purpose under heaven..."

(Ecclesiastes 3:1)

*I* was on the verge of womanhood. What would be my final year of college awaits. Once again, the new girl at a new school, living in new surroundings. Those apprehensions and insecurities of old reared their ugly heads; beset me as usual. For all intents and purposes, I might as well have been five years old, facing my first day at school.

Grace Solomon and I met on that day. She and I were assigned seats next to each other. *We clicked!* She was a year older.

Serendipity? Kismet? Call it what you will. In any event, we became firm friends. We were both 'only' children, but this is where the similarity ended. Grace lived in the house where she first saw the light of day. Raised by loving parents, she would always be her father's 'little girl'.

In one of our many heart-to-heart conversations, Grace laughingly confessed to having confided in her mother, "I'm going to marry Daddy when I grow up." She was four years old at the time.

My parents were still separated. I still had no permanent home. I had not seen my father in a month of Sundays, but my mother and I met for a couple of hours, two or three times each month.

Grace and I spent all our free time at school together. We grew close, like sisters, and, before long, I was spending my weekends at her family home in Lansdowne.

Her parents had practically adopted me from the outset. They contacted my mother after I had spent the Easter holidays with them and, with her consent, arranged for me to make my home with them. With a happy heart, I packed my belongings and left the school hostel with nary a backward glance.

Like her parents, Grace is open-hearted and generous. To a fault. She is outgoing, has a trusting nature. She's honest, naturally friendly, straight-forward, sincere, and supportive. I loved her long, straight, chocolate brown hair and coveted her catlike green eyes. She exudes a kind of energy that draws people to her. She almost always opens a new topic with the phrase, "The thing is…"

I am shy, but we share the same values and agree on important issues, Grace and I.

Mr. and Mrs. Solomon soon became Uncle Jacob and Auntie Miriam. Theirs was the kind of homelife I had secretly longed for and, what is more to the point, they treated me like a daughter. They were loving, supportive of my interests and progress at school, and not stingy in their praise of my achievements.

I learned to love them more than words could say. They loved me. Knowing this was akin to a gift that keeps on giving. In time, because of their love and support, I began to heal, as though from a disease. In time, it seemed the most natural thing in the world for me to make my home with them, for as long as was necessary.

*Home* is where people know you.

*T*he Solomon family have a few 'White' friends. Georgina Bailey being one such. A long-standing friend, and owner of *Georgina's Music Shoppe* in Claremont. She, at Auntie Miriam's prompting, offered me a job in her shop—working part-time—after school hours. This was a godsend; would be a stopgap until my schooling was behind me and I could fend for myself financially.

I loved music. I was delighted—in my element. I enjoyed working there; the work was straightforward, and I took to it like a duck to water.

Georgina is a good boss. She is flexible and understanding. Soft-spoken; fair in her dealings with her staff, but with an air of authority. It gained our respect.

Not only did working in the shop allow me some financial independence, it also broadened my musical horizon. Here, I was exposed to a wealth of music previously unknown. What a way to spend one's working hours!

Bittersweet memories surfaced whenever I came across some sheet music which he had chosen for me to sing at my primary school concerts. I'd find myself humming the tune and pictured myself back there, standing on that stage, waiting for my cue, while butterflies by the dozen seemed to be fluttering in my stomach!

Came the day when our schoolbooks could finally be closed, when Grace and I would don our school uniforms for the last time.

Grace was to start her nurse's training at Somerset Hospital in the new year. If I'd had my druthers, I would have loved to further my schooling to pursue a career in music. Oh! To be able to teach music all day and every school day…this dream would have to be put on hold. It was definitely not in the cards. For now. My job-hunting would have to begin in earnest.

Chop-chop!

The heavens must have been smiling on me because, in the new year, I landed a job in the offices of an international magazine distributing company in Cape Town. The department manager and staff struck me as being friendly and helpful. I was told there would be ample opportunity to advance within the company. I liked the sound of that. Plus, working a nine-to-five, five-day week, meant I could continue working part-time in Claremont.

Things had certainly changed for me. For one, I was now financially independent and had taken charge, in no small measure, of where I was headed. Now, tears had no place in my day-to-day existence. Best of all, since the Solomon family had taken me under their collective wing, I had become part of a 'whole' family; my roots had gone deeper. Grace's friends had become my friends. I felt in sync with my surroundings and colleagues.

I had carved out my niche. I belonged! Oh! What a difference *that* made!

Time moved inexorably on. Grace finished her training and accepted a nursing position at Groote Schuur Hospital. Because of the different shifts, travelling back and forth from her parents' home to work had become time-consuming and difficult.

My job with the magazine company in the intervening years had been on a steady, upward path. Pooling our resources so that Grace and I could find a flat closer to the hospital seemed the most sensible thing to do.

With some reluctance, her parents gave us their blessing, with the proviso that we turn to them if we ever found ourselves in a tight spot, financially or otherwise.

Some months later, we struck gold. We found a suitable flat in Wynberg. It was ideally located for both of us, in more ways than one. I worked in the city, so travelling back and forth on the suburban train was convenient. It worked well for those evenings when I went directly from my day job in the city to my part-time one in the suburbs.

With the help of donations in the form of unwanted furniture from various members of Grace's family, our little home was completely furnished when we moved into our separate entrance flat—a glorified garage, really—on a sunny day in June.

Our new home came with a tiny garden. I was overjoyed to have my own little patch of earth—even though it was overrun with weeds when we moved in—where I could plant and nurture my own flowers.

It's been many a long year since I first saw and fell in love with delphiniums. My father had pointed to a stand of these, on one of our Sunday excursions to the Botanical Gardens in Cape Town. There were some blue, some white, and others in various shades of pink. They struck me as elegant and stately. I guess this picture-perfect memory stayed with me.

After all our boxes had been unpacked, pulling weeds was one of the first tasks I tackled. Then, I lovingly planted and tended the seedlings and plants I'd bought (need I say some were blue delphinium?) and others I'd collected from Uncle Jacob's garden. I was richly rewarded for my efforts and pleasantly surprised at my success when, a few months later, my little garden came into bloom. A tranquil patch, mostly blues and whites.

Over time, blue had become my favourite colour.

*O*f all the seasons, my favourite is spring. Everything is new in spring! To quote Mr. Tennyson, "…In the spring, a young man's fancy lightly turns to thoughts of love."

It is early days in September now, and spring, newly arrived and bursting forth—lending wings to my every step as I make my way along the now-familiar route from home to a nearby bus stop—is all around on this delightful Saturday morning. The unmistakable, earthy smell of it is in the air I breathe. Every which way I turn I see trees in bud, some with leaves still unfurling, others already sporting leaves of brighter green. Leaves, which flutter airily in the gentle breeze and whispering, who knows what, to their many feathered inhabitants.

September may be newly arrived, but, in the new year, when January rolls around, I, Eve Emily Hanson, will be all of twenty-two years old.

Not a single, solitary soul is in sight as I stand at the bus stop, waiting for the bus to arrive. Ours is a friendly neighbourhood—a predominantly Coloured area in Wynberg. All is quiet, and not much seems to be stirring at this early hour. Even the dogs refrain from rendering their usual choruses. I feel as though I have this tiny part of Mother Earth all to myself.

As usual, the bus that takes me to my workplace arrives on time. Claremont, my destination, lay a good twenty minutes away. I have been making this Saturday morning journey for several months now, ever since Grace and I moved into our little two-bedroom flat.

Mr. Adams, the regular Saturday morning bus driver, seemingly also in tune with nature, whistles a catchy tune—albeit slightly off-key—between cheery greetings for each of his passengers as they board and alight.

Always friendly and polite to all his passengers, Mr. Adams had assumed the role of kindly uncle toward me from the first time I boarded the bus. As was his wont, he had a special parting greeting for me just before we reached my stop. With a smile in his voice as I stepped closer to the exit, he said, "See you next week. In the meantime, don't do anything I wouldn't do, young lady."

Once I'd planted my feet firmly on terra firma, I said, "I'll try, Mr. Adams. I hope you have a nice weekend with your family too…see you next week." I felt invigorated, and my steps were jaunty as I traced my route on the now-familiar Main Road.

The fact that I was wearing my new, and oh, so fashionable, wedge-heeled, multi-coloured sandals today added a decided bounce to my step. Quite snazzy, I'd say! They added a little "something" to the uniform which came with the job.

I love music and enjoy going to work on a Saturday morning and a couple of evenings each week. It was about a quarter to nine when I let myself into the shop. After unlocking the street door, I immediately raised the window blinds to let in the glorious sunshine and light. Once that was done, I stopped in my tracks, waiting to hear and absorb each familiar street sound to which I had by now grown accustomed.

There they were! Coming across loud and clear! The voice of the cocky young newspaper vendor calling out the headlines of the day to passersby; the receding, barely audible hum of motorcar tyres on tarred surface; the short, sharp sounds of a bicycle bell, tinkling stridently just as it passed the shop, then fading to nothing as the cyclist travelled on; the dull thud of a car door as it slammed shut somewhere on the street. Mundane sounds. Reassuring sounds. Sounds, which, since I had started working here nearly four years ago, had become a backdrop to my day. Sounds telling me all was right with my world.

It hadn't always been that way.

*I*ke Levendal, like me, is 'Coloured'. He is Georgina's full-time Stock Clerk/Salesman. Between us, we manned the decks in her absence. My duties as part-time Girl Friday are varied. Amongst other things, it fell to my lot to open the shop at nine o'clock on a Saturday morning, accept and check deliveries from suppliers, and advise customers by phone that the orders they had placed were now in stock—ready to be picked up. I did this whilst keeping an eye open for Ike, who usually showed up soon after.

Red-haired, tall, slender, and quite stunning to look at, Georgina is in her late thirties. She seems to float rather than walk. She's vivacious and utterly likeable. Heads turn when she enters a room.

She, by her own admission, was a confirmed 'party girl' and 'night owl', making the most of the weekends. For her, the weekend starts the minute she leaves the shop on a Friday.

"Expect me when you see me." Those were her usual parting words. So, that's what her staff had come to expect on any given Saturday morning. To give Georgina her due, whenever she put in an appearance, she more than pulled her weight; worked like a trooper during busy periods.

To set the tone before starting the serious business of the day, I loaded the turntable with records that were currently on the pop charts, interspersed with my favourite Mozart sonatas. I followed this routine religiously, took comfort in its sameness *and* the knowledge that my life was moving along in an orderly fashion.

To add to my feeling of well-being, soon after opening the doors, I accepted delivery of the expensive acoustic guitar and sheet music we had placed on 'special order' last week. This meant a sure sale for us. An auspicious start to the business day. Georgina would be pleased.

The hour wore on, with no sign of Ike, however. Still following a set routine, I leafed through the order book to locate the customer who had ordered the guitar and sheet music. Against an entry in Georgina's big, bold lettering, I came across the name Mike Moore, and a local telephone number.

Mr. Moore was "...*not available, so, you know the drill.*" Thus went the message I heard on the answering machine when I called his number. Acting on the premise that the customer is always right, I left him a detailed message, then placed the items in our stockroom. It would be just hours later that I would come face-to-face for the first time (across the shop counter, I might add) with my destiny in the form of Michael J. Moore.

Georgina breezed in minutes after I had returned from the stockroom. She made a beeline for her office but slowed down just long enough for us to have the following exchange.

"Good morning, Georgina."

"'Morning, Eve. Boy, am I glad to see you!"

"Why? What's up?"

"Ike asked for a few days off to go to a cousin's wedding in Mossel Bay, so it will be just the two of us today."

"Lucky Ike...perfect time of year for a wedding, hey? I wondered why he'd turned up missing this morning. When will he be back?"

"He should be back by Tuesday," she said on a sigh.

"Not to worry. Between us, I'm sure we'll manage just fine this morning. Thank goodness we close at one o'clock today. I just hope things don't get too busy for you on Monday."

"Me too...if it does, I can always get my sister to lend a hand for the day."

With that rejoinder, she closed the door to her office, and, mere minutes later, I heard her speaking on the phone. After a brief conversation, she was back, and I filled her in on all I had been doing since I opened the shop. I had barely finished, when a stream of customers entered the shop, and it seemed as if everyone wanted assistance at the same time. By the looks of it, we were in for a hectic morning!

The Saturday morning rush continued but slowed down considerably by noon. Georgina decided to take advantage of the lull—said she was off to buy herself a hat. She has a thing about hats and, over time, had made me the happy beneficiary of a couple, which, for her, had lost their appeal.

I was standing behind the counter sorting some sheet music when the doorbell tinkled. I looked up in time to see a man enter. His height, at a glance, easily five-feet-ten-inches with an athletic build. I judged him to be in his middle-to-late twenties. My eyes were fixed on him as he walked purposefully towards me. He had a spring in his step and, having reached the counter where I stood waiting, looked me squarely in the eye.

"'Morning. Someone from your shop phoned me earlier. I believe you're holding a guitar and some sheet music for me."

"That's right. You must be Mr. Moore."

"Guilty as charged. Was it you that phoned?"

Putting the sheet music carefully to one side, and imitating his tone, I said, "Yes. Guilty as charged. We have your guitar and music sheets in our stock room; if you'll just give me a moment, Mr. Moore, I'll fetch them for you."

On my way to the back of the store, I caught myself dwelling on his likeness: olive skin; well-shaped mouth and nose; incredibly long lashes framing tawny, green eyes with faint lines etched into their corners; a pronounced widow's peak; and dark brown hair cut short. His broad brow spoke to me of intelligence. These features were all seared onto my brain.

Returning with his order, I handed him the guitar for inspection, together with the sheet music, complimented him on his choices. The broad smile on his face and the way he ran his hands lovingly over the guitar told me he was well pleased.

The encounter was brief. On the surface, all business. Even so, during the transaction, I sensed a markedly un-business like gleam in his eyes each time they met mine. An unstated promise lingered in the air when he walked away from the counter with his purchases grasped firmly in his shapely hands. A promise, underlined in his parting glance—the 'glad eye' if ever I saw one—when he reached the street door and communicated in his oh-so-well modulated voice when he said, "*Totsiens.*" It left me with a strong suspicion that we would be seeing each other again.

The sparkle in his eyes and his confident bearing had not escaped me, and, to my way of thinking, he was the epitome of all things male. After giving it some thought, I decided I would not be averse to seeing more of Michael J. Moore in the not-too-distant future.

He must like music, I mused. I wondered how well he played the guitar, and if he had owned one before now. I pictured his fingers strumming the strings, bringing a sweet melody to life.

This image evoked a far-off memory, sent my thoughts to my early childhood and a happier interlude in a long-ago time and place—ten years ago to be exact. I was twelve years old then, soon to be thirteen. Knysna—my parents and I had been on holiday there. Together. One last time.

*C*laremont is a small community. Small enough, if one wanted, and, if the gods were in one's corner, to come face-to-face with almost any of the locals on the main road. Be it at the library, cinema, tea-room, or café. Some of us younger folk have also been known to bump into each other as we hiked the slopes of Table Mountain. My favourite hike was up Skeleton Gorge. I had noticed his athletic build. Who knows, maybe he liked to hike and also favoured this trail.

Two Saturdays later, as I was leaving the bakery on Main Street, there he was, up ahead and large as life, standing outside the chemist's window. He must have spotted me walking in his direction and was obviously waiting until I came abreast. When I had caught up with him, he grinned from ear to ear and looked directly into my eyes.

"Hello, there! Fancy meeting you here. How are things with you, Eve?"

Struck by the intensity of his gaze, I downplayed the excitement I felt on seeing him again. "Going well, thanks. Hello, to you, too. I see you remembered my name."

"Who could forget the name of a girl as pretty as you?" was his bantering comeback.

"Thanks for the compliment, but I'll have you know I'm not just a pretty face. Tell me, have you used your guitar yet?"

"*Ja*…couldn't wait. It's a beautiful instrument; if you'll let me buy you a cup of tea, I'll tell you all about it."

"Sounds tempting but now is not a good time. I have to get back to the shop. Chop-chop! We are short-staffed this morning, so my boss is on her own. Maybe some other time?"

"Too bad! If you like, I could walk you back to the shop instead."

Encouraged by my answering smile, he relieved me of the baked goods, then skillfully steered me in the direction of the music shop. I was not at all surprised at the ease with which he accomplished it. It felt natural, somehow.

Oh! The touch of his hand resting lightly on my bare skin... Electrifying! I felt an unexpected, warm, tingling sensation along the length of my arm. With the shop being only a stone's throw away, we just had time for small talk. When we came to a halt outside the shop, he spoke the words which lifted my spirits sky-high.

"I'd like to see you again. What do you say to a Coke when you finish work for the day? Failing all else, we could talk about my musical prowess."

Without any hesitation, I heard myself say, "Sounds like a good idea. I prefer root beer or Iron Brew, though. We close at one o'clock...I should be ready about quarter past."

Taking my packages from him, we smiled our good-byes. I stepped into the interior and waved as he passed the window. He waved back and I saw his lips frame the words, "'Til then."

On cloud nine, I made my way to the kitchenette at the back of the shop. I passed Georgina. Not much escaped her eagle eye.

"Eve, your smile is a mile wide. Did something happen that you'd like to share?" she quizzed, good-humouredly.

"You bet! The most incredible thing just happened, and I simply cannot wait for closing time!"

Her eyebrows shot up as if in question.

"Tell you all in a minute."

Skipping all the way to the kitchenette, I deposited my purchases on the small table and made tea for the two of us, my heart singing all the while.

Georgina left her position behind the cash till when she saw me approach with her tea and one of the cream doughnuts I'd bought.

Before she returned to her office, I handed over the tray and filled her in on my meeting with Mike and the date we'd made for this afternoon.

Georgina, my self-proclaimed guardian and mentor during working hours, aimed a few well-chosen words of caution in my direction. Other than that, and because she regarded me as a level-headed youngster, she gave me her blessing.

"Have fun!"

*I* had already phoned Grace to let her know of the latest developments. Having previously told her, at some length, I might add, about this Adonis, Grace was well aware that I had my eye on Mike, and how much I wanted to meet him again. We had even worked on a strategy and plan "B" to make this happen. Her excitement on hearing this latest development nearly matched mine. Notice, I said 'nearly'?

The rush had slowed down just before closing time. While waiting for the few remaining customers to decide on their purchases, my eyes were practically glued to the grandfather clock opposite the cashier's desk. Moving at a snail's pace—or so it seemed that day—its hands made their way to the top of the hour.

At precisely one o'clock, Georgina pointed to the shop window where Mike was waiting outside. She beckoned him in. After I'd introduced them, and knowing my state of mind, Georgina told me to finish up, even though there were still a few customers browsing through the racks and music stands. Not needing a second bidding, I collected my handbag and cardigan and said a hurried good-bye to her. I left with Mike in tow and nary a backward glance.

Mike suggested we catch a train to Kalk Bay and have a late lunch of fish and chips as well as the promised cool drink at his favourite fish shop near the harbour. We found lots to talk about on the train ride. For starters, amongst other things, we spoke of our respective families and hobbies.

The afternoon was far spent by the time we finished our lunch, but there was no talk of parting. We had already learned loads about each other. The subject of our mutual love of music and individual tastes was a given. He touched at length on his progress with the guitar. Next to music, his favourite leisure thing was pottering about in his garden.

We headed for the jetty when we left the fish shop and watched the fishermen unload their catch. The steady slap-slapping sound of the waves against the pier, together with the smell of sea and freshly caught fish, was at once soothing; heady. Those moments with Mike—unforgettable.

The sun was dipping down on the horizon, when, by mutual consent, we hopped on a train, Simonstown bound.

In a small Indian café, overlooking the ocean in Simonstown, we ate samosas and a fiery curry for supper, while watching the sun go down in a glorious blaze of oranges and reds. Day had turned inexorably into night, and we were still talking non-stop and laughing about a host of things.

We were the last to leave the cafe and it seemed the most natural thing to prolong the evening with a stroll along the moonlit beach. The night, tailor-made for the outdoors, was pleasantly warm. The smell of the sea was all around us and the waves of the incoming tide lapped gently at our bare feet—like a caress. Moon and stars shone at full wattage overhead in a navy sky; our surroundings conducive to imparting confidences as well as small talk and funny stories.

We continued our conversation about our childhood and shared some of our dreams and ambitions. Mike was open and had the skill and sensitivity to draw me out. To my surprise, I found myself telling him things I would otherwise steer well clear of on a first date.

There was nothing remotely resembling romance during our first time together. At one point, Mike reached out for my hand to help me over some rocks. Did that count? No, I said to myself. *He was just being courteous.*

Compared to some of my peers, I admit to being a tad inexperienced in the ways of the world. *He* found my unworldliness appealing and refreshing.

As for my looks "You are extremely easy on the eye."

That was how he put it to me. A compliment in no way deterrent—not by any stretch of my imagination—to what I devoutly hoped was a budding friendship!

All modesty aside, good looks *do* run in both sides of my family, and I was a beneficiary. Five-foot-two and shapely, with curly (bane of my life) brown hair that hung past my shoulders, dark brown eyes—big and wide-set—under slightly unruly brows, a come-hither smile (so I've been told), and an average sort of nose, about sums up the picture.

By most people's standards, I'd be described as pretty. Mine too. Not so, when I was with Mike, though. Seen through his eyes, I felt beautiful!

Mike exuded maleness. I was intrigued by this, also his insight into the ways of the world. Well-travelled, he had many anecdotes to share about the inhabitants of obscure places in South Africa and the northern parts of our continent. An interesting chap, outgoing too. All things considered, it added up to an extremely sexy package, in my opinion.

I was somewhat out of my depth at first and in awe of this man-of-the-world who seemed to have everything already going for him. He was the junior partner in a successful landscaping business that his dad's younger brother, David, had started some years back. Both were bachelors.

It was way past the witching hour when we finally reached my home. Before he left, though, Mike made sure that we'd have a second date. I had no objections. None what-so-ever!

As time would attest, this *was* the start of something good.

Mike had a wicked sense of humour and told a good joke. After having known him for a few weeks, if asked what drew me to him, I would have said, "Primarily, it's his 'take charge' attitude, his sense of adventure, and his innate sense of humour. I laughed a lot when he was around. He had a quick wit and even taught me how to laugh at myself. When seen through his eyes, irritating or embarrassing incidents took on another slant."

Like the time when we were at the beach, and I was enjoying a soft drink from a bottle without a straw. We were both was wearing bathing costumes at the time, and I had no pocket to hold a hankie. Somehow, the fizz went up my nose and came pouring straight out again.

There I was, spluttering, sans something with which to wipe my nose and some other parts of me, you know, those parts which jut out. By this time, the stuff was running back into my mouth where it should have gone in the first place, and me, with my face turning all shades of red. Mike, ever resourceful, offered me a corner of his beach towel so that I could mop up.

"Sorry about that, Mike. I just can't get used to drinking from a bottle."

"Don't give it another thought. Just imagine if it had been spaghetti!"

Who could fail to laugh at such pragmatism?

He was mild-mannered, affectionate, and gentle. There was a breadth to his shoulders that made him appear rock solid and able to take on any challenge. When, weeks later, mind, I leaned into his embrace for the first time, it felt as though nothing could harm me as long as he was holding me. With Mike, I felt sheltered; safe.

He was a far cry from the callow young men with whom Grace and I usually hobnobbed. So unlike anyone else I'd dated. He had *such* a way about him, possessed *such* a rakish charm. It drew me…held me captive. To my way of thinking, he was also quite sophisticated with loads of sex appeal; in a class by himself. Some time in the future, I was to find that ladies, in general, were of the same opinion.

I was falling for him in a big way! Fast! He made it extremely easy.

He was thoughtful, bringing me cuttings from his garden which he had rooted, planting them in my little garden—adding to my collection of blue blossoms. Mike was also extremely generous. He rarely came empty-handed when he visited. I've lost count of the many dozens of roses, boxes of chocolates, perfume, and other gifts he had given me.

Grace—who, at times, was also on the receiving end—told me, playfully, I must add, "I think he's perfect. I'm halfway to being in love with him myself."

Not at my best when on the receiving end of favours and gifts, I soon discovered not to let on to him when something caught my eye in a shop window because he'd promptly buy it for me.

When it became obvious that Mike was courting me, I honestly could not believe my good fortune. Me? Eve Emily Hanson? Young for my years, serious by nature, shy, intelligent...I was being wooed by this man who seemed to have everything already going for him.

I welcomed his attentions, found them extremely flattering. Who wouldn't? I ask you with tears in my eyes!

There was no disputing the fact. He was sincere in his desire to win me over. I was somewhat overwhelmed as he stepped up his pursuit of me. Still cautious, though, and not at all ready to hand over my heart at the drop of a hat. Many episodes of rejection to date, coupled with the feeling that this was almost too good to last, plagued me. A carry-over from my childhood that had left its mark.

When we were together, Mike's eyes always held mine with a soft intensity. They did not flicker with boredom, or dart around to check out the surrounding action. When he looked at me, it was the easiest thing for me to believe that, for him, I was truly the most important being in the world.

I saw the best of myself reflected in his eyes. Is it any wonder I was completely bowled over by him...that I had reached the point of no return?

*I*n the months that followed, Mike made me the center of his world. Few people, other than Uncle Jacob and my father in those far-off days of my childhood, had ever paid me this much attention or made me feel more valued as a person.

The stars were out in all their splendour on the night Mike used the magical, four-letter word, and made it clear just how serious his intentions were.

I was euphoric! I capitulated!

There was no way now that I could, or even wanted to, deny the fact that I loved him too, and was totally captivated. I did not have to put it into words. He knew.

"Because it's written all over your face!" was how he put it.

I said it anyway. With feeling. "I love you too, Mike!"

One could say my life was transformed when we became a couple. Mike was different, then. Then, as in the first few years of our marriage, he was relaxed and happy to be with me. It showed. In the way his mouth curved upward, and his eyes crinkled when he smiled at me. In the way his arms protectively encircled my body; his eagerness to be with me and open up worlds hitherto unknown to me.

Back then, it did not take much to make Mike smile or laugh in joyous abandon. His, a most infectious laugh. These, just a few of my favourite things, set Mike in a class by himself and endeared him to me more and more. As the weeks went by, I found myself waiting impatiently for the moments when we'd be together; when I could share my thoughts and feelings with him, hear him voice his opinions on world events, the latest movie, not to mention John McEnroe's latest tirade on the Wimbledon tennis courts.

Now, not only was Mike my Prince Charming, he put me front and center in all things—unwavering. In doing so, he was steadily filling the gaping void left when my father disappeared all those years ago.

Having this relationship with Mike was reminiscent of the times when I used to figure prominently in my father's world. I now figured even more so in Mike's. I'd regained that all-important element that had been missing from my life since I lost touch with my dad.

Auntie Miriam stopped by one evening to bring us some groceries and her homemade *Melktert*. She was not slow to notice the aura (*she*, named it so) which surrounded me. Always forthright, she came straight to the point while were unpacking the groceries.

"My child, you look positively radiant! Can it be you're in love?"

There was no use in denying the obvious. I expected a barrage of questions and was not disappointed. Under cover of stocking the cupboards, I tried to hide my flushed face.

"Auntie Miriam, I feel I could burst with happiness! I'm going out with a dreamboat of a man, and you simply have to meet him. He is charming, and affectionate, and kind, and funny, and generous."

"Well, I certainly look forward to meeting him. Soon. By the way, I notice you say man, not boy. Does he have a name? How old is he, this paragon of virtues?"

"Mike Moore. Twenty-five, or thereabouts."

"We'll have to have him over because you know your uncle Jacob will want to have the 'talk' with him and lay down some ground rules. I'm sure your mom would also like to meet him, so I'll invite her as well…make it a family affair! What do you think?"

"Sounds like a plan, Auntie. I'll find out when Mike's free and let you know. Okay?"

"Fine. I'll hold off on the arrangements until we can set the date. Meantime, I'll prepare Uncle Jacob for the fact that he's lost his place as your number one heartthrob.

"If this chap is as wonderful as you say, then I'm delighted for you, my girl. Uncle Jacob and I want only the best for you. You know that don't you?"

Between us, we arranged the visit for the following Saturday afternoon. I was nervous—as nervous as a mouse in a cat house—when I took Mike to meet 'the family' a week later. Understandably so. Mike, however, saved the day with his easy charm. My mother fell for him like the proverbial ton of bricks. On the spot! Auntie Miriam was a tad more realistic. She wanted time to make up her mind, be sure I was not being carried away—in love with the idea of being in love, so to speak.

Uncle Jacob found Mike extremely likable. Both men were well-travelled and could swap anecdotes of the various places they'd visited. Mike impressed him favourably on other counts as well. Uncle Jacob was a keen gardener and felt only respect for any man who earned his living by working with the soil.

It didn't hurt Mike's cause when he promised to bring some dahlia bulbs which Uncle Jacob had long coveted. He told me afterwards that Mike had a lot going for him as a person. I could tell he thought Mike and I would be a good fit.

Auntie Miriam did herself proud with the meal. Mike was not the only one to rave about her culinary skills.

The afternoon was a great success by anyone's standards. Mike was told, "Don't be a stranger." He was promptly invited to join us on Christmas day. Once he'd fulfilled his obligations to his own family, of course. He accepted the invite with alacrity.

The days leading up to Christmas were heady, to say the least. Grace and I did our annual, 'window shopping' tour of department stores. Stuttafords, Garlicks, and even one or two jewellers in Cape Town were high on our list. Our oohs and ahs were spontaneous when we looked at the beautiful merchandise which was so invitingly displayed. The Christmas decorations in all the shop windows on Adderley Street adding to the festive atmosphere.

What would I buy for Mike? There was so much from which to choose. I tossed out one idea after another: 'not quite his taste', or 'he already has one of those', and so on.

Dear Reader, I was now shopping for a man who has excellent taste. Finding just the right gift would be a challenge. One which I was determined to best, and, in the process, have loads of fun.

The last time I had looked forward to Christmas Day with this much excitement and anticipation, was when I was a child and on the receiving end of the gifts.

I eventually found a book at CNA titled *Creative Guitar*. It had a wealth of information about the history of the guitar, the various types of guitars, and information about things like chords, and tuning, and temperament. I further thought it would appeal to Mike because it also had a section that gave instructions on song writing.

Maybe he'd be inspired to write me the love song at which he'd been hinting. I added a set of three initialed handkerchiefs for good measure. When all is said and done, one can't go wrong with a set of hankies!

*T*o help Auntie Miriam with the preparations for Christmas Day, Grace and I had gone to her parents' home on Christmas Eve. Uncle Jacob was also expecting us to lend a hand with trimming the tree. My favourite task was setting the table in readiness for dinner the next day.

Auntie Miriam's trousseau had included a beautiful tablecloth that her grandmother had crocheted. This was always used at Christmas time and other such special occasions—lovingly laundered and packed away in tissue paper after each use—along with the fine china and cutlery, which she had also inherited from her grandmother. These would automatically be handed down to Grace.

I loved handling the beautifully-patterned plates and serving dishes. In these moments, I will admit to envying Grace. With both my grand-mothers having already gone into eternity, there had been no such heirlooms handed down to me.

Christmas Day dawned bright and beautiful. Grace and her family had been to Midnight Mass. After breakfast, each of us opened one gift. I went to church on my own, where I was to meet my mother. She and I would make our way back to the Solomons' home in ample time for dinner.

Including their other relatives and friends, we numbered sixteen at the dinner table. Dinner was most definitely something to write home about, and, when the votes were in, Auntie Miriam's trifle was voted second to none. Unanimous and loud!

Happy chaos reigned for a while after the sumptuous, traditional Christmas meal. There was much laughter and squeals of delight, as, one by one, the gifts under the tree were handed out. Each "thank you" and "ooh" and "ah" was accompanied by a hug and a kiss.

As in years gone by, some would have earmarked a favourite spot for a revivifying catnap, re-joining the group in time for afternoon tea. In the meantime, Auntie Miriam, along with her trusty helpers, tidied the kitchen. No sooner had it been done, when it was time to set out the tea things and the cakes, tarts, scones, and biscuits over which she had, days earlier, laboured lovingly.

After tea, anyone with even the slightest musical talent, old or young, would have a turn to perform and there would then be lusty singing of Christmas carols around the piano. Tales of Christmases past would be re-told whilst we pored over numerous photo albums. The festive atmosphere had been known to last well into the night. Some even stayed over.

*This family had a wealth of love to share. Could I be blamed for feeling blessed and privileged to be part of their inner circle?*

Mike arrived while we were having tea and in good time for the sing-along.

True to their thoughtful nature, Auntie Miriam and Grace had bought a couple of gifts for Mike. He reciprocated with chocolates and flowers from his garden for Auntie Miriam, a book on raising dahlias for Uncle Jacob, and a pretty scarf for Grace in her favourite colours—one that I had hand-picked.

I was impatient to hand over the gift I'd chosen for him and led him to a quiet spot for our gift exchange. To say he was touched and tickled pink when he opened my gift would be quite an understatement. I watched while he leafed eagerly through its pages.

Taking me in his arms, he said, "Thanks a lot, Eve. What a thoughtful gift." He jokingly added, "Just know, it will be on your head if I ditch my job and decide to turn pro."

When I, in turn, opened his gift to me, I was lost for words, overcome by what I saw. In a jeweller's box, nestled in a layer of white velvet, lay the most exquisite jewelry I had ever owned: a deep red garnet—my birthstone—beautifully cut, set in white gold, with a fine silver chain and earrings to match.

Mike slipped the chain around my neck and secured the catch. With trembling fingers, I put on the matching earrings. I couldn't wait to show off my exquisite present to the others.

"Thank you, Mike. I love it. I must surely be one of the luckiest girls alive," I whispered in his ear. We held each other tight for a long minute.

"I'm the lucky one, Eve! Make no mistake about that! Oh! By the way, my uncle Dave had Christmas dinner with us. I whispered that I had a date with 'my girl' for afternoon tea. I should have known better because he really set the cat among the pigeons when he teasingly said, "Well, now, Mike, old boy, it's not fair to keep this young woman to yourself. You should bring her here afterwards—introduce her to the family, and, at the same time, she can have a taste of your sister's fridge tart and Christmas pudding. So, if Eve has serious designs on you, she'll have a good idea of what she's up against in the cooking department!"

"As a result, I had to answer a wagonload of questions, and, to cut a long story short, my parents and my sister Iris insist we come around later, sometime this evening. How about it?"

"Sure, Mike. I *would* like to meet your family. In fact, I think this is the perfect time! There's so much going on here, I doubt we'll be missed if we slip away in a little bit. I should give Auntie Miriam the heads up, though…Oh! Dear…I promised I'd arrange a lift home for my mother when she's ready to call it a day. I'd better ask Grace if she will oblige."

Grace egged me on when I told her I had been invited to meet Mike's parents and agreed to see that my mother had a ride home. When I told Auntie Miriam about the impending visit to Mike's family, she insisted I not go empty-handed. Before Mike and I took our leave, she handed me one of her delicious date loaves, festively wrapped and beribboned, to take along.

"I don't want you to go there empty-handed, Sweetie," she said with a knowing wink.

Never at my best when meeting strangers for the time, I was a bundle of nerves all the way there, despite Mike's assurances that all would be well.

The ride to his parents' home in Greenhaven seemed to take forever. He has his own key, but, before we reached their front door, his mother was at the ready to let us in. She greeted me with a smile, then turned to Mike, her arms flung wide to embrace him. I noticed there was not much difference in their height and that he bore a striking resemblance to his mother—even to the shape and colour of her eyes. Her face was softer, though, and her hair, worn under a scarf, showed some grey strands.

We moved forward into a large, comfortably-furnished room where Mike's dad, Mike's sister Iris, and their uncle Dave were waiting to greet us.

Mike made the introductions. There were handshakes all round and "Merry Christmas" on everyone's lips. The age-old greeting served to break the ice. Still, meeting Mike's family for the first time was daunting. I held onto the date loaf as though it were ballast.

I could tell Iris was pleased to meet me and wanted to put me at ease. She stepped forward to shake my hand and to relieve me of the date loaf. I liked *her* on sight.

"What have we here?" She asked as she motioned to the parcel I was still holding.

"I hope your family likes date loaf, Iris," I said, handing it over. "This one was made by my good friend who is a champion baker, and, speaking of baking, Mike raves about *your* skill in that department."

"Why am I not surprised? He always does…I hope you won't be disappointed," she said, with a loving glance in her brother's direction, as she led me to a seat on a well-upholstered couch.

Seating herself beside me, she said, "Our family loves all things made with dates. Please thank your friend for the gift. I'm sure we'll enjoy it to the last crumb."

Meanwhile, Mike's mother took him aside. With an arm possessively around him, she held him captive while speaking in earnest to him. Uncle Dave, wanting to break up the tete-a-tete, jokingly called out to him, "Hey,

Mike, where are your manners? Offer Eve some punch and let's make a toast!" The ensuing back-and-forth banter took the edge off my nervousness.

As was the custom during the Christmas season, a table, set against one wall, was laden with all kinds of goodies. The ubiquitous trifle and Christmas fruit cake had pride of place, but I had a hard time choosing from the many pastries, biscuits, *konfyt,* and other delicious eats.

Their uncle seemed open to the opinion of others, and I found him easy to talk to. A younger version of Mike's father—the resemblance, without the spectacles, was striking—he wore a short-sleeved shirt which showed off his muscular brown arms. I put this down to the work he did outside in his landscaping business.

Mike's dad is of stocky build and sports a toothbrush moustache. Even though he is already quite bald, he is still a handsome man. His deep-set eyes, behind black-framed spectacles, are brown. Like coffee. Soft-spoken and not as voluble as the rest, he did not have much to say to me during my stay but smiled at me a couple of times, though.

As the evening wore on, I could not help but notice how everyone deferred to Mike's mother. She appeared to have strong opinions on everything. I would not be the least bit surprised to learn that she always got her way.

Mike's instincts served him well. His parents and his sister were friendly and hospitable. Uncle Dave was the life and soul of the party, and Iris's desserts were certainly deserving of all Mike's praise. I do believe the Christmas spirit added to the overall good cheer. My heart was lighter when we left.

*T*he old year was all but spent, and the excitement of Christmas day celebrations was history now. However, Grace and I would not have long to wait for the next occasion to make merry.

New Year's Eve was just around the corner. So too, my birthday. Two excellent reasons to celebrate. As this would be the first party the two of us had ever hosted, we decided to make it one which would go down in history! Grace, more than I, had kept in touch with the pre-Mike crowd, and she had invited them to our flat to ring in the New Year with us. Naturally, Mike was included.

A 'theme' party? We dithered. Should it be Indian or Hawaiian?

After much deliberation, we decided on an Indian affair. The girls were told to wear saris with lots of bangles and earrings, and the guys were to beg or borrow their outfits from their Indian friends. They were also asked to borrow a couple of Indian records to set the tone for the evening.

There was shopping to be done, phone calls to make. We had our work cut out and not much time in which to do it all. Mike offered to lend a hand, so Grace put him in charge of hanging colourful paper streamers, blowing up balloons, as well as choosing some party games. She also dubbed him Emcee and D J. for the evening. He was in his element and took to his tasks as though to the manner born.

Planning what food and drinks to serve was a challenge because there were so many delicious Indian dishes from which to choose. Grace said she would ask her mom to make some shrimp *breyani* and a pot of mutton curry. Our shopping list would include *rotis, samoosas, slangetjies,* and spicy mango chutney. These items would be ordered in advance from our favourite Indian restaurant.

Bowls of potato crisps and plates of savouries would round off our list of eats. Mike would contribute some chocolates and some peanuts with raisins, and he also gave us a killer punch recipe—one his family served whenever they had a *braai* during the summer.

We would also provide Pepsi, Stoney Ginger Beer, and my all-time favourite, root beer. Those, with a glass of champagne each to toast the New Year, would just about cover our drinks list. Luckily, our friends were on the quiet side and definitely not into the hard stuff.

I say "luckily" because Grace's parents would hit the roof were they to learn that our party—our first party, to boot—had ended up being of the 'raucous' kind! We also had our landlord to consider.

When all was said and done, our party was a huge success. Wearing traditional Indian finery, the girls provided the glamour, and the guys were a sight to behold in their borrowed plumes! Having the Indian music playing in the background was nothing short of inspired.

Auntie Miriam certainly came through for us. There was nary a rice kernel leftover from the *breyani,* nor a crumb of the *roti,* nor even the tiniest spoonful of the mutton curry as we rounded off our meal with the *koeksisters* the girls had contributed.

To show their appreciation, the gang kindly insisted on helping us with the clean-up. Such a nice bunch! So, with their help, our flat was beautifully tidy as we rang in the New Year together.

The next morning would see us up and out, bright and early to spend a day at the beach. Picnic style. A well-known, New Year's Day tradition! The Solomon family, like so many others in the Cape Flats, kept up this tradition each year.

We relied on Grace's dad to load their Kombi with all kinds of scrumptious eats and treats which her mom had packed, plus an assortment of rugs and cushions. Auntie Miriam liked her comfort! Beach umbrellas were a must because he knew neither Grace nor I enjoyed getting sunburned. We would definitely need protection in some measure from the rays of the scorching, summer sun.

Even though we'd had a late night with the old crowd, Grace and I were bright-eyed and bushy-tailed on New Year's morning. Mike picked us up and drove us to the beach where we would join Grace's parents.

We prayed fervently for the South Easter to lay low that day. No one enjoys even the odd grain of sand along with their chicken leg or hard-boiled egg!

Our timing was perfect because we arrived before the crowds descended on the beach and managed to stake our claim to a reasonably secluded spot.

Lazing away the day, frolicking in the waves to cool down from time to time, and stuffing ourselves with Auntie Miriam's picnic delights was the order of the day. More than content in each other's company, we laughed with abandon at Uncle Jacob's seemingly endless collection of van der Merwe jokes.

The gods smiled on us and the wind lay low. At day's end, we were sated with sun and surf and all kinds of goodies. A delightful day from every aspect ended too soon for our liking, but we packed up our belongings and headed home as the sun was setting on the horizon in a blaze of reds and golds.

*M*y birthday falls in the first week of January. Lucky me, our company gives each staff member the day off on their birthday. Mike wanted to spend the day with me, so he arranged to have the day off from work. When Mike told his uncle why he wanted the day off, his uncle gave him his unqualified blessing.

"What would you like to do on your birthday?"

I opted for a day at Kirstenbosch Gardens, knowing he and I would both enjoy being surrounded by nature. *Little did I know Mike would be proposing at the end of the day.*

Mike beamed from ear to ear. "That's a *lekker* idea. Let's do it!"

Dressed casually in blue jeans, a short-sleeved glad-neck shirt, and looking oh-so-sexy, he arrived at the flat shortly after nine o'clock on the morning of my birthday. He stood on my doorstep armed with the most exquisite red roses in a deep blue vase—blue, being my favourite colour. I buried my nose in the flowers to inhale their heady bouquet before taking the vase from him, but, before I could thank him, he burst into his rendition of the birthday song.

"Happy birthday to you, happy birthday to you, happy birthday to you, Eve…happy birthday to you!"

Our gazes locked. I went weak in my knees, listening to Mike's lovely voice. His accompanying embrace sent my pulse into high gear.

"Thanks a bunch, Mike…what lovely roses. I love their fragrance. It almost takes my breath away. I bet they are from your garden!"

"Yes, Ma'am! Lovely flowers for a lovely young lady. Let me introduce you to Mr. Lincoln, Eve…he's top favourite of all the roses in my garden."

"Thanks again, Mike. You and Mr. Lincoln have made my day!" I placed my vase of roses where it could best be seen and rewarded Mike for his thoughtfulness with a hug and a lingering kiss on his lips.

Earlier, I had packed a few of the snacks we both liked, as well as a flask of Rooibos tea in a knapsack. Handing it to Mike, then, with my handbag and sunhat in hand, sunglasses perched on my nose, we locked up and set off in his Morris Minor station wagon. It being a Thursday meant it was a workday for most, and, therefore, not much traffic on the roads at this time of day.

January is a beautiful month in the Western Cape; sunny, but sometimes too hot for my comfort. Today, the sun was hot; high in the sky. A welcome breeze swirled around us as we rolled down all the windows.

We arrived at Kirstenbosch in record time, there to be met with a breathtaking view of Table Mountain and the diverse Cape flora and fauna. Luckily, Mike found a shady tree under which he could park the van. With the knapsack safely slung on his back, we set off to discover the wonders which nature, in all her glory, had to offer.

Mike was in his element as we strolled, hand in hand, along the many winding paths, the air redolent with the fragrances of the many species in full bloom. The colours around us showcasing all the hues of a rainbow. What stood out for me were the tall stands of white delphinium and beautiful shades of blue. There were also palettes of pink and of mauve.

Kirstenbosch, a veritable paradise of plant life. There is so much to see. We oohed and aahed in the presence of a massive baobab tree.

The Sculpture Garden is a truly fascinating place. It houses Mambo stone sculptures in a beautiful garden setting. It's been said, the artists believe the stones have a spirit and life of their own.

The Water-wise Garden was of particular interest to Mike, so it followed we would spend a long time there. Mike was mightily impressed because it demonstrated how to create a garden that needs far less water and maintenance. He had high hopes of implementing some of the ideas in their business.

Mike's keen interest in all around him spurred him on to catch sight of what lay beyond the next bend in each path. He was considerate, though, and frequently asked after my welfare.

"How are you holding up—not too hot? Would you like to stop for a drink? It's your birthday Eve, so you're calling the shots," and so on.

"Not to worry. I'm happy to be doing this," was my answer to all his questions. Being out in the sun for long periods was not my cup of tea. Mike knew this. However, the shady spots were easy to find and we made the most of them. It was well after one o'clock when he suggested we go along the Fynbos Walk and stop for a break immediately afterwards.

"Are you up for it?"

"Sure. Then, after our lunch I'd like to wander through the Fragrance Garden, okay?"

Soon after, we found a bench under a shady willow tree and thoroughly enjoyed a leisurely lunch with a couple of stolen kisses slipped in for good measure. Magnificent Table Mountain, in all its grandeur, presiding over it all. There wasn't a single cloud in sight to mar its perfection—not even a fragment of the 'tablecloth' to be seen today.

The Fragrance Garden lived up to its name, teeming with fragrant flowers and aromatic leaves. We came across plants with familiar and not-so-familiar features, some with interesting textures and scents. This is one of the few gardens where visitors are invited to touch the leaves. Here, the plants are grown in raised beds, bringing them within easy reach for passersby to touch, feel, and smell. Mike was a fount of information on a lot of the plant life growing there. He shared what he knew with me.

So sexy!

Strolling hand in hand through this beautiful place was magical, even romantic! I felt close to Mike and, from the way he looked into my eyes, I knew the feeling was reciprocated. It was like our mutual love of nature was putting a special seal on our relationship.

Mike fairly oozed an air of pent-up excitement. I had sensed it at odd times throughout the day. When questioned, he just shrugged it off as though he had no idea what I could be talking about. At first, I thought I had been mistaken, but, as the day wore on, the impression lingered. It hung in the air—as though one could slice it with a knife.

Even though we'd covered much more ground than I had anticipated when I suggested this outing, I sensed a reluctance in Mike to call it a day. He was in his element in this botanical wonderland. So, under the watch of Table Mountain, we kept on walking. With no destination in mind, we followed the paths to wherever they might lead.

As luck would have it, we eventually found ourselves within sight of the restaurant. Since it was well after four o'clock by this time, taking a break to enjoy a cup of our favourite Rooibos seemed the right thing to do.

Having had our fill of tea and *koeksisters,* we both agreed it had been a day well spent, but, sadly, it was time to take our leave.

Little did I know, there would be more wonderful things in store. On our way to the parking lot, Mike told me he needed to stop in at his house.

"I would like your advice about a bookcase my uncle wanted to get rid of."

"How can I help?"

"I'll show you when we get there."

On the drive to his house, we both agreed it had been a lovely way to spend the day and voiced our opinions about our most memorable moments. Mine, without question, were the flower beds where the regal delphinium held sway. These striking wonders grew there in abundance…just too memorable for words.

While Mike agreed the flowers were exceptional, his most memorable moments, however, were those spent in the Water-wise Garden. Why was I not surprised?

It was late afternoon before we were finally ready to put an end to the day. Still, we lingered on our way out, reluctant to shake off the dust of this beautiful place.

*T*he sun had already dipped behind Table Mountain and a lavender twilight had extinguished the last light of day by the time we reached his house. Our drive to Mike's home in Diep River had been in bumper-to-bumper traffic.

After he'd let us into the house, we made our way to the kitchen. There, he unlocked the door which opened onto his back *stoep*. Reaching for my hand, he led me outside to where an old, wooden table he was restoring took pride of place. A few fold-up lawn chairs and a canvas garden swing provided the seating. With his arm encircling my waist, we looked at his garden by the light of the moon and stars.

"Mm mmm…the honeysuckle sure smells lovely," I said, as I set my bag and hat down on a nearby chair.

"*Ja.* It sure does, hey! Take a seat…make yourself at home, Eve," Mike said, waving me in the direction of the seating arrangement.

"When do I see the bookcase?"

"Later," came his smiling response as returned to the kitchen.

The early evening air was pleasantly warm as I made myself comfortable on the swing and listened to the crickets as they chirped their song in the background. The light streaming out from the un-curtained kitchen windows, and the light from the moon and stars, amply illuminated the backyard, allowing me to feast my eyes on the garden now bearing Mike's stamp. I had no idea what it might have looked like when Mike's grandparents had tended it. Now, it was a delight to see and smell.

When the kitchen door opened a short while later, I was surprised to see Mike bearing a tray with an unopened bottle of champagne and two flutes —beads of moisture trickled ever so slowly down its sides. Those drops glistened like early morning dew drops on a nasturtium leaf.

He placed the tray on the table but, before I could comment, retraced his steps and, in a heartbeat, reappeared with another tray. This time, bearing some savoury snacks and a box of Cadbury's Milk Tray chocolates which he also placed on the table.

Taking me by the hand, he silently led me along a path in the garden to a sweet-smelling rose bush. Its fragrance, not unlike the roses he had given me earlier. This bush, however, sported creamy, white buds instead of red.

"Choose one," he invited.

When I pointed to my choice, he promptly picked it and handed it to me. Looking deep into my eyes he said, "For the girl with the most amazing eyes I have ever seen."

"This day just keeps getting better! Thanks for the compliment, Mike, and the gorgeous rose. "What's up?" I asked as I hugged him to underline my appreciation.

"You'll see…'Patience is a virtue', remember?"

With those words, a wink, and his arm around me, he steered me back to the table. I looked on while he deftly opened the bottle and poured champagne into the two glasses. He then picked up the chocolate box, opened it and held it out to me.

"Would the young lady care to sample one of these?" His smile was mischievous.

I peeked into the open box, expecting to find only the Cadbury's assorted chocolates. Instead, I immediately caught sight of a ring so beautiful, it leapt out at me. Took my breath away. It lay in the hollow which had formerly housed a chocolate-covered Brazil nut.

Three garnets. They matched the ones on the necklace and earrings Mike had given me at Christmas. Set also in white gold, they were separated by two diamond baguettes. I stared at it for a long minute, feeling my jaw drop in total surprise, while my brain registered delight.

Mike removed the ring from the chocolate box and held it out for me to take a closer look.

"It's a beaut, Mike…I love it!" I barely heard myself say the words because I was choked up with emotion and unable, for a long moment, to take my eyes off the ring.

"This is music to my ears, Eve. I was hoping you'd be pleased. Allow me," with his eyes glued to mine, Mike reached for my left hand and slipped the ring onto my finger. Swept up in the significance and the unbridled excitement of the moment, I felt the tears welling up in my eyes. They fell. Mike saw them and tenderly brushed them away.

"Eve, the best thing that's happened to me is falling in love with you. You've grown on me, and I know you're the only one I want to share the rest of my life with. Please, say you'll marry me!"

The last thing I had expected today was a marriage proposal. I was thrilled! Elated! The smile on my face grew and grew until I felt it must be more than a mile wide!

"Yes! Yes! Yes! Was there ever any doubt?"

As I said this, Mike's arms encircled my waist. Holding me in a tight embrace he whispered, "I love you. You've made me a happy man, Eve."

"I love you, Mike."

"Let's not wait too long, hey?" He handed me a glass of champagne, picked up the other and raised his glass. "To us!" We sealed our pact with a lingering kiss.

"To us!" I echoed when our lips finally un-locked.

I believed him when he said I made his life complete; that I brought out the best in him; that he wanted to spend the rest of his life with me. He promised that ours would be a good life. I believed him with all my heart!

*Dear Reader, I ask you, "Would you fault me for placing my trust in this man?"*

We snuggled up on the swing and planned our future together by the light of the moon, while we munched on the chocolates and snacks which Mike had so thoughtfully provided. All the while, our favourite music played on in the background.

Later, Mike fired up the *braai* and served his version of *boerewors* on a bun. We toasted our future once again with another round of champagne. To top it all, Mike serenaded me with a couple of songs on his guitar. It was without any doubt, the happiest and most romantic time in my life—coming down to earth was the furthest thing on my mind!

It had been a day to beat any other I had ever experienced in all my twenty-two years. When Mike eventually took me home, I was reluctant to say goodnight. He shared my sentiments.

He held me close as he said, "Never fear, we'll have other days just as happy."

Grace opened the door just as I was about to put my key in the lock. Knowing I would be sharing my news with her made me less wretched to see him go.

In weal and woe, she and I always acted as a sounding board and support system for the other. I could not wait to show her my beautiful ring and share with her the excitement of what promised to be (at Mike's insistence) a whirlwind courtship.

"Did I hear right? Mike proposed? What did you say?"

"Yes, you heard right, Grace, and, to answer your last question, I said no!" This said with as close to a poker face as I could muster.

"But I thought…" she said, looking at me in disbelief. "I thought you *wanted* to marry him. Did something happen to change your mind?"

Unable to contain my excitement a moment longer, I held out my left hand for her to admire my ring, as I said, "Only joking, silly! Of course, I said YES! Get this! Mike wants us to get married soon. Gracie, I'm so happy; I think I'm going to cry."

I *did* cry and so did Grace. She was excited and happy for me and raved over my gorgeous ring. I knew she would—be happy for me and rave over my ring, I mean. She and Mike got on well together. This pleased me no end. It would have been unbearable if it were not so.

"Hmmm…Come to think of it, I'd like to hold out for a September wedding…what do you say?"

"Hey, Eve, you're 'preaching to the choir'. I say go for it! You know, spring has always been my favourite time for a wedding!"

"We're planning on going to your parents' house to-morrow to break the news and show off my ring. I hope you don't have anything on because you have to go with us, okay? Do you think your folks will mind if we include my mother? Kinda kill two birds with one stone, right?

"Come to think of it, I've used that expression a lot and just now realize it's not at all animal friendly."

"Do I ever agree! It really is an awful saying when you come to think of it. About your mom, though, you *know* you don't have to ask; your mom will always be welcome at my parents' place. Plus, announcing your engagement is huge, my girl! Your mom simply *must* be there!"

Mike's idea of a whirlwind courtship would be jettisoned, however. The next day, when he told Uncle Dave about our engagement and our plans to marry soon, those plans were laid well and truly to rest. In short order.

"First, let me congratulate you, Mike! She's a nice girl and I'm delighted for you both." Then, taking a deep breath, he rested a hand on Mike's shoulder. "As it happens, my boy, I have some pretty darn exciting news myself, but something tells me you're not going to be so happy when you hear what I have to say.

"You see, a great opportunity has just presented itself…landscaping jobs…out of the blue! In Canada, of all places. There's this guy, Sheldon Schwartz, a hotel magnate from Canada whom I met a few years back. Remember that landscaping job we did on the Milnerton golf course? Well, he was impressed with the work we did and sought me out at the time.

"So, to cut a long story short, when he went back home, we kept in touch off and on. He's back now, visiting family in Tamboerskloof. He phoned last night, and, like I said, he wants us to do some landscaping at his hotels in Canada.

"This is an opportunity of a lifetime, Mike…the work would last about five months. I've given the matter a lot of thought and I think you should oversee the project. If all goes well, you'll leave end of April and, if nothing gums up the works, be back by September."

"What? Uncle Dave, you're not serious, man!" Mike, having slowly and with great care, set down the cup of hot tea he was holding, went on to say, "This means I'll only have three months before I have to leave! Here I was, hoping Eve would like the idea of a June wedding. Man…this really throws a spanner in the works!"

"I know! I know! Of all times for this to happen…you see, his newest hotel in Vancouver, British Columbia, is nearly finished and he wants us to start work there in April. Plus, he and his wife Laura own a house there, which also needs some landscaping.

"Hopefully, come April, they'll have a decent spring. He says their summers are between June and August, with maybe some warm days in September. He needs us to make the most of this time. This guy also owns hotels in Ontario and wants the landscaping to be revamped on a couple of those as well. So you see, old chap, the timing is lousy, but we can't afford to turn down this opportunity. I'm depending on you to take charge!

"Sheldon has even promised to fix all the paperwork—work permits etc., as much as possible, from his end. What could I say, except commit to taking on the work? Plus, look at it from this point, it will be a feather in our cap, man. Remember, he knows people over here too. More than likely, he could put in a good word for us with local companies; you know, throw other jobs our way! I have to think long-term when it comes to the business, you know.

"So, think about it. Okay? Talk it over with Eve. She seems like she has her head screwed on right. I reckon, between the two of you, you'll come up with the right answer. What do you say?"

"Don't get me wrong, Uncle Dave, I can see it's a fantastic opportunity, but the timing, like you say, sure as hell is lousy! I'll talk to Eve this evening. Though how I'll find the words to break it to her, sure as heck floors me!"

"Before I forget, Sheldon told me you'll have a vehicle at your disposal over there. He reminded me to make sure you get your International Driver's Permit."

Later that evening, Mike stopped by to tell me about the job offer in Canada. His disappointment at this turn of events was unmistakable.

Leaning against the kitchen counter, he drew me into his arms while he relayed a blow-by-blow account of his conversation with his uncle.

"I had planned to twist your arm into having a June wedding, Eve. Now, by all accounts, we'll probably have to wait until October to tie the knot. I hate like hell that this has come up now. God knows, I see no way out."

"I'm all for a short engagement, Mike, but a wedding in June? This seems a bit soon. Hey, it rhymes! Did you hear that? *A wedding in June? This seems a bit soon!* I'm a poet and didn't know it! Anyway, it often rains in June, so, maybe the timing is all for the best, right? Tell me, how did you leave it with your uncle?"

"I said I would think about it and discuss it with you before making a decision. Come to think of it, you bring a good point about the weather, though. Are you sure you are okay with this development?"

"Well…I would have to say," nodding in agreement, "this is a fantastic opportunity all-round, no matter how you slice it! If push comes to shove, I'm in sync with the timing, but I'm not crazy about the long separation. Life won't be the same with you being thousands of miles away from sunny South Africa!"

He stroked my face with a featherlight touch. "Believe me," he said, "This is no little fling, Eve. We both know this to be true. What we feel for each other is real and we will work to make it last. Right? I'll miss you like 'sliced bread'. I don't particularly want to delay our wedding or miss out on the excitement of planning it all with you, but there's no getting away from the fact, this is a fantastic opportunity for Uncle Dave and for our future— yours and mine.

"I have to go, Eve. I know it's the right thing to do. I owe it to my uncle. Besides, distance is relative. We'll speak on the phone, exchange letters and photos. Okay, Sweetheart?"

Mike's words were comforting and sounded so sincere, I could not help but believe every word he said. So much so, I felt I could take everything he'd said to the bank.

"You better believe it. We will make it work. Here's a thought, Mike, while you are gone, I can get the ball rolling and still run things by you. It won't be the same as having you here, but I can keep you in the loop, and you can give me your opinion as things take shape. How's that for a plan?"

Grace, naturally, was the first person I turned to after Mike had gone home. I knew his emotions were conflicted and I had swallowed hard to hide the extent of my disappointment during his visit; but now I sobbed like a child on her shoulder, while unburdening myself.

Grace held me tight as tight could be. "The thing is, Evie, time might not hang all that heavy on your hands, you know. You'll miss him for sure, but you will have your upcoming wedding arrangements to focus on while he is away. You'll have long conversations on the phone, whispering sweet nothings and exchanging love letters. How romantic!" With those sage words, she consoled me.

Have I mentioned the fact that Mike is wildly attractive and could charm birds off trees? Having a long-distance relationship was new to me; I honestly did not know how I would cope with this separation. I would find the time apart quite unbearable. I knew this without a shadow of doubt.

Hardly a day had gone by since our first date that Mike and I had not spent together. Five months apart seemed unthinkable at this point and, as I've learned from all too many experiences in the past, life doesn't come with a guarantee.

So, despite everything both Mike and Grace had said, an annoying voice in my head insisted on making itself heard, *Will Mike change while he is gone? What if he does? Will you be able to tell? What if you change?*

*T*he hoopla over Christmas, New Year celebrations, and my birthday was history now. I was back at work, when, a few days later, Mike called with more news. Good stuff, by the excitement I could hear in his voice.

"Hey, Eve, I told Iris I had popped the question."

"You did? What did she say?"

"Naturally, my news threw her for a loop. After all, we've only known each other for a few months. She is all for throwing us an engagement party at my parents' house. She suggested you come for supper so that you can work things out together. Only if you agree, of course."

"I don't mind. As a matter of fact, I think it's terribly sweet of your sister to offer to give the engagement party. When will we meet?"

Well, seeing we had nothing planned for tonight, I figured, the sooner the better. We'll have a *braai*—I'll have you know my dad's a *Braai-master*. Afterwards, you and Iris can hash out the arrangements for the party. How about it?"

"Sounds like a good plan to me."

"*That's* my girl! I'll let Iris know."

"I hope your family accepts me, Mike."

"They said they liked you when we went there on Christmas evening. I told you they would, didn't I? So, not to worry, Eve. We'll meet by our spot after work?"

"I'll be waiting. Sure as God made little green apples, future Husband. Now, about the other thing...you know Mike, you say your family liked me. I was just your latest girlfriend then, That, my friend, is a far cry from their accepting me as the person you plan to marry, you know. So, while we're there, just stay close, okay?"

"Not to worry. I won't let you out of my sight, soon-to-be Mrs. Moore. By the way, Uncle Dave invited himself when I told him about my sister's plan for tonight. I know he approves. He thinks we'll make a good match, so he is happy for us.

"To quote him, 'I can't wait to congratulate the future Mrs. Mike Moore'. I've asked him and Iris not to mention our engagement to my mom and dad. I'd like the two of us to be together when we break the news to them. He's also going to tell my folks about the job offer in Canada."

Dear Mike, I could tell he was trying his level best to be reassuring. Still, having this meeting with his parents sprung on me at a moment's notice, so to speak, was most unnerving. I quailed at the mere thought of the upcoming meeting with my future in-laws.

Ask any bride-to-be who has met her fiancé's family only once. Chances are, she'll be like-minded.

The hands on my watch seemed to move at a snail's pace for the rest of the day. On the one hand, time could not pass slowly enough to suit me and on the other hand, I wished I could speed up time so that the evening ahead could already be played out.

The day passed as though in a lull before a storm. The fact that my desk was piled high with work which I needed to clear away before day's end was my saving grace.

I left the office straight after work, and my heart went boom, boom, boom when I saw Mike waiting for me. Catching sight of him across the street, or a crowded room had that effect on me each time.

Mike was his usual talkative self on the drive to Greenhaven. I, understandably, was a bundle of nerves and did not add much to the conversation.

The evening started well enough. Iris's welcome was all I could have hoped for, and she even gave me a knowing wink when I handed her my cardigan.

Her mother's friendly demeanour from before was noticeably absent after Mike announced our engagement, and her congratulations were decidedly lukewarm. As the evening wore on, it became more and more obvious she did not approve of Mike's choice. Mike's dad was also less than enthusiastic. Uncle Dave, however, insisted I dispense with all formalities.

"You'll soon be part of the family my dear, so, please don't stand on ceremony with me."

He and Iris did their best to smooth over the awkward moments by regaling me with Mike's youthful escapades. Mike, true to his word, stayed close, so, by and large, the evening was not a total write-off.

Having settled myself in the passenger seat of Mike's van at the end of our visit, I said, "Your dad certainly knows his way around a *braai*! I'll say this for him. Everything else was delicious too."

"Yep! Between the three of them, they always put on a good spread. Did you make much headway with the party arrangements, though?"

"Well Mike, first, I'd like to sum up my impressions of the evening. In all honesty, I'd have to say, your parents—your mom in particular—did not seem overly warm after you told them our news. I sensed both your parents were far from delighted at this turn of events. Uncle Dave's reaction was the exact opposite, however. Iris and I got on swimmingly. I felt she was trying to make up for your mother's standoffishness toward me. As for the arrangements, she and I have everything in hand."

"I agree with you, Eve. My mother did seem rather distant, but after all, you know, we did rather take them by surprise. So, how about we give my parents, especially my mom, a little time to get used to the idea? I think we owe them that much. Fair enough?"

"Fair enough!" I wanted to please Mike and I wanted his family to like me, but I could not shake the feeling that winning over Mike's mother would be an Augean task!

Waiting on news from Canada to advise that all documents were ready for Mike's departure added to my distress. All too quickly, the days turned into weeks. Before I was even remotely ready to say good-bye, we were into mid-April, and it was time for Mike to board the plane for Vancouver. Mike and I drove to the airport with his uncle Dave. They had the inevitable last-minute details to settle.

I badly wanted Grace by my side, but she was not able to change her shift. Thankfully, she would be home to console me on my return. What on earth would I do without Grace? Dearest, sweetest, Grace.

*S*pring had sprung by the time Mike arrived in Vancouver. He was in his element; waxing poetic about the gardens in his neighbourhood which were already flourishing. Many with beautiful tulips, impatiens, petunias, and gorgeous cherry-blossomed, tree-lined streets. In a word, 'breathtaking!' Much like our jacaranda-lined streets in Stellenbosch and elsewhere in the Cape, is how he described it.

"Some of these hydrangeas are an incredibly beautiful blue—as blue as the blue of our South African summer skies. They are huge, Eve, just as big as that blue and white fruit plate you guys keep on your kitchen table. Another thing, do you know that these people drive on the opposite side of the road? Now that I have a company van—here they call the thing a truck—at my disposal, I have to remind myself constantly and get used to it… Chop-chop!"

He went on to say he had already been promised a visit to Stanley Park. This is a huge public park which borders Vancouver Downtown and is almost surrounded by waters of the Pacific Ocean. The weather wasn't yet warm enough to hit the beach for a suntan, though.

I could tell Mike was eager to get started on his project; anxious, even. My heart went out to him because I also wanted him to be successful at his job.

"Good luck for Monday, Mike, honey! Don't worry too much, okay?"

"Thanks, Eve. I miss you already. I'll be thinking of you and wishing you were here to share all of this with me. Talk to you soon. Don't forget, I love you!"

"I love you too, Mike. I miss you like crazy. Hurry back!"

To give Mike his due, he called regularly during the first month or so, sticking to the times we had agreed on. We had long conversations, where I gave him a running commentary on the arrangements for our wedding I'd made so far. His comments were encouraging, and his input was helpful. He, in turn, filled me in on the project at hand. Workwise, things had started well. He was getting used to the Canadian way of doing things.

His boss did not stand on formality. He was a laid-back, generous man, known as "Sheldon" to his employees. In the short time since his arrival, Mike had already been to dinner at the Schwartz's home and was promised tickets to baseball games and the movies. There was talk of picnics on the beach as the weather turned warmer and other social gatherings during the time Mike would be working in Vancouver. It was obvious that Mike had become Sheldon's blue-eyed boy.

Whale watching, golfing, hiking, fishing and boating, and an upcoming wine festival were other activities of interest on the horizon.

The Schwartzes' beach house in Parksville overlooks the Pacific Ocean and sports an indoor swimming pool and a billiard room. Oh, and let's not forget to mention the television room where they screened movies on the current hit list. Mike certainly had his pick of new things to experience and a bird's eye view as to how the other half lives.

Sheldon and his wife Laura host a plethora of outdoor social activities. Year-round. Business associates and some staff members were invited on occasion. These gatherings were informal and, by all accounts, always ended up being quite large, with some guests at times spending the entire weekend. Apparently, the idea of all work and no play did not sit well with this couple.

Some weeks after his arrival, Mike was duly invited, along with some of the staff to spend a long weekend there. An informal affair, hanging out around the pool and playing volleyball on the beach. All were encouraged to let their hair down. The photos Mike sent, showed there had been no shortage of females. Attractive females.

Each August, the city is host to the annual Parksville Beach Festival. The week-long event catered to families and others. The highlight of the festival would be the sandcastle building competition. If so inclined, one could build a castle on one's own, or just stroll along the beach, collecting sand dollars.

Mike also sent me a couple of travel brochures. The one of Parksville showed long stretches of sandy, white beaches, and incredible scenery.

It was late June now, and it seemed as if Mike had been gone forever. It had become somewhat difficult at times to reach him by phone. We did not always connect when I called. Instead, I'd hear, "Mike Moore, please leave a message." This did not help my state of mind.

In the weeks following, I would come to detest those words. Instead of speaking to him in person as I'd anticipated, I'd have to leave a message and wait for him to return my call. Not knowing when he would return said call, was disappointing, to say the least. Frustrating too! Almost more than I could bear.

Mike had already been gone two, unbearably, long, lonely months. According to him, work-wise things were not going according to schedule. They had initially wasted some time because of delays with material deliveries and misdirected orders. This meant working overtime whenever possible. Sometimes, as long as daylight held out.

Now, not only did we have the time difference with which to contend, but there was also Mike's schedule which had become erratic. We used to speak on the phone every other weekday and on Saturdays as well as Sundays. Now, his phone calls were sometimes down to just one during the week, and there were times that we did not even connect on a Saturday or Sunday. This was a huge letdown!

Often, when we did make contact, Mike did not seem to have much to say and the sweet nothings which he was wont to whisper in my ear had dwindled, to almost nothing.

He seemed preoccupied; there was the odd time I imagined him giving a mental sigh of relief as we ended the call. It would seem the distance had indeed become a factor, and I had no way of knowing exactly what was afoot. He seemed to avoid lengthy talks of the wedding. What was I to think? I was sick at heart and reluctant to refer to wedding plans already in the works.

In an effort to be reasonable, I bent over backward, I told myself he had a lot to contend with at work—a lot of responsibility in a strange country. I put it all down to the long work hours—possibly frustration when things went awry—and told myself it was bound to take its toll.

If something was troubling Mike at this point, he was doing his level best to avoid any reference to it. Short of asking direct questions—which I was loath to do—about the women with whom he had been socializing, I had no choice but to lay my anxieties and suspicions to rest. I made a concerted effort and tried hard to convince myself I was overreacting because I was so lonely for Mike. I was mollified when, at the end of each call I heard him say, "I love you, Eve."

This being said, I will confess to owning an extremely active imagination. Suspicion insisted on having its way with me, but I usually ended up giving myself a good talking to—tried with all my being to hang onto the words he'd said to me before he left home to take on this assignment. After all, I told myself, *There's no percentage in having these dark thoughts.*

Grace agreed with me.

Uncle Dave stopped by our flat one evening towards the end of June to tell us Sheldon Schwartz was highly satisfied with the work Mike and his crew had accomplished. They were on schedule and Mike's stint in British Columbia was nearing its end. Mike and Co. could well be wrapping up operations within the next two weeks.

Next stop, Ontario, where Mike and crew were to revamp the gardens of four existing hotels—one each in Niagara Falls, Oakville, Mississauga, and the last one in Toronto.

Should this be music to my ears? I'd say so. But definitely!

Laura Schwartz also had nothing but praise for the work Mike and his crew had undertaken. Amongst other projects, Mike had designed an ornamental fishpond as a habitat in their garden for the many colourful, butterfly koi he had found. A decorative bridge straddled this picturesque and tranquil setting. Sheldon told Uncle Dave this feature had already become a conversation piece, and his wife makes a point of showing it off to both family and friends.

*V*ancouver was history. Finally! One leg of Mike's overseas stay had been completed, and he was now well and truly on his way to Niagara Falls. He phoned as soon as he'd settled himself in the house his boss had put at the disposal of the crew.

Niagara Falls, the ideal honeymoon destination! This was where they would start their next project. Then, onto Oakville, a couple of hours' drive from there—both big jobs, by all accounts.

Still, Mike had said, these would not be quite as taxing because he now had a good working knowledge of procedures and suppliers. He and the crew worked well together, and that was half the battle won.

He went on to talk about his plane trip, the different scenery and the breathtaking Niagara Falls, which he could see from his lodgings—not a patch on our magnificent Victoria Falls, though. He talked at length about the mountains of British Columbia—so reminiscent of our mountains in the Western Cape.

It struck me Mike still favoured neutral topics. I decided to test the waters and steer the conversation to our upcoming wedding. To my sensitive ear, it seemed as though he had not yet overcome his reluctance to comment at length on the plans I'd been making.

Alarm bells sounded in my head…blared ugly, unanswerable questions. Had the unthinkable happened? Was Mike cooling off? Pulling away? If so, why? Was another woman involved? I shied away from facing it head-on, but it was becoming increasingly impossible to deny the suspicions which had been eating away at me—like a cancer!

The big question was what could I do about it from this end? Do I probe or leave well enough alone and hope the situation, whatever it was, would resolve itself?

Grace was the only person I could talk to about my fears.

"The thing is, Evie, you should wait until Mike gets back. Talk to him eyeball to eyeball before you do anything rash. You know the old saying, *Least said, soonest mended?* Well, that's the road I would take."

She handed me this sage advice, along with a much-needed cup of tea.

I nodded in agreement, as I reached for the cup. "You're so wise, Gracie. Sounds like a plan…for now, anyway."

At the beginning of his stay in Niagara Falls, Mike's phone calls were still not as frequent as I would have liked, and he still seemed disinclined for long conversations; seemed pressed for time when we *did* connect. Consequently, after more weeks of frustration and feeling out of the loop, my imagination continued in overdrive.

Surely, I mused, no one could be expected to work all those hours and not take a break? Why couldn't he call me on his tea break or lunch break? What about when work was done for the day? Granted, there was a time difference, but I was willing to wait for late-night calls when he was off duty, and I offered this as a solution.

He took me up on this suggestion, and it worked. For a while. In no time at all, it seemed as though those late-night calls, when he was supposedly off duty, again became unpredictable and sometimes too short for my liking. Certainly not conducive to an outpouring of loving, sweet nothings.

Even though I was happy to hear his voice, my being tense already at the outset was par for the course. On edge, I anticipated those dreaded words, "Can't talk long, I'm waiting on a call from a supplier." Or these, "Sorry Eve, this is not a good time. I'm in a meeting and don't know when I'll be free."

Hearing Mike say those words left me feeling disgruntled, excluded; not always privy to what he was doing or with whom he socialized in his off-duty hours, especially since I knew some of his evenings and weekends were free. The way I see it, he made time to go to the movies, or played snooker, among other things. He did not say whether these outings took place in mixed company.

Would I be prying were I to ask? I was at a loss. My pride wouldn't let me, anyway.

I looked, again, for the umpteenth time, at the photos he had sent me from Vancouver, which showed a mixed company. Had one of those females set their cap at Mike? It would seem the opportunities to amuse himself and indulge in mild dalliance had not been lacking, were he so inclined.

*Had* he been so inclined, though? *This* was the million-dollar question that hounded me! Given his lack of warmth in our recent phone conversations, was I living in a fool's paradise for believing Mike had kept his promise? His almost non-existent interest in our wedding arrangements continued to disconcert me. Distress me. Oh! Those demons of doubt. How they beset me!

Even so, I missed him. I ached for him and wanted him beside me where I could reach out and touch him. I heeded Grace's wise words though, held my doubts in check, and, instead, poured out my longing for him in no uncertain terms when I wrote. I made sure, though, to keep the tone light and forward-looking to his return.

As is their wont, all things come to an end. Mike's stay in Canada had already reached the halfway mark. It was music to my ears when I heard he was to spend only about eight more weeks away from home.

My last letter must have resonated with him. He had been stationed in Ontario for a month when things appeared to change for the better. Our scheduled phone calls now came through without a hitch. Bit by bit, I was reassured by his tone and our chatty conversations. Also, the letters and the photos as promised. Photos, I'm happy to say, with nary an attractive female in the background.

O! Joy! My restraint was being rewarded.

*Had I overreacted initially because I missed him so much…let my imagination run riot? I could not help but wonder.*

To help me blot out all previous negative emotions, I read Mike's last letters to me; read them over and over again, replayed our latest phone calls in my head.

Now, with Grace's all-too-willing help along every step of the way, spare moments at hand were devoted to finalising wedding plans with renewed vigour and enthusiasm.

*I* was flying high now, but it was inevitable for my thoughts to sometimes turn to my still-absent father. It had been ten years, at least, since I'd last seen or heard from him, and I had no idea where he could be found. I wanted, with all my heart, for Dadda to give me away on my wedding day.

Like so many other milestones in my life, by the look of things, he would be in absentia for this occasion as well. It hurt! I cried. I turned to Uncle Jacob in my distress. He dried my tears.

"Eve, I cannot take the place of your father, but I would gladly stand in for him if you're sure you won't be able to track him down in time. You're like a daughter to me, my girl. It would be my privilege to 'give you away'. Just say the word!"

I had come to love this man as though he were kin. There was no way I could refuse this offer so lovingly made. The expression on my face must have said it all. With our arms linked firmly, we went to the kitchen to break the news to Auntie Miriam.

Meanwhile, Grace and I, with the help of her parents and my mother, had all the arrangements well in hand and my wedding day promised to be all a girl's heart could desire. Weather permitting, our reception would be held outdoors in the Solomons' spacious backyard.

Grace had been my anchor during the time Mike was away. My rock! She had commiserated with me when I could not get through to Mike on the phone and had rejoiced with me on those occasions when I managed to have a decent conversation with him.

Together, we counted the days until his return and religiously struck them off the calendar at night.

Mike finally called with the details of his return flight at the beginning of September. A day which could not come soon enough for me. I had no choice but to exercise patience until the day he stepped off the plane. Grace, with her down-to-earth approach, helped hold me in check.

*M*ike was back! The two of us were caught up in our reunion; caught up in simply being together. I was on cloud nine once more and I could not get enough of the feel of his arms around me, holding me tight—the arms of the Mike who set my pulses racing, not the one whom I had for so many weeks found emotionally distant and un-recognisable.

There was no indication, whatsoever, that something was troubling Mike. If it were so, he disguised it well. Not wanting to mar our reunion in any way, I made a concerted effort to lay my past suspicions to rest and finally convinced myself I must have been over-reacting at the time because I had been so lonely for Mike.

Slow, but sure, the months he had been away receded into oblivion. It suited me to sweep any troublesome, lingering doubts 'under the carpet', so to speak. Savouring his return and ironing out the fiddly last-minute plans for our wedding consumed all my thoughts and time now.

To be married on Mike's birthday would have been best of the best. October 10th, unfortunately, fell on a Sunday, so we opted to get married a week earlier.

Marry him, I did. On a gloriously sunny Saturday afternoon, roughly one year after our first meeting. Our wedding, a small affair—intimate—took place in the church where Mike had been baptized and confirmed. His mother had put her foot down!

The walk down the aisle to where Mike was standing with the minister seemed interminable, like one of those dreams where everything was happening in slow motion.

Uncle Dave had gladly accepted the role of best man. Grace, dearest Grace, did the honours as my bridesmaid. Who else, but Grace, would I have chosen?

Heading down the aisle, my throat seized up with emotion, and, in those moments, I truly had eyes for no one and nothing else but my bridegroom. I remember taking deep breaths to control the beating of my heart and to keep in step with Uncle Jacob.

The ceremony, incredibly beautiful and touching. I just know, in years to come, I will again see myself walking or, should I say, floating up the aisle on Uncle Jacob's arm to the altar where Mike stood waiting for me. See, again, his smile, wide as the sky, his eyes locked onto mine as I neared him. I will again hear the joyous strains of Pachelbel's Canon in D—loud and clear—reverberating throughout the church.

Never, in all my life, had I felt more committed to any one being than in those moments when I said, "I do!" Tears glistened in Mike's eyes. The conviction with which he repeated his vows assured me he felt as I did.

When it was time to sign the register, I could barely see the page in front of me. My eyes were swimming in tears of happiness, and sadness too. I wished, with all my heart, that my father could have been witness to this day; that he could have been on hand to share my joy and support me as I took my first steps on the road leading me into the future.

It was not meant to be! My 'family party' consisted of my mother—elegant as always—playing her role as mother of the bride to the hilt; Uncle Jacob, dapper and impeccably attired; and Auntie Miriam, stylishly outfitted. Seated in the row directly behind them were Georgina Bailey, her husband Tom, and their three children.

Also present were my minister, a few friends from my church, Ike Levendal, and a handful of my associates from work. Last but not least, the friends of my BM (Before Mike) days.

Mike's immediate family, their relatives, and close friends completed the list of those who witnessed our marriage.

The Solomon family had kindly offered to host our wedding reception in their enclosed backyard. Mike and Uncle Dave, lending their expertise, had made the setting as pretty-as-a-picture.

Georgina has a wealth of 'connections', even in the catering world. This proved invaluable because she had arranged for us to 'taste the menu' beforehand. A unique experience and lots of fun—so many choices! Mike and I wanted to select a menu to delight our guests. We had a hard time choosing, but, on the day, the refreshments were scrumptious and beautifully presented. The crème brûlée shared top billing with our delectable wedding cake, made by Auntie Miriam. Who else!

Family members and friends who had come to join in the celebration toasted us, the younger Mr. and Mrs. Moore. A cerulean sky served as our canopy on that memorable October afternoon. Bird sounds, high up in the trees, vied with those of clinking glasses, happy chatter, and laughter.

Much later, Mike and I drove off into the sunset (as newlyweds are honour-bound to do). This, to the dubious music of tinkling tin cans tied to the rear bumper, ringing in our ears, with one of the guests belatedly calling out, "May all your troubles be little ones!"

We would spend our first night as Mr. and Mrs. Michael James Moore in the house which Mike had so beautifully restored. Thrilling prospect for more than one reason! Even more thrilling, the moment when Mike carried me over the threshold and topped it off by handing me my own set of keys.

*How much more romance could a girl want?*

Next morning, sated with the intimacy of getting to know each other—in the biblical sense—and much too excited to sleep, we set off at dawn in my spanking new egg-yolk-yellow Volkswagen Beetle (Mike's generous wedding gift to me) for 'Destination Honeymoon'.

$\mathcal{K}$nysna bound, we drove at a leisurely clip along the beautiful coastline of the South African Garden Route, stopping for refreshments as the mood took us and topping up the tank.

Gorgeous jacaranda trees were in full bloom everywhere in Swellendam. They lined Main Street on both sides, made a virtual canopy of purple blossoms—a purple haze, no matter where one looked. Blossoms, more than one can shake a stick at, already spent, had fallen to the ground, carpeting the pavements. A sight for sore eyes!

Headed in the direction of Oudtshoorn, we agreed it would be fun to explore the famous Cango Caves. There, the majesty of those dripstone caverns opening into vast halls of towering stalagmite and stalactite formations simply take one's breath away.

The next leg of our journey led to an ostrich farm where we learned about the lives of those hardy, enigmatic creatures. The brave will sit astride on one, and the adventurous soul can attempt to ride one. Mike had been itching to catch a ride on an ostrich and show off his manliness.

His wish was granted. I could not resist taking a photo of him straddling one of those creatures while hanging on for dear life. *This* is one I would be sure to pass on to a future generation of Moores. Sitting on an ostrich did not appeal to me, but I was all for buying an egg or two as souvenirs. My first purchase, as Mrs. Moore.

Next stop, Knysna. The ever-popular seaside resort in the Western Cape. Knysna—home to The Heads—the place where I was born.

Visions of past holidays—days of my childhood when I visited with my grandmother and other family members in Knysna—flashed across my mind's eye. Halcyon childhood memories. God willing, Mike and I would make many happy ones while on our honeymoon here. Without a doubt, these memories will merge with those already in my 'love box'.

As familiar landscapes, known to me from my past, came into view, I felt an overwhelming sense of things having come full circle. I'd come back to the place of my roots. Being in this place, at this time, made me feel as though our union was doubly blessed.

I have many a lasting memory of my visits to Knysna. The one of my grandmother reading tea leaves for the ladies from the Women's Auxiliary in her front room, now sprung to mind. This was a ritual, routinely observed at the end of their quilting afternoons.

During my holidays there, Gramma called me in to help serve her delicious chocolate cake and *gemmerkoekies* while she poured the tea. I'd be privy, then, just briefly, mind, to these readings. As a treat, after the quilters had left, Gramma would pour a cup of tea for me and read my leaves.

I had felt special then, important too because I was allowed to drink from one of her best china cups. The tea-set was housed in an antique, stink-wood china cabinet and used only when company came.

During one such reading, my grandmother had told me, "One day you'll marry a kind man, but you will have to cross the ocean to do so. I won't live to see you go."

My reverie, however, was fleetingly tinged with sadness because my grandmother had long since died. The aunts and uncles had moved their families on to greener pastures. Now, there was no one left with whom I could reminisce about former times, or share my newfound happiness, or to whom I could show off my wonderful husband. I revelled in the thought that Mike also loved this part of the country—where I first saw the light of day.

Uncle Dave had arranged for us to stay with friends who owned a small boarding house. We had a spectacular view of the Knysna Lagoon from our bedroom windows. In the distance, I espied the outline of 'The Heads'—those two sandstone cliffs so well-known along this coastline. They rise majestically out of the water on either side of the channel from where the sea pours its sometimes-turbulent waters into the lagoon, and dramatically separates the tranquil lagoon from the pounding surf of the Indian Ocean.

I took Mike's hand and, with his arms encircling me, we stood, looking out in silence for some time, drinking in the tranquil scene. Myriad stars twinkled far, far above, in a velvety, navy-blue, night sky. I could see us coming back, time and again, wanting to recapture what promised to be a blissful experience.

Our hostess kindly served a candlelit supper in our room. The setting was oh-so-romantic! The smell of the ocean wafting in through the open windows, candlelight, twinkling stars in the heavens, all seemed a fitting prelude to a night that promised to be ideal in every way imaginable.

Dear Reader, everything we ate and drank must have been delicious but, please, don't expect me to pass on any details, because I was too caught up in my emotions and drinking in the reality of being Mrs. Moore.

It had been a long day. Both Mike and I were only too ready to have an early night. We moved the remains of our meal to a tea trolley and set it outside our door. With the closed door now separating us from the rest of the world, the long day notwithstanding, when we lay down on the big bed, sleep was the farthest thing from my husband's mind. Mine, too. With Mike exploring my body and I his, we learned how to pleasure each other.

We spent our first morning climbing 'The Heads' at our own pace, walking along the lower path to the water's edge, paddling in the shallow pools, lazing away the day, going just where the mood took us. We stopped only to enjoy light refreshments. Awesome vistas, from any which way one chose. Incomparable!

Toward sundown, we went on a leisurely cruise on the breathtaking blue Knysna Lagoon. Ah! The colours of the setting sun on the waters—words fail me. To see is to be mesmerised!

Alone in our bedroom at the end of each day, we shut out the rest of the world, sharing what lived in our hearts and continued our quest of how best to pleasure each other. His skilled hands moved over the length of me and awakened desires dormant and hitherto unknown. Not only did he know how to awaken these desires, he also knew how to fulfill them. Over, and over again. In turn, he taught me how to make his body come alive and thrill to *my* touch.

His hands—did I mention they were long-fingered, somewhat calloused but sensitive? Hands so competent when strumming the strings of his guitar were now working their magic on every part of me. Taking me to heights from which I was loath to descend. Each time we made love, it seemed he had come to know my body just a little better and found new ways of pleasuring me.

This was how we spent our nights.

During the days that followed, we sometimes drove aimlessly along the coast, just taking in the sights. Other times, we lazed in the sun and frolicked in the surf with childish abandon. It was on one such drive that we found ourselves in Plettenberg Bay. To our delight, we witnessed some bottlenose dolphins leaping in and out of the water while the rest of these amazing creatures surfed the breakers close to shore.

On another day, we walked hand in hand for miles along the beautiful, sandy beach. Later, with the westering sun just setting in a riot of reds, we headed for one of the cafés, our empty stomachs propelling us there.

Mike bought a fishing rod for me because I'd said it looked like fishing might be a fun thing to do. I gave it a trial run but did not have much success. I badly wanted to land my first big catch and made him promise to take me fishing once we were settled in at home.

This was how we spent our days.

Our honeymoon was all I could have asked for. Like all good things, however, our travels were destined to come to an end. After two weeks of sightseeing, lazing in sun and surf by day, and nights of seclusion where Mike and I found yet new ways to pleasure each other.

Regrets at having to leave these idyllic surroundings vied with the excitement of starting the next phase of our lives together but we did not really wish for a longer holiday. After all, our life together was to be one long honeymoon.

That was the plan as we headed for home with a host of happy memories. Ones we would always treasure. Did he carry me over the threshold again? I'll leave it to your imagination, Dear Reader.

Number sixty-three Gordon Road in Diep River is a single storey house, set well back from the road, on a large, pie-shaped plot. Mike had spent innumerable hours renovating it after his grandparents' death. During our courtship, he often spoke of the work he still needed to do and sometimes called to change our plans. His reason, "I'm sorry to bail out, Eve, but I want to finish tiling the kitchen," or "I plan to start laying the crazy paving in the yard tonight," or "I have to be on hand when the electrician comes," and so on…

He had taken me on my first tour of inspection two months after we'd met. I fell in love with everything I saw that day. He had exceptionally good taste, and there was absolutely nothing I would have done differently. As Mike pointed out, there wasn't much left to do on the inside, only a few minor details, such as finding a few suitable light fixtures, or tracking down the odd piece of furniture and curtains for some of the rooms…things like that.

After he proposed he always referred to it as 'our' home. It followed quite naturally that he should then seek my advice and take me along when he went scouting for the above-mentioned items. I was thrilled to be asked and more than happy to put my stamp on things. I wanted to be his wife and live with him in this lovely place. I knew this, without a doubt!

He had held onto some of the furniture which he'd inherited from his grandparents. We both felt those pieces would blend in well with the ones he had collected over the years and those we had acquired together during our brief courtship.

Both Mike and I loved the look of the Cape Dutch architectural style. He had employed artisans in the Moslem community, those highly skilled in their craft, to restore the outside of the building to its former beauty. With plain gables at either end of the house, the decorative, ornately sculpted gable at the front of the house was deservedly a focal point and contributed largely to its character.

Equally eye-catching, the *Broekie lace* running the length of the covered, front *stoep*, the roof of which was supported by two stately white columns…so reminiscent of the house in Riversdale where my dad and I had spent six carefree, happy months of my childhood.

Both the exterior and interior benefitted from Mike's handiwork. The gardens, back and front, would become his pride and joy over the years. I was more than happy to work alongside him in the early hours of the morning or in the cool of the evening.

I pulled weeds with the best of them, and when he finally called a halt, we would sit back and admire our handiwork. Sometimes, with a glass of South African wine. Mike had a plethora of ideas to improve on what I already thought of as perfection.

*G*race met her Prince Charming soon after Mike and I had celebrated our first wedding anniversary. Tall, well-built, handsome with clear gray eyes, he and Grace go well together. I thought they would have beautiful children. I said so to Grace.

She blushed but did not contradict my thinking. Methinks she'd already pondered this!

Claud Theunissen was a doctor at Groote Schuur Hospital. They'd met at a house party given by a staff member on New Year's Day. I was ecstatic for my friend! Somewhat opposite to Mike in character, Claud was quiet and more than content to let others do the talking.

He obviously adored Grace. It showed, for all to see. Like a beacon on a dark night. He was attentive and affectionate in public. He struck both Mike and me as a dependable person with a depth of character. A gentleman, worthy of our friend.

Auntie Miriam and Uncle Jacob admired Claud immensely. They felt their daughter had found someone who would be a welcome addition to their family; one who would cherish her.

Just as Mike and I had done, the couple announced their engagement mere months after they met. Grace was in love. She had found the man of her dreams and she saw no reason to dilly-dally. Wedding bells would be ringing for her before long.

*I*n the interim, Mike and I were blessed with twin boys. Our bonny babes arrived eighteen months after our wedding. Benjy, baptized Benjamin after my father, and George, named after Mike's dad. Beautiful, perfect babies. We doted on them, even before they were born!

Mike was in awe of our newborn babes. He epitomized the proud father, and I was proud of him for the way he pitched in—feeding and bathing and burping his sons. He needed no second bidding when they demanded attention in the middle of the night. We often had to tend to both babies at the same time. I appreciated his help.

We had many sleepless nights and grew accustomed to dealing with baby paraphernalia in what seemed like every corner of the house. Two of everything.

Hard work but oh-so-rewarding, to see them grow and develop their personalities day by day. They were special, like no other babies, and they brought about big changes in our home and our way of life.

We were fascinated by our twins, so was Boomer, the German sausage dog—Uncle Dave's gift to the twins on their first birthday. More often than not, the dog could be found lying on the floor next to their cots while keeping a wary eye on all who came through the doorway.

With nary a cloud on our horizon, our life was perfect. Just as Mike had promised it would be.

*Little did I know then, he had a dark side to which he would someday give full rein.*

*G*race was in the throes of planning and shopping for her wedding, whilst I was adjusting to being the mother of twin boys. It was a hectic time for our little family. This meant I could not always visit the shops with her.

She included me in all her planning, though. Together, we pored over fabric swatches. Discussed the merits of shantung and shot silk over guipure lace. We matched shoes and veil—all the accoutrements which go hand in hand when fitting out a bride in royal fashion.

Grace's delight in choosing cake decorations and flower arrangements knew no bounds. Auntie Miriam, always at the ready for consultation, proved to be a mine of information and good ideas.

I was to be Grace's Matron of Honour.

Time and tide wait for no man, as the saying goes. Spring had sprung! I knew Grace had always dreamed of a spring wedding. Her dream came true. Their wedding day dawned on a cloudless, sunny day. Blue skies as far as the eye could see.

"Happy the bride the sun shines on..." Walking Grace down the aisle, Uncle Jacob personified the image of 'proud father of the bride'. He was quite content to 'give his daughter away' to the man whom he held in such high regard. The day went without a hitch. All weddings should.

A veritable dream wedding! The weather, the bride's gown, the flowers, the music, the venue, the reception, the wedding cake, the speeches. Absolutely everything lived up to Grace's expectations.

Perfection, on every level!

The newlyweds left on their dream honeymoon amid a flurry of well-wishes, and it was high time for Mike and me to be heading home. Our infants, who had been on their best behaviour all day long, needed to be bathed, fed, and bedded. Strictly in that order.

Grace had kept the flat we had shared before my wedding. She and Claud planned to live there until they found *their* dream house. Their son Christopher was born before that became a reality, and, barely one year later, they found their dream house two streets away from where we lived. She phoned to tell me even before she broke the news to her parents.

"...I'm so excited, Evie. The house is perfect. It's newly renovated and ready to move in. The thing is, the people who are selling want to vacate as soon as possible because her mother died so they are going to live with her father. Her dad has dementia and needs someone to look after him. We can move in as soon as all the paperwork is done. Best of all we'll be living practically on each other's doorstep! What could be better, hey?

"We'll have three lovely sunny bedrooms and the kitchen is huge! I want you to see it as soon as possible and you *have* to help me measure for curtains, okay? Claud loves what Mike did to your place and told me he wants Mike's advice to fix up our garden in the front and also the back yard... only, if Mike's not too busy, of course."

"Gracie, it goes without saying, I'm dying to see your new home. Of course, I'll help with the measurements! Believe me, I'll even make time to sew your curtains if you want me to. Mike's not busy over the weekends, so I'm sure he would like nothing better than to show off his expertise in the gardening department!"

"You are a brick, Evie! I hear your babies calling you, so we'll talk later! Squeeze those twins real tight for me. Okay?"

When moving day dawned, I was keen to help my best friend in any way I could. We measured, sewed and hung curtains, lined cupboards, and unpacked boxes together, while the men dug the soil, moved stones, and planted away outside. Auntie Miriam and Uncle Jacob were in their element as our go-to and trusted babysitters.

By Grace's calculations, their daughter was conceived in their new home, just weeks after they moved in. Their Kathleen, a perfect little angel, was born on my birthday. Amazing timing on the part of her parents! I envied Grace her daughter—in a good way—but mightily consoled when they asked me to be godmother.

I loved having Grace so nearby and the thought of having our children grow up together. We would be like one family and our children would have what both she and I had missed out on…siblings. Since we now lived a mere stone's throw apart, it followed that we would once again share fully in each other's lives.

*O*ver the years, the landscaping business had been growing steadily. Uncle Dave and Mike worked hard. Some of the business, as Uncle Dave had so wisely foreseen, was due to the recommendation of his Canadian friend, Sheldon Schwartz. Mike was working longer hours and there were times when he even spent some nights away from home because the jobs were quite a distance away.

The Mike I knew of old had been a 'social drinker'. More and more of late, when he came home after a long day at work, I thought I could smell liquor on his breath when he leaned in to kiss me.

Mike was changing. The changes were gradual. He became moody, easily angered over trifles. I became somewhat concerned after a while, because, other than an increased workload, I was at a loss to account for the changes.

My concern was brushed aside as though I were making mountains out of molehills!

The twins would be thirteen years old come their next birthday. Teenagers. We had put our heads together and planned the party to end all parties! Friends and family had been invited. Both boys had put in requests for their favourite party food and other treats.

Mike and I had decided to surprise them with a new bicycle each, and, since they both loved building things, we figured adding a couple of model airplane kits to their growing collection would be just the thing.

We agreed to let the boys have the responsibility of decorating with balloons and coloured paper streamers in preparation for their big day. They also put a lot of thought into the party games with which to entertain our guests, young and old.

'Musical chairs' was just one of their choices for inside. "In case it rains, Mom!" Said in mock exasperation. For outside, there would be the inevitable 'blind man's buff', 'hide and seek', 'soap bubble contest', and another game involving inflated balloons.

We held our collective breath for a sunny day. Lucky us! The weather cooperated and we had the perfect day for a party in our back yard. We ended up with a nice turnout of family and friends.

The party was a blast! The food and drinks we had set out were a big hit and the games the boys had arranged went down well. They went wild over their new bikes and enjoyed unwrapping their gifts after blowing out the twenty-six candles on the two-tiered chocolate cake Auntie Grace had baked for them. They had included her in the preparations. To have it any other way would be unthinkable.

"I can't wait to sink my teeth into that chocolate cake!" This, from George, who always praises Auntie Grace's baking to high heaven.

It had been a long afternoon and, when a couple of the younger children became a tad fractious, it seemed best to call a halt to the day. The Theunissens, bless their little cotton socks, were the last to leave. Grace, my trusty helper from start to finish, pitched in with the cleanup while Mike and Claud were supposedly helping the boys restore order to the chaos in our living room. From the shrieks and laughter coming from there, I'd venture to say there was more horseplay than anything else afoot.

The twins were thrilled with their gifts and could not wait to ride their new bicycles, could not stop talking about the Scalextric racing set from Auntie Grace and Uncle Claud.

When Mike made his way to the garage after they had left, I sat down in the kitchen with the twins to read their birthday cards, but I could see they were anxious to get a handle on all their newly acquired loot, so I shooed them out of the kitchen. They needed no second bidding and left faster than the speed of sound waves travel through the air. Boomer, hot on their trail.

The sun had long gone down before Mike came back into the house. Supper was a non-event—everyone agreed they had had too much ice cream and cake earlier. The boys enlisted their dad's help in setting up the Scalextric. A perfect end to their day.

$\mathcal{M}$ ike's dark side finally surfaced a few months after the twins' birthday party. Another Mike took over—the mean one; the one who would disgust and intimidate me. His drinking bouts became more frequent and did not deal kindly with his temperament.

There had been signs along the way, but I chose to downplay them— made allowances for Mike, telling myself he had a lot to contend with at work—unwittingly enabling him. Things finally came to a head though, and all pretense of 'social' drinking went out the window. Increasingly, he made excuses to be with his buddies on Saturday afternoons.

These, later turned into weekend drinking sprees, with him staying out all of Saturday night…a harbinger of troubles looming large. A destructive pattern had emerged.

Our social circle had always been small, intimate. Now, because of Mike's unpredictable temperament when he had been drinking, we'd gradually stopped seeing people—all, excepting Grace and Claud. They were still kept in the dark, though—I was too embarrassed to let on that Mike's drinking had become a problem. Oh, he'd retained those qualities which went 'skin deep'. These were always on display for the benefit of neighbours, friends, my in-laws, and other family members. My mother included.

On the now-rare occasions when we had company over, he was still a charming host. He appeared to be a loving, considerate husband. Alone with him, and especially in the privacy of our bedroom, the old, loving, and lovable Mike had become an elusive creature; I began to compare him to Dr. Jekyll and Mr. Hyde.

When necessary, communication with friends mostly took the form of phone calls and greeting cards. Of course, attending family birthdays, anniversaries and festive holidays were somewhat obligatory! There were occasions, however, when it became my task to make excuses for our absences even from some of those.

In times past, Mike's touch had invariably aroused me—I had always responded spontaneously and ardently until I encountered the other Mike, the one who resorted to abuse. Verbal and physical. I now find myself cringing at the mere thought of being close to him or having him touch me; my stomach heaves when I recall his brutish behaviour and coarse language.

My once-ardent desire for him was fast waning, and so, too, my deep love for him. I was disgusted and intimidated by his behaviour. I had lost respect for him. At times, even when sober, my husband turns me off, but, to keep the peace, I disguise my negative feelings.

I felt demeaned when our children were around to witness their father's loutish behavior. There was no way I could cover for Mike, even if I'd wanted to. They were old enough to realize what was happening and I could tell the strain they were under when he stayed out late. On these occasions, they kept to their bedroom as soon as they heard his van screech to a halt in our driveway.

Mike always avoided them for a few days after an incident, and then, a few days later, when he did come face to face with them, pretended nothing untoward had happened.

When he was sober or I thought it an opportune moment, I would broach the subject of his unacceptable behaviour. Usually, he would be at a loss to offer an explanation and claim he had no recollection of the incident, bristled at my well-meant efforts to curb his drinking. It took my sometimes-bruised body parts to convince him. He was always contrite and then, for a couple of weeks, things would appear to settle down.

Until the next time he'd had one too many drinks. Then it would be business as usual.

Things were going from bad to worse on the home front. I was becoming resentful and angry; our once perfect life was being disrupted, turned inside out. My perception of myself had reached a low ebb; I felt unwomanly, undesirable, unappreciated. I questioned myself. What should I be doing differently? Could it be my fault Mike was acting this way?

Sooner or later, this issue would have to be fully addressed. Resolved. I decided to stop pussyfooting around Mike. It took a lot of willpower to confront him and put a name to his excessive drinking. He would have none of it, however. No surprise there!

"I'm not addicted to booze. I can stop drinking any time I choose."

This was his mantra. I knew better.

"Please, get help, Mike!" I implored. He refused. I vocalized my frustration. Big mistake! It gave him the excuse he needed to storm out of the house; be with his friends and drink even more.

"You're nagging me. Again. I'll be damned if I'm going to stay here and listen to your preaching." These were his go-to parting words, the perfect exit line. Time and again.

*We had reached an impasse.*

The ongoing tension between us finally spurred me on to find relief.

It's been more than a year since our boys had had their thirteenth birthday party.

*There was no way to escape this glaring fact. Our marriage, once the envy of our friends, is a sham.*

There, I've said it! If only to myself.

Dreams, and hopes alike, lay crumbled about me like so much rubble, but the fighter in me was reluctant to 'down tools' until I'd exhausted all avenues which might change our situation. I needed to take another stance. One that would help me get through to Mike. I owed it to my family and myself to find a solution.

After much soul-searching, I decided that the Al-Anon support group was the answer to my prayers. I made up my mind to attend their meetings which were held in a nearby school building on Saturday afternoons. The timing was fortuitous, seemed tailor-made for me since Mike now religiously spends Saturday afternoons and evenings with his drinking buddies. Somehow, I'd find a way to attend without letting Mike know. For now.

*I*t was a Saturday in May. One, that I would long remember for the impact it would have on my life down the road. Mike had done his usual disappearing act after breakfast. Earlier in the week, Grace had invited the twins to spend the day at their house, so I walked them over around mid-morning. Boomer, of course, tagged along. Doing his doggie routine. Sniffing the ground on the way.

Claud was playing with their children in the backyard when we arrived. Benjy and George didn't need second bidding to join in the fun. Next to their dad and Uncle Dave, Uncle Claud was their all-time favourite male.

As soon as my boys were out of earshot, Grace, who could always read me like a book, held me in a tight embrace and demanded to know what was troubling me. Her arms, like a warm blanket around me, took the edge off my distress.

"Come. Come, sit by me," she said, pointing to the padded seats of their breakfast nook."

Shamed. Embarrassed. I had not yet been able to tell her I was being abused by my husband—admit my marriage was in dire straits. Now, my defenses crumbled and, in the quiet of her kitchen, over a cup of tea, I confided my woes to her, told her I was toying with the idea of attending my first Al-Anon meeting later that day.

I never doubted for a single moment that Grace would be a sensitive, supportive listener.

"Why didn't you do something before now, Evie? Why didn't you come to me?"

While keeping an eye on our children playing in her backyard, I said, "Believe me, I wanted to tell you…tried to, many times, but the words would not leave my mouth, Gracie.

"Anyway, Mike is always remorseful and begs forgiveness when sober, promising he would not lay a hand on me again. Unfortunately, there was always a next time, and I *did* think long and hard about leaving Mike. Where would I have gone, though?

"To leave home and uproot the twins was unthinkable! I know, only too well, what it's like to come from a broken home. Besides, I kept hoping things would get better if I just rode it out; kept hoping it *would* be the last time."

She, understandably, was appalled at the thought of Mike abusing me. Not only verbally, but emotionally and physically as well. Such behaviour was foreign to her. By contrast, her marriage and her parent's marriage were happy and stable. In a word, blissful.

"I won't belabour the obvious questions, but the thing is, it looks like you keep setting yourself up for more of the same…you certainly can't go on like this. I just hope you find some answers at these meetings, and it had better be soon!

"Once you've made up your mind to attend Al-Anon meetings on a regular basis, Evie, I'll gladly go with you to future meetings. We can go whenever Mike chooses to spend a Saturday with his friends. That way, should he ask, you will be telling the truth when you say we spent the afternoon together. I'll have to tell Claud. Okay? He won't let on to anyone."

Grace had just thrown me a lifeline. Her support meant the world to me

I rose from my seat as I said, "I *will* take the plunge and go to the meeting today. It's getting late, so I'd better be on my way…call you when I get back."

Grace called Claud and the children in to say good-bye to me, and as usual, the two of us walked arm-in-arm to the corner of her street then waved until we lost sight of each other.

The house was quiet on my return. There was no sign of Mike. A welcome relief because it gave me time to think, get my ducks in a row, so to speak. The unpleasant memories of all those past incidents demanded I take some kind of action.

I sat down at the kitchen table after I'd prepared a light lunch for myself. My resolve grew by leaps and bounds. Still, the thought that Mike might return while I was gone, threatened to make me lose my meager lunch.

A little voice inside my head urged, *Mike has gone off, leaving you to your own devices, so why not make the most of this opportunity. More than likely, he would already be holed up with his drinking buddies. Given his routine over the past year or so, his family's whereabouts would be the last thing on his mind.*

I *would* go to the meeting today, and, to ward off confrontation for now, other than Grace, I'd keep my own counsel. Then, when I was more informed, I'd broach the subject at home. It would give me an edge, one, which might well serve to deflect Mike's anger when I eventually told all.

*"Please, Lord," I implored in silent prayer, "don't let Mike find me out."*

*T*he sun was still high in the heavens when I stepped outside. I locked the front door and walked with determination in my every step to where my car was parked in the driveway.

I kept reminding myself why I was taking this step and the benefits for all concerned. If I learned how better to cope with the situation at home, it could mean our marriage stood a better chance at survival. A stable marriage would translate into a happy home for our family—a winning situation all round!

Still playing 'devil's advocate' I found myself thinking, *what, if, by some quirk of fate, he saw me on the road? What explanation could I give that would not spark off an argument? He might hurl the old, unfounded accusation that I was sneaking off to meet another man at me.* These thoughts jostled each other unrelentingly; vied for prominence on the short drive to the school where the meetings were held.

*"Please, Lord," I asked again in silent prayer, "don't let Mike find me out."*

I arrived early, impatient for the meeting to begin. The sooner we started, the sooner I could head back home. I was nervous and tense, albeit hopeful that these meetings would help me find a way to cope with my husband's ongoing drinking problem and loathsome, destructive behaviour.

Desperate, too, because nothing I tried on my own had worked so far, and, at this point, I was willing to try almost anything that would give me an insight into the monster which emerged from time to time, creating havoc in our home.

*Another chance.*

Here, please God, I would find the key. Quite frankly, I was at my wits' end; had all but lost the motivation and the desire to keep trying to save my marriage.

Colourful flowers growing in tidy beds lined the path which led to the entrance of the school building. As I made my way forward, I stopped to inhale their fragrances and almost applauded the aery dance of the butterflies winging their way gracefully from shrub to shrub and flower to flower.

Finding the classroom which had been set aside for the meeting was easy. Seating myself towards the back of the room, I took stock of my surroundings. The distinctive smell of chalk dust lingered in the air.

Letting my gaze travel around the room, I zoomed in on the childish drawings and collages covering almost all of the classroom walls. It looked as if this room was used by young children. Innocence shone through in the cheerful scenes depicted and the bright colours they'd used.

I pictured those little artists at work on their projects, crayon poised over paper, each expressing their own ideas and vision. I could almost hear the silence in the room while their young minds were hard at work; pictured their faces, each a study in concentration, little tongues protruding here and there.

In contrast, I felt used up and dull.

Because of Mike's constant abuse, my self-confidence had plummeted almost to zero, my belief in myself—that I was a good person—corroded. I was on the brink of despair and had confided this to the secretary of the organization. She had been sympathetic, understanding, and told me the more meetings I attended, the more I would learn to trust my own judgment again.

The urge to stand up and be counted, dormant for so long because of Mike's bullying, would grow strong. She also said the members supported and rallied round each other like family.

I needed answers and mental strength as much as I needed my daily bread. God willing, I would find it in this place. People were still filing in, but a lot of the seats remained unoccupied. No doubt, some were long-time members and others, newcomers, like me.

As a child, I disliked being center stage with a passion. Still today, I am reluctant to attract attention to myself. A throwback to the time when my dad used to make sure I was one of the participants on stage, singing a song, reciting a poem, or doing my tap-dance routine.

Advertising my plight to a roomful of strangers would not come easy.

Just thinking about the way my husband had changed over the years, how brutal and coarse he became after a drinking bout tied knots in my stomach. I just knew I would not be able to stop my tears when my turn came to speak out—if I dared speak out.

On the other hand, having battled solo for so long, opening up to people whose situations resembled mine could be cathartic. Hearing their stories, how they overcame the odds could be just what I needed to shore up my busted morale...impart much-needed hope that there *is* life after alcoholism.

It would suit me better if, today, I just listened to other people's experiences. I'd focus on taking charge of the tumult raging within me, focus on controlling the fear and feelings of helplessness that had overtaken me over the past years.

For now, resorting to my favourite game of people-watching seemed like a good idea. It might serve to calm me down. A simple game where I singled out one or two people close by, and then speculated about their lifestyle, occupation, hobbies, marital state—a handy conversation opener too.

The room was beginning to fill with people as I began my little game. Letting my gaze wander across the room, I prepared to study those around me but stopped in my tracks when my eyes came to rest on a tall man who had just entered and was abreast of the row where I sat. He looked straight at me. Our eyes locked.

Before I could avert my gaze, he smiled a friendly greeting. I responded by nodding my head but quickly looked away to discourage further contact.

It had the effect I was aiming for, and out of the corner of my eye, I saw him take a seat closer to the front, though still in my line of vision. From my vantage point, I continued my aborted observation of him, my eyes lingering on his profile. All thoughts of 'people watching' had now evaporated into thin air. He had made quite an impact on me, this tall man.

His hair was a light brown, graying at the temples, and showed signs of having been recently barbered. His dark brown eyes, narrowed as though always gazing into the distance, were set in a face which, at first glance or stretch of the imagination, could be described as beautiful or even handsome. Inscrutable, maybe. Later, on closer acquaintance, I would discover that his features, taken singly, were unremarkable. Yet, the impression of beauty would persist.

Beautiful. Not a word I would generally ascribe to the male of the species. Nonetheless, on knowing him better, this was how I would describe him. He was dressed casually but tastefully and his stature upright, impressive. My thoughts remained centered on him, and I felt a quickening of my pulse. An undefinable attraction.

In retrospect, a secret self, deep within me must have tuned in to the impact we were destined to have on each other. Oh! The irony of it. I came here to find a solution to my problems. Instead, in a wink, I find myself having to examine an inexplicable attraction to a total stranger.

The room had filled by this time and those in charge signalled the meeting was about to begin. After the welcome address, we joined in an opening prayer. The Serendipity Prayer. All formalities having been dispensed with, people took turns to stand up, introduced themselves to the group, and talked openly about their experiences. I could relate to most. It was as if they were telling my life story. I certainly did not feel isolated anymore.

I plead guilty to hiding Mike's bottle on more than one occasion in the past. It did not bode well for me when he found out. Someone in the meeting admitted to doing the same thing. They went on to say it sparked a violent episode. I learned then, hiding the liquor was not the answer.

More of my problems were reflected in the stories told by those present. Others told how they had resolved similar episodes. I was filled with hope that my situation could also change. If it were up to me, it certainly would, and I determined to change my modus operandi right away.

I could not summon the courage to speak out but, with a full heart, joined in saying The Lord's Prayer when the meeting ended. I did not linger, but made my way quickly to the parking lot, fearful that my luck would run out and my husband, having had a change of heart, had returned home earlier than had been his habit.

All the way home, I mentally replayed what I'd heard in the meeting. It made a lot of sense. More so, when compared to the methods I had previously used as I tried to curtail Mike's excessive drinking.

*Had I unwittingly contributed to the problem? Had I, in my ignorance, hindered rather than helped?*

*D*usk was falling as I drove through our quiet suburb. Children's shrill voices could still be heard, as they played in their backyards, reluctant to put an end to their games and the day. On entering our cul-de-sac, I set my sights on our driveway. Relief beyond words washed over me when I saw no sign of Mike's van. Except for a few teenagers lazily tooling their bicycles ahead of me, not much else stirred.

Once inside the house, I hurriedly changed into something more casual. Heaven forbid, Mike should come home and find me 'all dolled up'. I phoned Grace to let her know I was home and relayed the gist of all that had happened at the meeting.

"It sounds like you made a good choice to go to the meeting today… like you've spent a profitable afternoon."

"You bet! I want to put what I learned to good use. It won't be easy, especially when Mike is determined to pick a fight. Gracie, you just cannot imagine the hell he puts me through after a drinking session with that crowd with whom he runs around. Anything and everything is an excuse for him to act out."

"The thing is, Evie, judging by what you've told me, you now have a better way to handle Mike's episodes. I just wish you had taken me into your confidence sooner. Just thinking about what that monster has put you through makes me want to wring his neck!

"We go back too many years, you and I. Nothing will convince me you deserved to be treated so cruelly; no woman should be expected to take abuse lying down. I don't want you to keep me in the dark any longer…you're like a sister to me, so just tell me what I can do to help. Promise?"

"I promise!" She was sad and concerned for me. I could tell. "I knew you would stand by me, Grace. Things just seemed so complicated. I did not want this side of my life exposed. In some weird way, I thought to distance myself from you and others because I wanted to hide the fact that Mike was out of control, and that our marriage was crumbling. He calls me a loser, you know."

"You, a loser? Not in my book!" She scoffed. "Step back for a bit, Evie, consider the many curve balls you've had to field and the difficult choices you've had to make on your own. Even when you were just a kid. I've always admired your spirit and the way you worked at besting the fates instead of just wallowing in self-pity."

"I want my old life back, Gracie...a stable home life. One where Mike doesn't make drinking and hanging out with his cronies a priority over the weekends. It has been ages since he spent a Saturday at home. The boys and I have been left pretty much to our own devices on a Saturday. Sometimes he even sleeps out.

"You know, I was ashamed of what I had come to view as failure on my part to provide a happy home for my husband. Afraid, too, that people would look down on me. I guess, by keeping things to myself, I felt I could hold onto my dignity."

"The thing is, it looks like Mike has serious problems, and the sooner he faces up to them the better it will be for all concerned. In my opinion, he can't face his weakness, so he's making you the scapegoat!"

"Having you on my side makes all the difference now...I can't thank you enough. Moving right along, will you let the kids know I'm home? Tell them to hustle, will you? I'd like them settled in before Mike comes home. See you soon."

"I'll tell the twins you're home. Take care of yourself, okay?"

Benjy and George, with Boomer making up the rear, arrived soon after I put the phone down.

Because we were on our own, the boys and I had our favourite meal of fish and chips with lots of salt and vinegar. Listening to their happy account of their day took my mind off my problems.

An incident from some years back popped unbidden into my head. The four of us had gone to Zuurbraak to spend a few days with my father's family. Chickens and geese roamed free on their property. They also kept a couple of pigs in a pigsty. Well, the twins, about five years old and unattended at the time, decided to let them out, thought it would be fun to ride those animals. The pigs, however, were not used to this kind of treatment. Their frantic squealing alerted all and sundry to the fact that something was sorely amiss.

I'll have you know, Dear Reader, by dint of scrubbing with lots of soap and water, we were finally able to get those boys as fresh as the proverbial daisy.

George, after having seen those chickens running around in the back-yard all morning, declined the chicken wings he was later served for his dinner. On being asked the reason for his sudden aversion to something he had formerly enjoyed, this five-year-old, with a straight face, declared, "I won't like it because the chickens sweat under their arms!"

It took a lot of convincing and many months after our visit before he would agree to have another chicken wing on his plate.

The evening wore on and the house was quiet again. Later, when I'd looked in on them in their bedroom, the twins were each with nose buried in a favourite book. I lingered in the doorway, cast my mind back to when, at their age, I, too, loved reading in bed until sleep claimed me.

Now, on tenterhooks, I worried for them while I waited for Mike to come home, ears cocked for telltale signs of his mood. The screech of brakes as he rounded the corner on our street would be a dead giveaway, a sure sign he was on the warpath, spoiling for a fight.

There was no way Mike would be sober at this hour.

It was well after nine when I checked on the boys one last time. I straightened their bedding and gave Boomer the tummy-rub he adores. More than half asleep, they wanted to know whether I'd heard from their dad.

I saw no reason to give them cause for concern, so I simply said, "It's still early. He'll probably be home soon, so sleep tight and don't let the bed-bugs bite!"

Before leaving the room, I switched off their bedside lamps and heard them giggle at our little bedtime joke. Gazing at them by the glow of the passage light, I felt my heart swell with love and pride. They were good boys. Handsome boys—lovable, intelligent, and funny too. Both can lay claim to Mike's sense of humour.

Their well-defined, straight eyebrows favoured his side of the family, and, when I looked into either of the boys' eyes, it was as though I were looking at Mike's tawny green ones, framed by long lashes. They also have the same broad brow and widow's peak.

There was no denying they were Mike's offspring. Some other features, however, were definitely passed on from my side of the family. Both have my father's swarthy complexion. Benjy has a curl in his hair like mine and liked it kept short, whereas George's hair is straight and worn Beatles style.

My heart ached when I thought of the stress they sometimes had to endure because of their father's uncontrolled, drunken behavior—not the ideal role model for our growing sons. Our boys should not have to be exposed to such ugliness.

I prayed they would not succumb to alcohol cravings like their father.

Well-armed with my newfound resolution and insight, I planned to circumvent his abuse tonight—verbal or otherwise.

I waited. The evening stretched before me, and I had a feeling it would be a long one.

It was well after midnight when I finally gave up and headed for bed. Mike had not come home, nor had there been a phone call summoning me to the police station or hospital.

I looked in on the twins one last time before making my way to my bedroom farther along the passage. Standing over their beds while they slept, I felt a profound wave of concern wash over me. What if I failed to muster the courage to take a stand against their father's destructive habits? What if he, in one of his rages, harmed me and I could no longer care for them—what then?

Now I prayed that Mike would *not* come home. Better that he'd collapsed in a drunken stupor and stayed put than have him come stumbling home in the wee hours to shatter the peace with his foul-mouthed yelling and cursing. Or worse. We'd been down that road before. Time without number.

My prayers were to be answered.

I slept fitfully throughout the seemingly endless night, tossing and turning—plagued by mental images of my husband involved in an accident, being arrested for drunken driving. This would not be the first time. As a result, I overslept, but, in those first, waking moments, I had thoughts only of Mike. I left my bed, going headlong from room to room in search of him. I even went outside.

*Maybe he was sleeping it off in the van.*

There was no sign of the van in our driveway or garage. Mike hadn't made it home.

*W*e were in a mad rush to get ready for church. After a hurried breakfast, we set off. Still no sign of Mike. George, of the two, always the more concerned for his father's well-being, wanted to know whether I knew where his dad was and why he hadn't come home.

Ben, who had sized his father up long before this, simply shrugged his shoulders and said, "Guess there's not enough action at home. You know Dad. He likes to be where there's action!"

I steered the conversation into safer waters.

It was a glorious morning, one so typical of autumn in the Cape; truly the kind of day which makes one glad to be alive and in tune with one's Creator. Despite my concern over Mike and his whereabouts, I *was* glad to be alive. Thankful for many things, not least of which the fact that my boys were with me. Thankful, too, that we could spend a peaceful hour in church and find renewed strength.

The sermon, as it turned out, was mainly about the importance of tolerance and forgiveness. *Is this a sign?* I felt it must be because it dovetailed so beautifully with what I'd heard in yesterday's meeting.

On the way home, the boys opted for ice cream from Mr. Parker's Cafe. George, ever the keeper of the peace, said, "Let's take it home in case Dad's back."

As luck would have it, or *not*, I saw Mike's van parked in the driveway as we rounded the bend in our street. My pulse raced, and my palms became sweaty in apprehension.

*What awaited us inside? What sort of mood would he be in?*

"Dad's home!" yelled George. Grabbing the carton of ice cream, he made a beeline for the front door as soon as I had switched off the engine.

Ben, who had until now been quiet more than was his wont, observed, "Well, at least the van is parked on Dad's side of the driveway."

I rubbed his curly head as we headed towards our front door and said, "Guess we should be thankful for small mercies, right?"

I could tell he was nervous, so I gave him a reassuring look before we stepped into the house, where Boomer greeted us in his usual frenzied way.

As I entered the house, I was met with the aroma of grilled meat and sounds coming from the kitchen at the back. It told me Mike was cooking our Sunday dinner. A dead giveaway that he was in a contrite mood. My pulse steadied as I said a silent, fervent prayer of thankfulness because today, at least, there would be no belligerent bully to battle. This, I could live with!

At yesterday's meeting, amongst other things, I'd learned it was imperative to display a positive attitude and to offer praise when and where it was due. I planned to put it into practice at the first opportunity.

*Remain calm, I told myself—meet him halfway and make a point of letting him know you appreciate the fact that he was fixing lunch.*

Walking through the house to the kitchen seemed to take forever. Mike and I came face-to-face in the passage leading to the kitchen. Not knowing what to expect, he appeared hesitant.

I, on the other hand, with all the confidence I could muster, sailed right in and smilingly said, "Something sure smells good! What are you cooking?"

His relief at my friendly greeting was palpable. It showed on his face. Were I able to touch his expression, I imagined it would feel like velvet. Soft and smooth like the lamb's ear plants growing in our garden. He was wearing the Chef's apron I had made him the first year we were married.

"I made the salad earlier; the *boerewors*, chops, and potatoes are on the *braai*. George showed me the ice cream you bought. We put it in the freezer. How about ice cream on a cone after lunch for everybody?"

"Sounds like a plan to me, like you have everything under control. When do we eat?"

"There's time if you want to change. Pity if you did, though. You look lovely!"

"Thanks, Mike. It's a new outfit. I *should* change because I'd hate to get grease or something else on it…won't be long, then I'll come and sort out plates and stuff."

He did not follow me as I made my way to our bedroom. Relieved that he was safe—and in a good mood, to boot—still, I simply could not face an intimate moment with Mike right now; could not bear to have him touch me as though everything was hunky-dory between us.

Another time, I would immediately have berated him for his weakness, as I saw it, and expressed the feelings of disgust I felt for his lack of self-control. Now, I gave myself a talking-to.

After yesterday's meeting, I knew better. I'd learned, dwelling on negative issues was natural, but counterproductive. I'd also learned alcoholism is a disease and my husband needed my support, not evidence of my loathing for the person he had become. Mentally, I put myself back in the schoolroom where others, with worse circumstances than mine, had found hope for the future and were fighting to hold on.

Chiding myself worked! By the time I left our bedroom, I was composed and ready to face my husband with a changed attitude. This resulted in a resurgence of the old, familiar desire to fight back and beat the odds stacked against our becoming a happy family once again. I was going to give Mike yet another chance to do right by us.

The meal went off rather well. Mike was a competent cook and when the mood took him, loved pottering about in the kitchen or firing up the *braai*. Later, when he had caught up with everything the boys had done the previous day, they joined the neighbouring kids in a game of cricket on the big field across from our house. Boomer and I applauded their efforts.

To round off the day, we played a few games of Scrabble after supper. I, as usual, beat them hollow! I was reluctant to end this stress-free family time, but it was getting late, and there was school to think of the following morning.

"Okay, guys, we've had a long day. Time to hit the sack!"

Our kids are pretty good about knowing when to call it quits, so off they went, without a murmur, to the bathroom. After much splashing, and crying out, and laughter, they finally emerged—scrubbed clean, and ready for bed.

Together, Mike and I settled them for the night, listening to them as they decided which had been the best part of the day. Mike's eyes met and locked with mine across their beds, as we tucked in our sons.

Now, for *our* moment of truth—his, and mine.

With bedside lamps turned low, our bedroom was a cosy place; the colour scheme, furnishings, and accessories we had so lovingly chosen, conducive to relaxation and intimacy. Mike reached out as we prepared for bed. Holding me in a tight embrace and burying his face in my neck, he begged forgiveness for his latest lapse. His apologies to date were legion and his words predictable. I knew them by heart.

What would make this moment different from the ones that had gone before? My new-found attitude! Determined not to be sceptical, I *would* be compassionate, *would* accept his apologies with grace. My altered perception of my role as supporter would stand me in good stead.

Mike released me and looked into my eyes as he said, "Eve, believe me, I only had a couple of drinks with the boys but, because I was tired after the hectic week at work, plus, I hardly slept the night before, I just passed out. When I came to, it was way past your bedtime. I felt sick and much too ashamed to come home, so I figured I'd just stay put, sleep it off, and go home to freshen up after you had gone to church.

"I know you must have been worried. I'm sorry. I've made up my mind to quit. I know I've said this all before, but this truly is the last time. I swear! I want to live a sober life and I need one more chance to prove I can change. Please, sweetheart!"

There was an urgency to his plea I had not heard before, making it well-nigh impossible to doubt his sincerity.

"You *can* change, Mike. It *is* time you did, but you should change because you want to, not only because you think it's what I want. While we're on the subject of quitting, do you think it might be a good idea to speak to Doctor Edwards? Ask him if there are tablets he could prescribe? Does that sound like a plan?"

"Sounds like a capital plan to me! You know, I used to think I could lick this on my own, but it looks as if I do need help after all. I'll speak to Dr. Edwards to-morrow and get this show on the road."

"I've wanted to hear you say that for a such long time, Mike, and it does my heart good to hear the conviction in your voice. Our boys are growing fast. They need a sober role model; need to spend more time with their dad, especially over the weekends.

"Think of taking them camping again. They miss you and look for you to cheer them on at their cricket and rugby matches. They don't complain, but I know they are always disappointed when the other dads are on the field and you're *not* there."

Taking his hands in mine and looking deep into his eyes to give weight to my words, I continued, "They're elated when they're on a winning streak— they want to share their success with *you*; have *you* commiserate with them when they feel they've let the team down."

"Like I said, I'm sorry, and I promise I'll make it up to them and you. If counselling will help, I'm willing to give it a try."

With this last remark, he drew me into his arms again. Hearing the ring of sincerity in his voice left me without any defense and I went without hesitation into his embrace.

His admission was long overdue, but having finally owned his weakness, and having coupled it with a willingness to seek help, made Mike a bigger person in my eyes. I could tell he was also aware how far we had drifted apart. His tone left me in no doubt that he wanted our old relationship back.

This is what I'd been waiting to hear, and I believed him with all my heart when he said he intended to seek help.

Compassion flooded my being for this man whom I had once adored. I felt hopeful for our future. He was tender, yet passionate as we made up. Made love in the most real sense of the word. I felt wanted, needed as a woman; unlike other times, not just another body to satiate his selfish, male urges. This, taken together with Mike's humility (a quality that had been sadly lacking of late), created an intense desire to pleasure my husband. Set the mood for me.

Fully aroused now, I conveyed this to him in soft murmurings. The tempo of his lovemaking changed. My ardour and unbridled response created a ripple effect and together, we discovered a new plateau of intimacy and fulfillment.

It's been an eon since I'd been this moved when making love with Mike. I wept. He dried my tears and promised this was to be the turning point in our lives; holding me tenderly, as though I were something precious.

I was content. With Mike's strong arms encircling me in exactly the way I liked, I was on the verge of sleep, when a new thought flashed through my mind and drove all thought of sleep away.

*This intimacy was not to be taken lightly, it would be a work in progress; sustaining it would require constant work and commitment from both of us— I would give it my all. One day at a time.*

This was another lesson I'd learned at yesterday's meeting.

Sleep was elusive now, fled as I mulled over the life-changing road we were on. I lay awake long into the night, praying that we had indeed reached a turning point.

Like his mother, Mike is hung up on the 'family name' and, until now, both of them had been in denial about his weakness. Formerly, he would have preferred me to emulate her—sweep his peccadillos under the carpet and make excuses for him. So, having Mike agree voluntarily to seek counselling was a watershed moment indeed—prayers answered.

As good as his word, he consulted our doctor the next day and, by the end of the week, it seemed the medication which had been prescribed was kicking in; counselling would start a week later. The days following Mike's visit to our doctor passed with a surprising and welcome lack of tension.

I was relieved. He appeared to be genuinely committed to making the change to sobriety. When he started his counselling sessions, Mike was open about the details, giving me a lengthy account of the proceedings. I felt pangs of guilt because I had not yet told him about my one and only Saturday afternoon meeting with the Al-Anon group.

"Eve, I've read the stuff the doc gave me. Doc was emphatic! I have to take it one day at a time. *One day at a time.* I mean to hang in there and see this through. Doc warned me, if I ever think I can drink like 'normal' people, I'll for sure end up right back at square one! You should read it too, and I think I should go to my folks and also fill them in."

Thank goodness Mike was not as obdurate as his mother had been. What would she make of Mike's decision? This thought crossed my mind now. I'd confided in her; looked in vain to her for support. She'd been outraged at the time, and totally against the idea of asking for our doctor's advice. To quote her, "It was tantamount to airing our dirty linen in public."

*S*ome weeks have gone by since Mike started counselling and our lives seem to be on an even keel. Mike stays home and has picked up his old Saturday routine of spending time with the twins. On Sundays, he goes to church with us.

Today we had an early lunch and my three 'guys' were looking forward to spending the afternoon at the Newlands Rugby Stadium. They were going to watch a match between our national team and a visiting overseas team of some renown. This match had been highly publicized, and the boys did somersaults when Mike announced he had managed to get tickets. He had even bought tickets for Claud, Christopher, and little Kathleen.

Claud had offered to pick up Mike and our twins and chauffeur them to the stadium. George tailed his dad the whole morning; kept his dad in his sights until the Theunissens showed up. I guess he was afraid if Mike were to leave the house, something would happen to keep him away. We had, after all, been down this road many, many times before.

Mike, however, showed no signs of leaving the house all morning and, when Claud arrived with Christopher and Kathleen, they left for Newlands— highly excited, *happy as pigs in a puddle.*

*U*ntil now, I had only been to the one Al-Anon meeting because Mike no longer hung out with his buddies on Saturdays. Grace knew I felt a burning need to return because I wanted to learn more from this group. I also wanted to let them know they'd had a positive influence on me.

As promised, she accompanied me to the meeting and even offered to drive us there. I was grateful for the way she stood by me. Keeping Mike in the dark, however, did not sit well with me.

I hated telling lies.

On the way there, the face of the tall stranger I'd seen at the last Al-Anon meeting swam before my mind's eye, unbidden. The image, not unwelcome. He had captured my interest.

Once there, we seated ourselves. I found myself scanning the room for him. He was nowhere to be seen, but I did not have long to wait. I did not see him so much as sense he had entered the room.

I turned around. Our eyes met. He immediately approached me and asked whether the seat beside me was taken. When I indicated it was not he immediately sat down and introduced himself.

"Hello, there! I'm Jonathan James du Preez. When my mother calls me by my full name, I know I'm in trouble. Mostly she calls me Jamie. I am 'J. J.' to my friends."

This was said with a hint of laughter in his voice. The hand he extended, cool to the touch and incredibly soft, held mine in a firm grip that lasted just two breaths longer than I might have expected.

Grace was first to volunteer her name in return. I followed her lead and in doing so, had the perfect opportunity to discreetly study his face. I discovered that his features, taken one by one, were quite unremarkable. Many moons later, I would get to know him well and I would find my first impression to be a lasting one. To me, he would always be beautiful, however you sliced it.

In a voice that was well-modulated, warm, and intimate, he made small talk while we waited for the meeting to begin. I was all too aware of his nearness, and the incipient attraction I felt for this oh, so charming stranger. As a result, I did not say much. Grace obligingly stepped into the breach.

The magnetism, I concluded, was in his eyes; they drew me, looked deep into mine as if they could, at will, uncover every secret I'd ever had and lay bare my every emotion. I, strangely enough, wanted this man to know me and read my every thought.

Soft-spoken and reserved is how I would further describe him.

He had aroused my interest. Inexplicably. I sensed the feeling was mutual, at a time when my sense of self-worth had been at its lowest ebb.

Dear Reader, I am not averse to noticing a well-turned-out male, and there were those of the species, other than my husband, whom I had admired (discreetly, from a distance, of course) from time to time. Warm blood still coursed through my veins, after all. Nor am I oblivious to the admiring glances directed my way sometimes.

I was flattered, that's all. Here, though, I sensed a pull by a thread so fine it was gossamer-like but still strong. Insistent.

*Dangerous waters to be treading,* I admonished myself. Admittedly, leading up to the present, I had often been sadly neglected by my husband, sometimes even abused, but Mike had stepped up to the plate now; he and I were working at restoring broken trust and healing the rifts in our marriage.

Guilt assailed me.

Spurred on by Grace's presence, when the meeting began, I was one of the first to introduce myself to the group, eager to recount my experiences since my previous visit but at the same time, anxious to regain my seat and obscurity.

Slow to start, I explained how, after having heard their experiences, I gained new insight into my problem. Also, how hard I'd worked at changing my attitude. I told them how my changed attitude had encouraged my husband to seek help. Help, which, until then, he had resisted. I searched for just the right words to convey how hard I'd been fighting all the negative feelings I'd lived with for so long.

With many a break in my voice I told my story. Tears threatened to overflow but I held them back as I thanked them for being my inspiration.

There were many more stories told that afternoon. Some, again, mirrored my own.

Then there was Jonathan, a regular at these meetings because his wife had a history of alcohol abuse. This group had, to him, become akin to an extended family. Sadly, his story today told of yet another setback. Still, he firmly believed in the adage, *While there's life, there's hope.* Our hearts went out to him. We promised to pray for each other. It was time well spent.

> *God, grant me the serenity to accept the things I cannot change,*
> *Courage to change the things I can,*
> *And wisdom to know the difference.*

The meetings ended with the group saying this prayer.

Well aware the rugby match would still be in full swing and knowing our 'gang' would stay to the bitter end, Grace and I agreed we needn't rush home. We felt free to linger awhile, to mingle after the meeting but would leave in good time to be home before our rugby fans.

This, after all, was a special time for the group. People chatted over a cup of coffee or tea and bonded. Lifelong friendships were forged. Troubles halved. Soulmates found. The warm atmosphere, conducive to all of the above.

To my surprise, I spotted some old friends of ours with whom we'd lost touch. My first instinct was to avoid them and spare myself embarrassment until it dawned on me that we were all in the same boat. No need to hide when you were amongst people who cared and were non-judgmental.

Grace and I walked over to join my friends. Introducing her proved to be all the icebreaker I needed. Before long we were swapping stories of our involvement with the group and catching up as old friends are wont to do.

Words of encouragement and hope for healing just naturally found their way into our conversation. I told them in confidence that Mike was unaware I had become involved with this group and attended these meetings. They promised to respect my wishes but, with one voice, urged me to tell Mike before someone else inadvertently let the cat out of the bag.

"Take care. God willing, see you next week." These were the parting words on their lips.

Grace and I became separated. For a few brief moments, I found myself alone. This gave me a chance to mull over what had been said at this meeting, as well as everything I'd learned from the pamphlets I'd been reading.

For some time before today, a little voice in my head had been whispering I was not to blame for Mike's actions in any given situation. He had choices to make. Each time he showed poor judgment or lack of self-control, he alone should be held accountable.

It was here, in this moment, that I had my epiphany! *Mike's problem was due to a flaw in his makeup. Somewhere along the way, concepts like integrity and loyalty to our sons and me had gone south.*

During Mike's 'dark' period, when an opportunity presented itself, he did not hesitate to gratify his own needs; more often than not, with scant regard for the consequences or thought for how it would impact his family. When confronted, he invariably shrugged off responsibility for his actions.

I faced these facts squarely and it only strengthened my conviction that I should not take responsibility for Mike's weakness.

Support him. By all means. Be compassionate and refrain from judging him. This had been emphasised in the literature with which I'd armed myself at the first meeting. I also learned that a counsellor's job is made easy when patients admit when something has gone wrong. However, a counsellor cannot create qualities that are lacking, or instil qualities patients do not wish to own.

I felt purged; relieved of a burden which, for years, had been mentally weighing me down. Just then, Jonathan fell in step alongside me. Unable to contain myself, I blurted out my thoughts.

"I'm delighted for you, Eve. You seem to be getting your house in order. Does this mean we won't be seeing you anymore?" He smiled but there was a sadness in his eyes.

*His house was not yet in order.*

"Oh, no…you haven't seen the last of me. This group is my lifeline and I plan to attend the meetings as often as I can. I need to be here for myself as well as for Mike. As for getting my house in order, it's early days yet. It depends on my husband's continued commitment to sobriety."

I also wanted to let Jonathan know I empathized with him and understood the hurdles he and his wife were facing. On impulse, I reached for his hand. Clasping it in both of my own, I said, "I believe strongly in the power of prayer. You'll be remembered in mine."

"Thank you, Eve. I would appreciate that…" His voice trailed off but not before I detected the pent-up emotion, though; saw the pain in his eyes. The answering pressure in his grip wordlessly told me my prayers would be reciprocated.

I felt a definite fluttering in the region of my stomach before he released my hand, and, in that moment, I felt wholly connected to this man—a virtual stranger. I became keenly aware of stirrings in my body. Stirrings that caused the heat to rise to my face. They unsettled me—would have to be ignored.

"Oh, there you are! I hate to cut this short, Evie, but we really should be heading home soon." Grace's voice created a most welcome interruption, giving me an excuse to turn away from Jonathan and bury the emotions which I knew were written on my face.

"For sure! Thanks, Gracie. We were just finishing our conversation." With my composure restored, I turned to face him again.

"I look forward to seeing you next week, Jonathan. Meantime, look after yourself, okay?"

"You too, ladies." With a firm handshake for both of us and a lingering backward glance in my direction, he walked slowly toward the exit.

*G*race and I were each immersed in our own thoughts on the way home until she raised the subject uppermost on *her* mind.

Alcoholism.

Even though she was appalled at the unpleasantness some families and friends of alcoholics have to endure, she echoed my newly-learned compassion for the addicted.

I'd had Jonathan on *my* mind, replayed the sound of his voice—deep, distinctive, and even seductive. I could not help but wonder…was he drawn to me the way I felt drawn to him? Did he feel what I'd felt when our hands touched?

Had he sought me out at the end of the meeting, or had our paths had crossed by sheer coincidence? Intrigued by him, I sensed he was a man of strong character, albeit a lonely one. My heart went out to him.

I berated myself; shook myself mentally to dislodge these totally inappropriate wanderings of my mind. Disloyalty to Mike was foreign territory to me. I should rather concentrate on what Grace was saying. Moved to tears by the stories she'd heard this afternoon she gave voice to her thoughts.

"I'm saddened beyond words by the trauma that alcoholism creates in the lives of people's families and friends. I treated countless women with bruised bodies and faces when I was on duty in the hospital. Knowing you and the twins have had to endure it too, makes me doubly sad!"

It was at this point she broached the idea of the two of us becoming personally involved in the existing campaigns against alcohol abuse—finding a way to make a difference in the lives of women and children in abusive situations.

Grace even suggested we have fund-raising drives of our own.

A wonderful idea if we could get it off the ground, but, in all fairness, I'd first have to tell Mike about Al-Anon—make him understand my reasons for attending these meetings. Only then could I feel him out about the idea of committing myself to further involvement.

*Get him on board,* as they say.

For now, though, our project would have to be put on hold. The timing was all wrong. My situation, as I explained it to Grace, had me hog-tied. Mike had only just begun facing his demons and started counselling sessions. I simply could not start on the project without his knowledge and finding the right moment to tell him might not happen overnight.

Keeping my involvement with Al-Anon under wraps, however, continued to weigh heavily on my conscience. It went against the grain! Anathema to me! Sooner or later, I would have to find the courage; brace myself for the fallout. Until I do, Grace and I couldn't bring our ideas out into the open.

A "Catch 22" if ever there was one!

What's more, were I to reveal our plans to be actively involved in this project, I suspect he would be livid, see it as a betrayal; rail against my decision to have any part in it. This, coupled with the fact that I'd taken Grace into my confidence, had told her about his drinking problem, would be adding insult to injury.

As sure as God made little green apples!

In my heart of hearts, I could not be sure there would ever be a right moment to 'fess all.

Whichever way I played it, I'd be seen as a traitor. Taking his mother's stance, he would resent me for having attended the meetings and keeping him in the dark; say I was humiliating him by broadcasting our private affairs to the world. There could be repercussions. Should he feel the need to reach for the bottle again, this could well be the trigger, and, knowing Mike, he could easily pin the reason for his lapse on me. At this point, I could not jeopardize his commitment to sobriety.

We continued to discuss our plans, Grace and I, and eventually reached a compromise. I would hold off telling Mike. To keep our objective in view, however, and remain motivated, we decided to collect as much information as we could until we could both openly commit to our project.

We named it Helping Hands.

Grace would be the keeper of all information gathered. Unlike me, she knew she could count on *her* husband's unequivocal endorsement and promised, faithfully, not to let Mike get wind of our plans until I had cleared the decks at home, so to speak.

She accompanied me to Al-Anon meetings whenever her clan and mine went to a sports event. Even though it was often on my mind, I could not yet bring myself to tell my husband I'd been attending the meetings or fill him in on my decision to work alongside Grace concerning victims of abusive partners. Just thinking of the ways he might react intimidated and unsettled me.

Thoughts of my Saturday afternoons spent at the schoolhouse were synonymous with thoughts of Jonathan. They followed as naturally as day follows night. I sensed he was a man of strong character, albeit a lonely one. My heart went out to him.

I found myself reliving our last encounter and the way I felt, just being in the same room. I reminded myself, these thoughts should be kept at bay. Better left!

Life on the home front continued, on a fairly even keel. Weeks had come and gone, *and*, before I knew it, Mike had been sober for three months. He came across a tad edgy on the odd occasion. I put this down to stress and dealt kindly with him—praying he would remain strong and not stop the treatment or give in to the cravings.

Mike had—to the best of my knowledge—been taking the tablets prescribed by our doctor and was still seeing his counsellor. Lately, though,

I sensed he was keeping me in the dark about some of the details. He seemed tense, reluctant to discuss his progress with me, said he was doing what he'd agreed to—follow doctor's orders—and added, irately, that was all I needed to know.

We appeared to have reached an impasse. This was not good. It distressed me because I saw it as his way of shutting me out again. If he were making genuine progress, shouldn't he be over the moon? Eager to share with me? Could it be, he felt his hold on sobriety was tenuous? I began to doubt whether he still went for counselling.

I kept these troubling thoughts from Mike. Instead, found ways to let him know just how much I appreciated his ongoing efforts. I prayed long and hard for the Mike who had courted me to regain the upper hand over his demons.

It would seem the gods were on my side, when, a mere two weeks later—as though he'd had a change of heart—Mike started opening up about his progress again. My prayers had been answered, and my fears laid to rest.

Even though I dreaded the negative ways in which Mike could react, keeping my secret was no longer an option. The constant threat that someone could inadvertently let the cat out of the bag kept hanging over my head—much like the proverbial sword of Damocles—loomed ever larger. This possibility became too much for me. I must speak up. Soon!

*W*hen Friday dawned, I decided to take the plunge. I would tell him no later than this evening. There! The decision had been made!

I needed a captive audience; needed to set the scene and choose the right words. The timing was perfect because the twins had been invited to a birthday party and would be staying over at the Arendses' home until Sunday.

Grace and her family would be leaving later today to spend the weekend with Claud's parents. I decided to phone and fill her in on my plan. In her trademark, warm, supportive way, she backed me up and said she would pray for Mike to see reason. Still, I sensed the concern underlying her words.

"Let me know how it turns out, Evie."

"For sure. You guys have a *lekker* weekend, hey…give love to Claud's parents."

Mike and I would be alone tonight. I *would* have my captive audience. Setting the scene posed no problem. Choosing the right words, however, would be the challenge. I would present my case lovingly and appeal to Mike's sense of fairness. I decided to lay the foundation for success with a special meal and a romantic setting.

I associate cooking Mike's favourite meals with happier times—intimate times. Times when we had something special to celebrate or times to just set the mood for a romantic evening.

Mike's mom had given me a list of his favourite foods soon after our wedding. *Bobotie,* with all the trimmings: yellow rice with raisins, chutney, sliced banana, and shredded coconut ranked high on this list. I've cooked it for Mike countless times over the years, and it always went down well. I decided to prepare it for our meal tonight. I would also make a tried-and-tested *malva pudding*, using another recipe that my mother-in-law had passed on to me. Of course, there would be custard to go with it.

While preparing our meal, I mulled over how best to break the news to Mike later tonight, kept thinking of the various ways in which he could respond after I'd made a clean breast of my ongoing involvement with Al-Anon. It could all blow up in my face. This gave me pause for thought. Although I wanted to be optimistic about his reaction, doubt lingered. I longed for our former, uncomplicated life. I confess, at times, I *had* taken it for granted.

In those far-off days, when we spent an evening alone, it had always turned out exactly as I had envisioned—beginning with a lovely meal I'd gone to great lengths to prepare. We would linger over a glass of our favourite wine, and our mutual enjoyment of the magical music of Richard Clayderman completed the scenario. The evening invariably culminated in hours of intimacy.

Tonight, however, there would be no wine.

While waiting for Mike to come home from work, I set the table in the kitchen with our good dishes and cutlery, and flowers from our garden. The result was inviting.

Mike was touched that I'd gone to so much trouble. After tasting the first mouthful, he whispered across the table, "You make the best *Bobotie*, Evie. Don't tell my mom I said so, okay?"

The air was relaxed while we ate, and we looked into each other's eyes often during the meal. Mike liked to tell me about his day at work. Tonight, was no exception. I always encouraged him and lent a sympathetic ear when, for whatever reason, a job had not gone as smoothly as planned.

Reluctant to say anything at all that would put a damper on our evening, I kept my contributions to safe subjects. I commented on Mike's relationship with the twins and how much their school marks had improved since he began sitting in on their study hour after supper each night. I broached the idea of taking a holiday when the boys were home from school in December.

Mike left his seat and walked around the table to where I sat. Lifting me from my seat he took me in his arms.

"Eve, it's been the highlight of my day coming home to you and the twins. Your support, especially over the past little while, has meant the world to me. I admit I've been foolish beyond words, to let the drink get the better of me. Going for counselling helped. I can see it's a huge mistake to think I can drink like 'normal' people. Taking my first drink *will* undo all I've accomplished, and I'd end up at square one.

"Believe me, I've been down on myself many times for being so weak. I know you guys didn't deserve the hell I put you through, and I thank God you stuck by me and got through to me when you did. I want to spend the rest of my life making things right with you and the boys. One day at a time!"

His words were charged with emotion.

What could I do, other than hold him tight? I ask you! We tidied the kitchen together after he'd helped himself to a second bowl of dessert. On the way to the front room, he smacked his lips appreciatively in anticipation as he carried the tray which held the chocolate cake I'd baked and the paraphernalia for our tea.

After putting the tray down on the coffee table, he took my hands in his and drew me down to sit next to him on the couch.

"What a treat! First, *malva pudding*, and now chocolate cake too? You're spoiling me, sweetheart…hey, I'm not complaining!" His voice tapered off as he smacked his lips once again.

"Well, we can do a stint in the garden in the morning. I think that should take care of those pesky calories. Right?"

Our front room was furnished with a mixture of old and new. Old, being some of the furnishings his grandparents had left him. Among the pieces Mike had chosen to keep was the large carpet in muted shades of blue and beige. This covered the greater part of the parquet floor. I quite liked the carpet; it had determined our choice of curtains and the colour scheme in this room.

Also inherited were three oil paintings: one large landscape depicting a mountain range and autumn foliage hung over the mantel; two smaller ones, each of a complementing olde world garden scene, graced either side of the mantlepiece—Mike had done a handsome job of restoring the fireplace to its original beauty. Taken together, these lent visual interest to the room. A focal point, as it were. A fire was laid, but it's been ages since it was last lit.

To round off the décor, we had bought a couch, two armchairs, a coffee table, and end-tables complete with reading lamps before we married. Our choices were eclectic but all-in-all, made for comfort and a look all its own. Quite pleasing, or so we both thought!

One last piece that Mike had kept was an oval gilt mirror—its frame beautifully decorated with sprays of flowers. "It's Victorian." he'd said with pride when we hung it in the passage, over the half-moon table that I'd brought from the flat all those years ago.

Much later, after we had leisurely enjoyed our tea and cake—a hefty slice for Mike—by the soft glow of candlelight, and the seductive voice of Doris Day in the background, I turned to face him. Looking deep into his eyes, I spoke lovingly, giving him credit for turning over a new leaf; stressing how much the tension at home had eased because of his continued abstinence.

I let him know just how proud I was of his efforts and his progress; reassured him that my concern would always be for his welfare and harmony in our household.

Mike was in a mellow frame of mind at this point. More to the point, he was stone-cold sober. Those tablets he was taking to control his urge to have a drink were spot on. Keeping his mood on an even keel for the rest of the evening would be another matter altogether.

There was a good chance that the lingering ambiance could well be lost. This, I knew full well, but I took the plunge. It was now or never!

I'd set the scene as best I knew how. Now, I prayed the time was right, that Mike would be in a receptive mood. With a leap of faith, I segued into the dreaded topic…my involvement with Al-Anon. I had been sitting back against the couch cushions before. Leaning forward, I took both his hands in mine, and held his gaze steadily.

With many a false start and monitoring his every expression, I told him my changed perception about alcoholism stemmed from having attended a few Al-Anon meetings and having gained firsthand knowledge of how others coped with situations much like ours.

By the time I had begun outlining the plan Grace and I were working on to help women in abusive situations, I saw Mike's expression had changed. It had taken on a decidedly wooden look, a sure sign he was fast losing it. My worst fears were being realized. I felt the ground under me beginning to crumble like old, dried leaves underfoot.

All the while gauging his reaction, hoping desperately that I would be able to stem the tide of his anger, *and* with as much diplomacy as I could muster, I persevered, tried to make him see how much this project meant to Grace and me. I continued in my effort to explain how badly we both wanted to be of service in the community. It was to no avail, however.

By this time, his stare was as blank as the eyeballs of the dead, and I felt his body stiffen before he withdrew his hands abruptly from mine. Silence had settled over us while Mike sat motionless beside me during those tense moments. Now, it was the other Mike—the hateful Mike—whose face I saw. He was livid! It showed in his flushed face; showed in the long, cold stare he levelled at me. His body, taut, like one of his guitar strings, tightly strung.

In split seconds, incidents from the past flashed through my mind, had me anticipating physical violence. Talk about skating on thin ice; I felt as though I were about to fall in—began to dread the almost inevitable backlash to my revelation. I was nervous and my palms were sweaty.

Glancing at my watch, I saw that it had been mere minutes since I had started unburdening myself, but it seemed as if an eternity had passed, as if time and the world must have come to a standstill in the meantime. He saw me glance at my watch, and, as if this were his cue, ejected himself from his seat in a single, forceful movement. Without a backward glance, my husband stormed out as if he meant to remove himself from me, mentally and physically.

In all fairness, he *had* heard me out, but had not spoken a single word to me, nor had he interrupted me once in all the time it took for me to tell my story. Now, his body language told all. Boded an unhappy outcome. Told me I had taken a gamble and lost. Abysmally.

I had hoped against hope and with all my heart for a positive reaction. Instead, a chasm that was a mile wide and twice as deep appeared to have opened between us. It would seem my earlier apprehensions were justified. Unable, for the moment, to form a coherent thought, and utterly dismayed by the outcome, I stayed sitting a while longer where he'd left me.

As if from another realm, I heard him making his way to our bedroom; heard sounds coming from our en suite bathroom. Familiar sounds telling me he was preparing for bed registered somewhere in my subconscious.

My world had bottomed out. It felt as though my heart were drowning in misery. I was left with the certain knowledge that we had reached a watershed, *and*, for what seemed like an eternity, I was rooted to the spot; drained by his reaction and unable to summon up the energy to go after him. On some level, I was afraid Mike would raise his hand to me if I followed him.

Myriad thoughts flitted through my mind, tumbling helter-skelter over each other as I tried to anticipate how this situation would be resolved. Not in my wildest dreams could I have anticipated the feeling of utter despair that would engulf me; I could only pray Mike would continue to remain sober after this.

Too late now to question the wisdom of having bared my soul to Mike, and also my timing.

What's done is done!

Tears stung my eyes, blinded me, but I managed to hold them back. On the edge of caving, I took a deep, calming breath.

No way would I let my husband intimidate me at this point! I believed in our project. My purpose and my desire to help others in distress were larger than Mike's ego. Any other time would have seen me going after him, placating him to keep the peace. Not now, however. A principle was at stake. So, too, my rights as an equal partner in this marriage.

My determination was renewed tenfold.

I *would* stand up and be counted! *Mike's ego be damned.*

I doused the candles, faintly aware of their lingering, smoky smell, carried the left-over cake and dirty dishes to the kitchen, washed them, and left them to drain. Putting away the cake was one more thing I bid myself do, all the while telling myself to call it a day and go to bed.

Procrastination personified!

When I could find nothing more to keep me there, I turned off all the lights and headed resolutely for our bedroom where Mike was already lying under the covers. As I lay down beside him, I could tell he was not sleeping. I touched his face lightly, in a loving gesture, and said goodnight.

He flung off my hand as though he could not bear my touch; giving me the cold shoulder—it would seem the path of anger is easier to travel than the road to forgiveness.

Sleep eluded me for most of the night as I lay in our bed behind my husband's unyielding back. There might as well have been a brick wall between us, and every moment of silence was like another brick that had been cemented down until the wall became insurmountable. The emotional distance between us appeared unbridgeable.

I must have drifted off in the wee hours, for I woke the next morning to the sound of the garage door being slammed shut. I opened my eyes to find that Mike's side of the bed was empty. He had left our bed and the house without waking me. Minutes later, I heard him drive off in his van—it was barely five o'clock on this Saturday morning.

I doubt he had slept much. His total silence since the night before, combined with his early morning exit, did not augur well for a peaceful weekend. I quailed at the thought, and, as the first fingers of dawn crept slowly into my bedroom, every vestige of sleep took flight. There seemed to be no point in my staying abed any longer.

I rose and, in zombie fashion, made my way to our bathroom where I breathed in the remnants of his aftershave fragrance. Its fruity, floral, spicy notes took me back to mornings when we were on our honeymoon. By my count, now just shy of seventeen years when I got my first whiff of Old Spice and became familiar with the smell of Mike when freshly shaven.

I used to love the smell of Mike at any given time, even when he came in from having worked all day in the soil; the rich smell of the earth still clinging to him.

The smell of stale alcohol on his breath, however, had the opposite effect on me. Turned me off. Would, that I need never smell it on my husband again!

A long, relaxing bath was what I needed just then to start my day. A bath plus my morning cup of Rooibos tea, taken in my favourite spot in our secluded backyard, would not go amiss.

*W*inter is on its last legs on this late August morning and the sun still climbing in a blue sky. I welcomed its warm rays as I made my way to the garden at the back of the house. The puffy, white clouds floating by overhead put me in mind of cotton balls and untoasted marshmallows.

Our front and backyard gardens were Mike's pride and joy. Mine too, for that matter, because we'd both put many companionable hours of loving, tender care into its creation and upkeep. We loved working side by side out here. He had styled it after an English country garden with well-filled perennial borders mixed with colourful annuals and bulbs.

Hosta plants grew in profusion no matter how many times Mike divided them. They had spread themselves all along the perimeter of our backyard. He often shared them with family and friends and sometimes used them in the landscaping business.

Mike's experience and artistry in landscaping shone not only in our garden; it was his field of expertise, how he earned his living. It had also earned him the coveted title of 'Best Gardener' in the local gardeners' club for the past three years. The three trophies were on display in his small office, off our bedroom.

On any given day, pulling weeds was one of my favourite things to do, next to deadheading the flowers and watering the garden. I found these tasks extremely therapeutic.

Having donned my once elegant, wide-brimmed sun hat, I stepped onto the paved pathway and set my mug of fragrant, warm tea on the wooden picnic table near the huge jacaranda before turning on the sprinkler system that Mike had installed.

Watering the garden seemed like an excellent idea just then. We hadn't had much rain this winter, so this mundane task would serve a double duty today—it would give the plants some needed refreshment and serve as a distraction at the same time.

As I sipped my tea, I spied a couple of gorgeous butterflies fluttering about and lost myself in the sound of cheerful birdsong and bees humming. Our backyard was a tranquil place just then. A sweet-smelling retreat, where fluffy, fragrant peonies bloomed profusely.

A treasure trove of roses greeted me as I left my seat and wandered over to the sweet-smelling white ones cascading from the wrought iron pergola. As I ran my fingertips lightly over their satiny red petals, I was reminded of painted, raw silk. Making my way around the entire backyard, I inhaled the heady fragrance given off by the hedge of white and pink oleanders, also still in full bloom.

The delphinium seedlings which Mike had planted were doing well. Shaded from azure to almost navy blue; under Mike's care and his green thumb, they would become tall and stately.

Unbidden, a far-off childhood memory played itself out in my mind's eye. A memory of my late-lamented father, pointing to some delphinium plants on one of our many Sunday afternoon visits to the Cape Town Gardens on Government Avenue. Their perfection had all but taken my breath away.

Unbidden, also, the words of a certain song came to mind, "…only God can make a flower grow…" I reasoned, if He can make a flower grow, surely He will help me in this time of need?

I spent a long time deadheading the plants, as I moved from one flower bed to the next, but, as the morning wore on, a stiff breeze had sprung up, making my task a tad uncomfortable. I decided to head back into the house where I busied myself with my usual Saturday chores and fielded a few work-related phone calls for Mike.

When midday came and went without any word from him, alarm bells started ringing in my head. I hoped against hope that he had not gone on a drinking spree, using my 'disclosure' as an excuse to slide off the wagon.

It was hours later now. I'd been wandering aimlessly from room to room and finally ended up facing the picture window in the living room. Sunshine was streaming into the room as I kept a look-out for Mike's return; looked out the window for the umpteenth time, yet taking in nothing of the outside scene. Try as I might to shun them, negative thoughts persisted and, in their wake, the fear that my earlier apprehensions were justified.

The still-warm, late afternoon rays of the sun travelling across a cloudless blue sky, stroked my upturned face as they journeyed into the room; caressed my being but failed to warm me. Neither did they help to dispel the gloom that immobilized me.

Having kept my pent-up emotions in check until now, my equilibrium was in danger of becoming a thing of the past. Tears kept pooling in my eyes, kept blotting out everything in sight, but I wiped them away and turned my back to the window.

I had earlier, perforce, put aside all thought of leaving the house. Now, I sat down and paced the rooms in turn. Endlessly. Like a caged animal. Hour after weary hour.

"*Saturday night is the loneliest night of the week...*" these lyrics, from a Frank Sinatra hit, float across my brain. How apt! I can totally empathise with the author of those words. In former years, Mike and I had always spent Saturday nights together. Now, it has become the norm for him to be out with his cronies, with me stuck at home, wondering where he could be and when he'd show up.

Night had fallen! It had crept stealthily into the room where I sat.

Still waiting for my husband's return.

I was about to run a bath, prepare for an early night when I went to answer a knock at my front door. I had earlier switched on the *stoep* light. Now, before opening the door, I saw the silhouettes of two people through its glass panels. Somehow, I was not surprised to see two policemen on my *stoep* when I opened the door...it was as though I already knew why they were there.

One of the policemen looked young, in his early twenties and the other, much older. Closer to retirement age. I invited them in, led the way to the front room with a calm that belied a sinking sensation in my chest threatening to suffocate me. They brought news of Mike's accident. He had been injured in a motorcar accident. They offered to take me to the hospital.

The dreaded scenario which had been living in my head for years had actually become a reality! While the older man explained what had happened, I broke out in a sweat, my hands felt clammy, my mouth went dry, and my tongue seemed swollen, making it difficult for me to swallow. I stood before them as one shell-shocked, trying to make sense of the words being spoken.

"This can't be true!" To this day, I don't know whether those words actually came out of my mouth or whether they were locked in my brain.

The policemen, seeing my distress, were kind and considerate; the older one led me to a chair while the other suggested a drink of water. In that moment I was incapable of forming an answer. Their news had devastated me.

"Can I get you a glass of water, Miss?" the young man asked. Again.

"Yes, please. The kitchen is down the passage." I had recovered somewhat but my voice sounded far-off in my ears.

Did I want to call a relative or friend and have them drive me instead?

"Please, just take me to the hospital to see my husband," I managed through tears and trembling lips.

The older one asked, "Would it help to have someone meet you at the hospital?"

I was desperate for a shoulder to lean on. Literally and figuratively. When I was able to put two thoughts together and come up with a name, the only person, other than Grace, who could fill this need would be Mike's uncle Dave. Thankfully, he lives only twenty minutes away.

"I should call my husband's uncle. He'll know what to do."

I tried dialing Uncle Dave's number, but my hands shook like leaves in a storm.

"Let me." Gently removing the receiver from my cold hand, the older man made the call. On seeing my distress, took it upon himself to apprise Uncle Dave of the situation when he answered his phone.

The officers made small talk on the way to the hospital. Asking questions about our children, their schooling, and hobbies. I can only assume they did this to keep my mind off the ordeal awaiting me. Their compassion had a calming effect.

In between answering their questions, I pleaded with God to watch over Mike.

The short distance to the hospital appeared to stretch into eternity. A godsend, on the one hand, because I had no way of knowing just how bad Mike had been injured, and I was terrified of the unknown. Somehow, felt I had to be prepared for the worst.

On arrival, I was told Mike had been taken to emergency. He was in a coma and had not yet regained consciousness. Doctors were attending and assessing his condition. I hadn't seen him. In a way, it was a huge relief as it would give Uncle Dave time to join me before I did. I dreaded having to see Mike on my own.

"A write-off!" This was the older policeman's take on Mike's van.

The younger man kindly stayed with me while I waited for Uncle Dave to arrive.

The time leading up to my arrival at the hospital had become a big blur, and I panicked because I could not remember locking the front door or whether the windows were shut, or whether I'd fed the dog.

Uncle Dave arrived post-haste. Oh! The relief to have someone share my burden. His mere presence was a comfort. I found myself describing, in detail, what had transpired last night, pouring out my pent-up misery.

"...Mike left home without saying good-bye to me this morning, and I've had no word from him all day. He was probably still angry when he crashed...I've been worried sick all day and afraid he would be under the influence and lash out at me when he did come home. Instead, the police showed up. They said he was under the influence and the car's a write-off... he was speeding and drove through a red light into a bus!"

"Don't take this on yourself, my girl. I know Mike's been sober for some time, but anything could have tipped him over the edge, so I don't blame you for having feared the worst today, Eve. Now we can only pray that he'll come out of this in one piece, and, hopefully, after this accident, he will come to his senses. Once and for all. I sincerely hope it puts the fear of God into him!"

One of the nurses came to tell us, "Mr. Moore had been brought in by ambulance. We've taken x-rays and various tests. The doctor will be along in a little while with more information."

The wait for news seemed interminable. I'd already been at the hospital for more than two hours when a doctor brought us news of Mike's condition. An older man. He was empathetic in his dealings with us, and I appreciated his common-sense approach in letting us know what Mike was up against.

Looking directly at me he said, "Mrs. Moore, your husband hasn't woken up. This is quite significant. He has not responded to stimuli. This leaves little room for doubt that he has sustained extremely traumatic brain and spinal injuries. At present, it would be unwise to hold out any hope for a full recovery.

"Rest assured, his condition will be carefully monitored at all times, and staff will do everything needed to ensure his comfort."

Stunned, I felt a shaking of the ground I was standing on. Or so it seemed.

Uncle Dave was my rock. The news must have been equally shocking for him, but he asked all the questions I was unable to formulate.

Some time after the doctor left us, and once Mike had been moved to Intensive Care, we were allowed to visit him. He lay motionless, hooked up to an intravenous tube, his head swathed in bandages. What could be seen of his face was not a pretty sight. His bruises, a rainbow of colour. When I first laid eyes on him, I ached. When I thought of his pain, I shuddered. I felt sick to my stomach. I did not want to believe it was my husband lying in that bed.

Still as death! Close to death?

*What were you thinking, Mike?* This thought ran like a refrain through my mind as I clung to what bordered on the last vestiges of my self-control. Uncle Dave caught my eye, shaking his head as if in total disbelief at the sight that confronted us. From the look on his face, I could tell his thoughts and mine were totally in sync. *What were you thinking, Mike?*

Uncle Dave stayed in the room and, after a little while, left me alone with Mike.

"I love you, Mike. Wake up, Mike... Please, wake up!" I implored. "You left home without saying good-bye, and I know you were angry with me when you left this morning. Please get better so that we can set things right. We want you to come home…we need you."

I took his hand and closed both my hands over his while I spoke, hoping to feel some response. There was nothing. No inkling that he heard me.

Uncle Dave returned after a while. We stayed until the nurse suggested we leave and come back in the morning after we had rested. My concern now was for the twins. How would it affect them to see their father in this state? How would they cope with this image of him? Maybe, for the rest of their lives? How was I to tell them their dad might not make full recovery? What would that mean to them? How could I comfort them and make it all better?

I turned to Uncle Dave, who, seeing the abject misery written all over my face and my slumped shoulders, read my thoughts, offered a reprieve. "Let's leave the twins undisturbed for the night. We'll pick them up in the morning and take them to the hospital once we've broken the news to them."

It was close to ten that night when we left the hospital. Uncle Dave's thoughts centered on Mike's parents. They should be told right away, but how best to break the news to them?

Relief washed over me when he offered to break the news to Mike's family.

*U*nderstandably, the family's initial reaction was shock and disbelief. Mike's mother was beside herself with grief. I felt more sorry for her than I could ever put into words. When I went to embrace her though, she would have none of it. She pushed me away with all her might.

"Do you know Mike came by for breakfast this morning and told me how you went behind his back to join that group? I warned you! I warned you long ago not to get involved with them. Didn't I? You went ahead anyway, and this is the result. My son is in hospital now and it is all your fault. You drove him to it. He was furious when I told him you knew I was against it from the start.

"Mike made no bones about it. He vowed he would put a stop to it.

"*That's* what my son thought of your precious Al-Anon and the rest of your plans. Now, I want you out of my house! I never want to see you again!"

Near hysteria and blinded by the tears which fell heedlessly during the verbal onslaught she directed at me, she stumbled out of the room. A truly broken woman. Mike's dad stayed just long enough to tell us they'd be at the hospital first thing in the morning before he hurried after his wife.

Iris stayed until we had answered all her questions—her grief, plain as daylight but, unlike her parents, she showed empathy for Uncle Dave and me.

Our visit was brief. As we closed the front door behind us, I could hear unmistakable, heartrending sobs coming from Mike's parents' bedroom, farther down the passage. They were distraught. My heart went out to them, but keeping my distance was best for all concerned.

When Mike first introduced me to them, his mother had been cordial. However, I noticed a shift in her attitude when we announced our engagement and plans to marry. From then on, she showed no inclination to warm to me as a person. She had been quite vocal about her disapproval, more than once over the years. My father-in-law was like-minded. He walked in her shadow.

I had wanted her approval, but my efforts largely fell on stony ground. In my humble opinion, had she been able to choose a wife for her blue-eyed boy, she would probably have chosen a girl from within their social circle— one whose parents were well established and well-to-do.

Having just learned I'd gone to the Al-Anon meetings against her advice added insult to injury and alienated her even further. It was unfortunate because I had simply followed my heart and done what I thought best for my family.

Being blamed for Mike's accident was another matter entirely, an unbearably hard pill to swallow. I don't know how I am going to live with that. She now had the perfect excuse to sever all ties with me.

Uncle Dave supported my faltering steps as we walked to his car. He apologized for the unfeeling behaviour evinced by his brother and Mike's mom's outburst. It comforted me somewhat.

My mother-in-law's last words pealed in my ears as we drove to my home in Diep River. Once there, we went straight to the kitchen where Uncle Dave thoughtfully made tea for us.

Heartsore and in acute mental distress, I sat at my kitchen table with my head in my hands, while I waited for the tea to brew. The image of Mike, as he lay motionless, swathed in bandages in the hospital bed, would not go away. Compared to what Mike was suffering, a raging headache seemed like the least of my problems; a Grand-Pa powder would most likely take care of it.

How on earth would I make it through the night? How face the coming days? What news of Mike would they hold? One thing I did know for sure, breaking the news to Benjy and George would be indescribably difficult.

Where would I find the words, the strength? How do I comfort them? They were both close to their dad. More so, George.

"I don't like the idea of you being alone tonight, Eve. You should have someone close by."

His offer to stay the night was a blessing and I accepted it with alacrity. For now, I could look to Uncle Dave for help. Being familiar with Mike's weakness, he'd had no scruples before when it came to reading Mike the riot act. Unlike Mike's mom and dad.

My thoughts whirled around in my head, and my brain just refused to make sense of this long night's train of events. Somewhere, in this maelstrom, surfaced the names of people who should be told of Mike's accident in the morning.

There was my mother, who had always been so fond of Mike. It was unthinkable to disturb her at this hour. Grace and Claud too. They would want to know. Sooner, rather than later. Auntie Miriam and Uncle Jacob were overseas on holiday…I'd ask Grace to let them know.

The clock in the kitchen said three o'clock! Uncle Dave had, by this time, finished his tea. Numbed, but by dint of habit, I cleared away the tea things and set the kitchen to rights. We said goodnight as he made his way to the twins' bedroom and I, blinded by my tears, to the one I shared with Mike.

I lay on my bed, fully clothed, lacking the will to get undressed. My thoughts were out of control, going hither and thither. It seemed like only yesterday I'd first decided to join the support group, yet more than half a year had already gone by. So much had happened since then. Our marriage, for one, had seemed to be heading in the right direction once again, and Mike had been spending his free time at home with us. We'd even begun to socialize with family and friends.

Now, anger set in; anger, at Mike's lack of responsibility—his selfish disregard for the consequences of his reckless behaviour. The impact on his family, however, would be long-lasting.

It wasn't fair! It wasn't fair! I fell into a fitful sleep to this refrain as tears dried on my cheeks.

*T*he dawn crept into my room through the open curtains, and the sun cast a rosy glow in the sky. I saw it all through tear-filled eyes as I lay on my bed. My first thought was of the twins.

I called the Arendses' home around eight. Sylvia answered the phone; I could hear her boys and mine talking nineteen to the dozen in the background.

"'Morning, Sylvia. It's Eve. I'm afraid I have some shocking news. Please don't let on to the twins…Mike's been in an accident and is still in hospital."

"Oh! My dear, how terrible! I am so sorry. How bad is he?" What can I do to help?"

"It's bad, I'm afraid. I'll tell you more when I pick up the boys in a few minutes. Sylvia, dear, you and Don have already helped by having the boys over yesterday and last night. There is nothing much anyone can do now but pray for Mike. His uncle is with me and will be driving me over to pick up the twins.

"It's a godsend they were at your house last night. You have no idea how much that helped. At least they were able to spend the night in ignorance. Thank you for always being so good to them. I'll see you shortly, okay?"

She said she would be waiting for us and then hung up.

Don met us in their driveway. Out of earshot of the twins, he immediately voiced his concern for our family. He said the children were playing in the backyard and Sylvia had sent him to keep an eye open for our arrival.

I introduced the two men as Don led us toward the house. Sylvia stood in the open doorway to welcome us.

We followed her to the kitchen, where we could see the children through the window. Uncle Dave, wanting to spare me, did most of the talking and told the Arendses what we knew about the accident.

Almost in one voice, they offered their support.

"Don't hesitate to call on us. Night or day! Promise?"

Since they knew we were anxious to be alone with the twins, Sylvia led us to their front room, while Don went to call them in. He did not come back but stayed outside with his children. To give us the privacy she thought we'd need, Sylvia also left us alone. Her footsteps echoed as she quickly made her way along the passage to join her family.

When Benjy and George came into the room, they were still playfully jostling each other, their faces flushed and happy. I, wordlessly, reached out to embrace them. As if sensing something was amiss when they saw that Uncle Dave, not their dad, was with me, they stopped dead in their tracks.

They would be crushed, no matter how carefully I couched the news of their father's accident and told them he was in the hospital. Loath to shatter this carefree moment with news of Mike's accident, I hesitated but could think of no way to soften the blow. What I was steeling myself to tell them might as well have been written on my face, because Benjy immediately blurted out, "What's wrong? Where's Dad?"

The truth had to be told but it was more than his sons should be asked to bear! As gently as I could, and with my arms holding them both close, I said, "There was a terrible accident late yesterday afternoon. Dad is in the hospital. He was still unconscious when I phoned the hospital earlier this morning. Uncle Dave will take us there now so you can visit him."

I was still holding them close because I could not bear to look at them and see the shock and disbelief etched on their faces. I heard the sharp intake of their breath and felt their trembling.

"Have you seen Dad, Mom?" Benjy asked, burrowing his head into my shoulder; his voice distorted by the tears he was holding back. Clearly, he was trying with all his might to be brave. They both were.

"Yes, Benjy. Uncle Dave and I were with your dad until late last night."

"Is it bad? Is he in a lot of pain?" George wanted to know. His voice was hoarse with emotion. His eyes locked onto mine, as though entreating me to take away the uncertainty. The fear. "Dad *is* going to be alright, isn't he, Mum?"

"George, Dad is in Intensive Care. He is in a coma, my boy. This means he is unconscious. Doctor says his condition is serious."

I hated the sound the words made when they left my mouth. To me, they were unyielding and flat, holding out little promise.

I hated the way the words affected me. They left me despairing. More to the point, how will those words affect the twins once the enormity of what I'd just told them hits home?

Now, I can think of nothing other than to hold them even closer and whisper, "I wish with all my heart that you did not have to deal with this. It's going to be rough on all of us, but we *will* have to be strong for your dad. Uncle Dave and all the rest of our family will help us. Auntie Grace and them too. I promise!"

George's next question, "When will Dad be coming home?"

"We don't know yet, Son, but we'll pray for Dad and take it one day at a time."

I turned to Uncle Dave, who had been standing to one side, and beckoned him to come close. They made a beeline for his outstretched arms. Holding them tight, he spoke in a soothing, soft voice to them. In turn, they clung wordlessly to him, as though to a lifeline. We left the house with the twins holding onto both of us for dear life.

The Arendse family was waiting in their driveway to see us off. Their children looked dazed. Stunned and sad. Each said a subdued good-bye as we made our way to Uncle Dave's car.

"Everything of the best, hey. We'll pray for Mike and your family. Let us know how Mike is doing." These were Don's parting words as he handed me the twins' belongings.

Almost choking on the words, I managed to say, "Thank you. We will."

Neither of the twins had been to a hospital before, so, on the way there, I thought it best to prepare them, tell them about the ICU where Mike lay. Uncle Dave enlightened them.

"You know, guys, when someone has been badly hurt or is seriously ill, they are taken to a special section of the hospital. It is called the Intensive Care Unit. There they have all kinds of wonderful machines and instruments. Patients are hooked up to monitors around the clock. For now, your dad is hooked up to several of these.

"Your mom and I realize that this will be scary and upsetting for you at first, but you shouldn't be scared because this is what you dad needs now. We think it is best you see your dad for yourselves. Doctors and nurses on duty will be there if we need any help. They will also be able to answer our questions. Your mother or someone from the family will be with you all the time."

Benjy needed to know, "Mum, can we talk to Dad, will he hear us?"

"Yes, Benjy. We can talk to your dad and the doctor says he can hear us. The thing is, we must try not to be sad while we're with him; try to be brave. It's okay if you can't think of anything to tell your dad today. Just say hello. Say you're sorry he is in pain. Tell him you hope he gets better soon. Say you miss him.

"When we get home, you could each write him a letter about stuff that's been going on while he is in hospital. You can write about what's been happening at school and the latest trick you taught Boomer and so on. Then, the next time you visit, you can read the letter to him. I'm sure he would love to be reminded of all the great stuff you used to do together. You can give him the latest cricket scores. He'd love to hear all about that."

"How long can we stay with Dad, Mum?"

"Maybe only for a few minutes at first, George, and only two of us at a time. Ma, Pa, and Auntie Iris will also be there. We all have to take turns. So, here's what we'll do…I'd like to be alone with your dad, just for a few minutes, then I'll take Benjy in with me. Uncle Dave will take you in to see Dad after that. Alright, guys?"

We stopped by the nurses' office before heading to Mike's room. They informed us there had been no change since we'd been in the night before. I was given Mike's personal effects—wedding ring, wallet, wristwatch, keys, appointment book, and clothing.

We found Mike's father and sister in the waiting room at the end of the corridor. They were distraught. I saw the anxiety stamped on their faces and felt the tension in the room. I led the boys over to their grandfather and aunt. Iris held out her arms to console me, but Mike's dad barely nodded a greeting in my direction. He embraced the boys and gently stroked each head in turn while he spoke softly to them.

"Have you been in yet, Iris?"

"No, but my mother is with him now."

"I'll go in now, unless you would like to, Pa."

The old man shook his head in answer and waved me in the direction of Mike's room. I made my way there slowly. His mom was sitting by his bedside. I greeted her. She did not return my greeting but left the room abruptly. Her eyes, however, glinted like shards of broken glass, as she flashed me a fleeting look of pure hatred.

I sat down in the chair she had vacated. Mike's eyes were still closed, and his hand was cool to the touch when I took it in my own. It was just as the nurse had said, no change!

Hoping with all my heart for any kind of response, I leaned in. "Mike, sweetie, it's me, Eve. It's Sunday morning. An ambulance brought you to the hospital yesterday because you've been in an accident. Your parents, Uncle Dave, the boys, and Iris are also here. They're all waiting impatiently to talk to you.

"Benjy and George went to the movies with Don and Sylvia's children yesterday and slept at their house last night. Uncle Dave and I just picked them up from there. They sent you their love and said they are praying for you. We're all praying for you, Mike."

I continued with encouraging words and snippets of news that would have interested him on any normal day.

I stroked his hand gently; the one which did not have the IV needle stuck in it. I cried inwardly for him, for the condition he was in; for our collective pain having to watch him lying in that bed and, because we had no way of helping him. I could not bring myself to touch his ravaged face, afraid I'd inflict more pain.

While Mike was in the hospital, we kept a constant vigil at his bedside, even though he never once responded to touch or voice. Our minister visited Mike often and prayed with family members present...a tower of strength!

There were occasions when Mike's parents' visits and mine overlapped. When they did, his mother's face was stony, like a blank canvas. She looked right through me, so to speak, and, when we happened to be in the room together, her attention was focused solely on her son.

Uncle Dave remained my ally. His support meant the world to me. Balm of Gilead. He and I had been open with the twins about Mike's condition. On the advice of the medical team, we told them their dad was in a bad way. We hung onto the hope that the doctors could be wrong, tried to stay positive, speaking to Mike of happier times, willing him to come back to us.

*T*he thought that I had driven Mike over the edge bedevilled me. Hindsight *would* have it that I should have waited—at least until he had firmly entrenched himself in the counselling program.

I poured out my heart to Grace. When she saw I was blaming myself for Mike's accident, she put the events leading up to it into perspective.

"Al-Anon," she said, "had been a lifeline for you; it also opened your eyes and mine to the plight of others in similar situations. The project we have in mind can only benefit them. If you ask me, Mike was his own worst enemy. He *could* have tried to understand and *chosen* to be supportive."

More than any other person I knew, she, was my saving grace. Kept me grounded.

With her unique brand of thoughtfulness and caring, she kept the twins at her house, brought them to the hospital, and looked after them while I sat by Mike's bedside—day after day, and often at night.

I missed connecting with my husband, longed to hear his voice, see the excitement on his face as I tell him about his favourite rose coming into bloom in our garden, hear his rumbling belly laugh as I share the latest joke about *van der Merwe*.

"Mike, please wake up, sweetie," I entreated him. "Please, talk to me, say you're not still angry with me." I willed him to open his eyes, to talk to us, longed for him to say, "I love you, Eve." One more time. It did not happen. Mike did not come out of the coma and died from massive head injuries and spinal trauma two weeks later.

*M*ike was dead!

A tragedy! It should not have happened. It *could* have been avoided.

*If only he had not given in to anger when I gave him my reasons for attending the Al-Anon meetings and my desire to help others. He and I would have gone to bed together that last night and woken up together and spent Saturday together…if only he had not been speeding! If only he had not been driving while under the influence.*

Instead, he had left home in a foul mood that morning, resorted to alcohol—his old and familiar crutch—on that fateful day.

My heart was heavy. A heavy rock. Its weight exhausted me. I felt old, bowed down by my grief. An inner voice asked, *would he ever have accepted my decision to attend the Al-Anon meetings?*

A moot question.

Mike was dead! I mourned a half-lived life.

As if losing my husband and dealing with my grief, conflicting emotions, and stress were not enough of an ordeal for me, my mother-in-law's acrimonious tirade on the day of Mike's accident continue to haunt me. I was no less a pariah in the eyes of his dad.

Iris had adored her brother; would have given her life for him. However, she also knew his weakness and faced it head-on. Now, as in the past, she commiserated and supported me in private. Uncle Dave continued to be a rock I could lean on; despite the unpleasant scenes and the criticism he must have had to endure from Mike's mother and father.

Benjy and George were inconsolable, but they knew the whole truth about their dad's drinking and resulting vile behaviour. They were my staunchest allies and stayed close to me.

When we left the hospital that evening, they insisted on sleeping in my bed. There was more than enough room now that Mike would not be sleeping next to me again. I welcomed the feel of their warm bodies snuggled up to me, found a modicum of comfort in consoling them and laying some of their questions to rest.

We leaned on each other in the days to come, the twins and I. Each sensing the depths of despair with which the other had to cope; the sorrow attached to losing a beloved father, a beloved husband.

Over the years, our little family had made many, many happy memories. Mike had seen to it. Now, the twins and I would work at banishing the negative and celebrate the good ones together. They had grown up fast since the day they were told of Mike's accident. I was justifiably proud of them. So, too, would their dad have been.

*S*pring was new!

I awoke to a cloudless, blue sky. Reminiscent of the day Mike and I were married. There was a crispness in the air, though, and, as the day wore on and the sun warmed the earth on its way across the heavens, the smell of newly mown grass lingered and intensified.

Mike would have loved being outside today. On a day like this, he would have been in his element, pottering about in the garden, and I could easily make myself believe he was at work; that he and I would be going to see a movie or play cards with the Theunissens after supper.

The illusion would last for just a fraction of time, though. Instead of being involved in any one of those innocuous, mundane activities, Mike would be buried later this afternoon. He had not come out of the coma—he had slipped away without saying good-bye.

*That* was the horrible reality!

A devastating time for us. I had lost my husband. My sons had lost their father. I mourned a life cut short, mourned the promises he'd made. Promises we had made each other. Promises not kept. Mourned the many dreams we'd shared that would now also come to naught.

I kept a tight rein on my feelings before, during, and after the funeral. My children grieved. Outwardly. Naturally, their need to be comforted and supported would be uppermost on my mind. Today, and in the many days and months to follow, seeing them through this ordeal would be my priority.

Family, close friends, and the landscape company's employees were the only ones expected to attend, but the word must have spread. The numbers were swelled by others who came to pay their respect. Surprisingly, these included several business acquaintances, members of the Garden Club, neighbours, and an overwhelming show of support by my Saturday afternoon Al-Anon group. I was moved to tears. Tears, I tried in vain to hide.

I came face-to-face with Basil and his brother Reggie for the first time that day. They introduced themselves, but I had no idea who they were. Later, I found out from Uncle Dave that they were two labourers who worked under Mike. In that moment, I realized that they were the ones with whom Mike used to spend his Saturdays—his drinking cronies, as I had always referred to them.

They offered their condolences and went on to say, "Missus, we could see he was out of sorts the whole time. Me and my brother, we wanted him to stay and sleep it off, but nah, no dice! He wanted to go.

"If he would of only listened to us, he would of been okay. He was in one of his stubborn moods that day…he just got in his van and buggered off…never even said good-bye to us."

Our minister committed Michael James Moore's body to the earth and his soul to God's keeping in a most touching and comforting service.

*Ashes to ashes and dust to dust!*

Birds twittered in nearby trees.

Dirt hitting a wooden casket as it is being lowered into its hole makes an awful, haunting sound. The sound of the last handful of earth, as it fell on Mike's coffin, made his passing final. *This* was the point of no return. We would never again look into his eyes, see him smile, or frown, or hear his booming laugh, or see the laughter lines making creases around his eyes. Never again would I have the chance to say, "I'm sorry." Or "I love you." Or "Thanks for making lunch."

Or the myriad other things I used to say to him in the course of a day.

With Grace's help, I had arranged to serve refreshments at our home after the service. Our Minister extended the invitation. All but Mike's parents and his sister showed up.

I felt honoured to introduce Jonathan and other Al-Anon members to my sons and others present. This show of solidarity was extremely touching. Before he left, we talked awhile—he and I. Mostly about my sons and how they were coping.

My broken heart felt somewhat eased when he put his arms around me. His embrace, purely, that of one friend comforting another, was akin to a haven. I felt I had arrived at a safe place I could not bear to leave.

I had no choice but to leave that haven. I had to mingle; accept condolences; find the right words to express my thanks and appreciation to all who had come to pay their last respects to Mike and show their support for the family.

Mike had always been extremely well-liked wherever he went. Today was proof positive. It must have something to do with the aura which Grace had attributed to him when they met for the first time, all those years ago.

Today, as always, she was my tower of strength; attuned to my needs. Every step of the way. She, who willingly took over the role of hostess when she saw I was fading. She, who, when everyone had gone, dried my tears, held me tight and spoke words of comfort. She, who insisted I retire for the night and stayed with us while the twins and I prepared for bed.

She, who made my home secure, left for her own home only after the sleeping tablets our family doctor had prescribed for me had taken effect. Those tablets were to become a crutch for me in the days, weeks, and months to come. I would need them to summon sleep at night until, in time, sleep claimed me naturally.

Iris phoned the next day. "I'm so sorry I had to leave straight after the service. I'm sure you understand, Eve. My parents are heartbroken. My mother is distraught. She barely made it through the funeral service. I wanted to be with you, but I felt my place was at their side, to be on hand to comfort them and take care of them. Will you explain things to the twins?"

"Iris, my dear, please, don't give it another thought. Under the circumstances, I'm sure I would have done the same. You should not feel bad when you so obviously had to put your parents' feelings ahead of your own and even ours. I'll make sure the boys understand why you had to go straight home. How are your parents holding up?"

"Eve, it will be a long time before my parents come to terms with their only son's passing. Especially the way he died. Mike had always been their blue-eyed boy. I know they have been hard on you, but I can see your side of things.

"I apologize on their behalf. You only did what you thought would be good for your little family. So, in a few days, when things have settled down here, I'll slip over for a visit. If it's okay with you."

"Sure, Iris. Anytime. Let's not be strangers, hey!"

Friends and family kept in touch by phone and frequent visits to our home. When Jonathan phoned, he called it, "My good deed for the day."

In the days following, I began to look forward to his visits by phone. Mainly because our conversations did not revolve solely around my bereavement. Amongst other things, I told him about the project which Grace and I had discussed before Mike's accident, also that we had shelved it because I feared Mike would not have approved.

"I think it an especially worthwhile project, Eve. When you focus on helping others, it goes a long way towards assuaging your own pain. The lingering remorse surrounding your husband's untimely death will pass. Regarding Helping Hands, I'll gladly join forces with you. Just let me know how I can help."

Grace and I agreed our project would benefit from his input.

The condolence phone calls had finally dwindled to nothing, but the postman still delivered sympathy cards. I received cards from members of the Al-Anon group, from Jonathan and his wife, also from people in Canada with whom Mike had exchanged cards at Christmas over the years. Sheldon Schwartz had phoned to sympathise the day after Mike died. I was touched when I opened a card from him and his wife.

For now, the names and messages were mostly a blur.

I will read them properly—sometime later—maybe, after to-morrow…

*I*t was Monday, and another new week had begun. Long days and nights had passed since we'd buried Mike. Seemingly unending days and nights. Nights where I had lain awake and repeatedly rehashed the sequence of events that had brought about his untimely death.

*Might I have pressed too hard to make Mike stop drinking? Would the feeling of uncertainty ever go away?* Then again, I reasoned, *Even though he was angry, he should have acted more responsibly!*

It's been rough at home! Unbearable at times, for the three of us who were left behind. The boys and I were trying to bring a sense of normalcy into our days. I don't know for how long it will hurt or how long it will be before we stop grieving.

Nowadays, each mealtime was a quiet affair for us. Desperately wanting to break the silence, inject a lighter tone, I told the boys what I planned to do while they were at school and encouraged them to talk about their favourite classes, the ones in which each of them excelled. I told them about Al-anon and the members who had come to their dad's funeral.

We naturally talked often of Mike; recalled memories of times past.

The chair at the head of the table—Mike's chair—remained empty. No plate, no cup, no cutlery was set out for his use. His footsteps and his voice would never again be heard as he made his way to the kitchen after a day's work.

Many's the time when he came home from work, he sat in that chair, took a load off, and told me about his day while I served our evening meal. I'd served him his last meal.

Never again, would I serve him a glass of my homemade ginger beer or a drink of cool water on a hot, summer day. Never again, would he smile his thanks and stroke my hand as I handed him the glass. Even so, it seemed like the three of us were waiting, ears cocked. Force of habit, one might say.

They were going back to school today. When it was time for them to leave for school, we left the house together. I walked with them to our front gate to see them off. When they were out of sight, I decided to spend some time in the back garden.

It had rained the day before and during the night. Now, looking up at my mountain in the distance, I noticed the sky was a pale gray. Clouds were hiding the morning sun; a sharp contrast to the day when we buried Mike.

Just thinking about that day and the ones leading up to it still made my heart hurt like it was being squeezed in a giant fist. My eyes became blurred with unshed tears while my feet felt weighted down; leaden, as I walked slowly on the stone-flagged path leading to the back of the house where Mike's favourite plants were flourishing. It was as if he still had a hand in keeping things alive.

No, not Mike. It was Uncle Dave who had come by, faithfully, each day, to tend to the garden which had been Mike's pride and joy.

I immediately spied the new dahlia Mike had planted—he had traded a cutting from a favourite rose bush for this bulb. The flower was about to open and showed just a hint of the vibrant red it would produce when it finally came into its own. Alongside it, the deep pink cosmos bushes were now in full bloom.

*Phone Mike, tell him…*this was my immediate reaction. In the excitement of the moment, for just a few, split seconds, the fact that I would never talk to Mike again had been wiped from my consciousness.

This momentary memory lapse proved too much to bear. Staggered me. Had sorrow washing over me anew; pounding me like so many waves crashing against boulders at high tide. I wanted to flee from the garden; find a place where I could shuck my pain.

Then it hit me. Forcibly! I had nowhere to go because the sound of Mike's laughter, his smell after a hard day's work, his touch on my face, the feel of his arms holding me close was only in my head. In my memory bank.

I passed the water fountain on my way towards the kitchen door. Mike's latest project, begun, but not finished. It resembled the story of Mike's life… not enough time. I craved oblivion from this stark reality.

In the kitchen, I made myself a cup of tea and swallowed a sleeping tablet before heading to my bedroom. Knowing the boys would be at school for hours yet, I lay down on the bed I'd shared with Mike until the night before his accident. Mercifully, the sleeping tablet worked its magic and, almost before my head hit the pillow, I'd fallen into a deep sleep.

I was awakened sometime after midday by the sound of a bell ringing. Heard it as though from afar, as if it were part of a dream I was dreaming. Its strident ringing did eventually penetrate my subconscious, forcing me out of my drugged sleep.

I identified the sound, but the ring tone which signified an overseas call did not register immediately. Still groggy, and slow-moving, I fumbled with the receiver and answered the phone.

"Hello."

"Oh! Hi! I'm calling from Vancouver, in Canada. Can I speak with Eve Moore, please?"

"This is Eve Moore." *A call from Canada?* Mentally shaking myself further awake so that I could respond coherently to this unexpected caller, I asked, "Who is calling?"

How could I know the ensuing telephone conversation would bring more misery and disrupt, even further, the lives of those who had been close to my husband?

"My name is Lisa. Lisa Shapiro." The mental fog was lifting, and my brain was sluggishly inching its way out from under.

"Lisa Shapiro?" I repeated after her. "From Canada…I'm sorry, your name is not familiar. The only person I know in Canada is Sheldon Schwartz."

"Sheldon's my boss. He told me Mike died in a car crash. First off, I want you to know I'm really sorry about Mike, but I'm also really worried because I need to know how he left things for our daughter Michaela. You see, his lawyers, they never got back to me when I left a message. So then I decided to talk to you."

Her words shot like hot needles all through my brain. Gone was the lethargy which had clouded it in those first moments of waking. Did I just hear this stranger say she has a daughter, and my Mike is the father?

What she had just told me was shocking. It can't be true! It's obscene! Crazy! I rejected her story instinctively, out of hand!

Wishing with all my heart for this to be part of a horrible dream, I said, "Mrs. Shapiro, I'm sorry, I don't recognise your name. Are you sure you have the right number? How do you know my husband?"

"Uh-huh! I know I've got the right number. Sheldon, my boss, gave it to me because he knows about Michaela...that she is Mike's child, I mean. I'm not married. You can just call me Lisa.

"You see, I first met Mike in the office when he started working for Sheldon here in Vancouver, and sometimes the staff used to hang out after work. Mike already knew I was pregnant when he went to work in Ontario. When he left Canada to go back to South Africa, I was already in my first trimester and Michaela was born in March the next year. She is fifteen now.

"He gave me money from the day I told him I was pregnant. When he went back to South Africa, he sent money every month and promised he would also pay for her education after she graduates high school next year. You see, I really don't know what I'm going to do if there's no money coming from Mike anymore. She is a smart kid. Mike knew it. I really need to know what will happen now that Mike is dead."

Her tone had become abrupt, and her voice had risen considerably since she first came on the line. I sensed that she was embarrassed and becoming fed up with having to explain her situation to me—a total stranger.

"Listen, it seems like you don't know about the fact that Mike is the father of my child, so I really feel bad for springing this on you, but I must look out for Michaela. She never knew her father, but I figured you must know about her, that Mike told you about our child. I have her birth certificate with Mike's name on it."

I'd heard her out in stunned silence, incapable of speech, mentally reeling from the shock, struggling to contain my emotions. All the while I was listening to her, my heart was racing faster and faster, threatening to knock the breath out of my body.

The words she'd spoken seemed to be floating around in the room, around my head. Up and down. Round and round. Mixed up and out of sequence, like a kaleidoscope that has been too vigorously shaken. All things considered, I had to admit, her words had an unmistakable ring of truth. I believed them; slowly came to grips with their meaning.

"Lisa…I realize that you must be worried for your child's future, but you should know my husband never once mentioned your name, or that he was the father of your child. This phone call, out of the blue…it's just too much! Believe me, I do not mean to be rude…I just cannot talk about it now. I'm sorry…I'll speak to our lawyer and ask him to contact you."

"Well, it really is too bad Mike didn't have the guts to tell you himself. I'm really sorry you had to hear it from me. So, then, I'll wait to hear from your lawyer…I need help. Don't let me down, eh!"

This is how the conversation ended. I hung up abruptly, couldn't put the phone down fast enough. Then, I lay back on my bed just staring blankly up at the ceiling.

Not for long, the blank stare, though. All desire for sleep was now gone. Gone, like yesterday is gone. So, too, the lethargy which had clouded my brain in those first moments when I was awakened by the ring of the telephone. Never had I been more fully awake!

*T*he woman's disclosure had been galvanizing. The sound of her voice finally faded to nothing in my head, but her words had me recalling the conversations Mike and I had had, from the day he left for Canada until he returned. Those were embedded in my memory. I could replay them at will.

In the beginning, the tone of Mike's phone calls had been enthusiastic about his work and complimentary about his boss and his co-workers; he had talked freely about the people he had met during the course of the day and how he spent his free time. Plans for our wedding, of prime importance.

I remember, connecting with him by telephone had gone without a hitch for several weeks. Then things changed. He wasn't as forthcoming about his activities during his free time anymore. I could recall in an instant when, at times, I'd had a gut feeling—it seemed Mike's answers were not spontaneous, he seemed to be carefully choosing his words. A little voice in the back of my mind had told me there was reason to doubt Mike's candour. He bypassed talk about our wedding.

*What lay behind this change? Absence supposedly made the heart grow fonder. Could Mike's resolve, his commitment to a future with me, be slipping?*

Doubts *had* plagued me at the time.

Red flags had waved like banners when he had not returned any of my calls for almost a week, and other times I'd called, only to hear, "Mike Moore's phone. Please leave a message."

How I'd come to hate that recording! Hated it with a passion! It had left me dangling, disappointed, dejected. Then, when he finally phoned me back, his apologies had been abject.

"Things have been crazy around here!" That's the explanation he had sometimes given. Relieved to hear his voice and unwilling to put a damper on the moment, I just left it at that.

Then there were those times when we did connect, but he'd say, "Can't talk long, one of the blokes need my help with…blah, blah, blah."

Another time he'd say, "This is not a good time—Sheldon and I are in a meeting and we're going for a drink afterwards, so I don't know when I'll be free."

Those responses and others came flooding back. I was frustrated and edgy back then, but pride made me hold back from voicing my disappointment. I did not want to sound clingy.

Negative thoughts, however, rattled around in my mind when we said good-bye, and I remember thinking at the time, *I know Sheldon is his boss, but, for Pete's sake…can't Mike excuse himself, for just a few minutes? Why can't he call me during their lunch hour? During his morning or afternoon tea-time? Surely, no one can be expected to work all those hours without personal time off!*

I also mentally replayed the calls I had made when he had supposedly been off duty; how the calls had sometimes been quite short because there was an unexpected emergency to be taken care of. I remember every one of those occasions. Remember them well. They had left me with the feeling that Mike had other, more important fish to fry, and was impatient to get off the phone.

*At the time, I had wanted to believe in Mike; believe he was being true to me in every sense of the word.* Those shortened, unsatisfactory calls had concerned me…now, in light of Lisa Shapiro's revelation, it would seem my suspicions at the time had been all too well-founded.

*B*ack then, Mike had told me that he—along with other staff members—had been invited to spend the Canada Day weekend at the Schwartzes' beachfront home in Parksville.

Now, as I lay on my bed, this all went through my mind at lightning speed.

*Could this have been one of their rendezvous?*

No need to wonder any longer. No matter where or when the affair had started, Mike's chickens had well and truly come home to roost! Clearly, my instincts had been spot on, and my fears back then had not been unfounded. Mike had been involved with another woman and had successfully managed to keep that part of his life under wraps.

The ugly, unvarnished truth, like flashing neon lights, could not be ignored! I was tortured by the knowledge.

My thoughts and emotions were all over the place. Torn. In tatters. Like a garden struck by a tornado.

My mind whirled! I felt I was going crazy. I wanted to scream; smash something—Mike's head, preferably—to vent the indescribably deep hurt, and anger, and jealousy, and frustration, and disappointment, and feelings of betrayal and shame. To crown it all, I could not turn to him for answers or lash out at him.

Mike is dead!

Before answering Lisa's life-altering phone call that had so rudely awakened me, the feelings of loss and regret had been uppermost in my mind.

In every waking moment! Before she phoned, I had been consoled by the fact that Mike and I had regained some of the earlier magic.

Now, because of a few ill-timed, inexpressibly hurtful words I'd heard from another woman—this stranger—the happy memories of my marriage had been tainted.

Question after question assailed me, clamoured for attention.

*Had my husband ever regretted marrying me?*

*Just how often had Mike and this woman made contact over the years?*

*Had he ever thought of fostering a relationship with her after their daughter was born?*

*Had he longed to see this child in the flesh and wished for a close relationship with her?*

*How had he coped with the fact that he had fathered a child, and kept her existence hidden?*

*Who else knew about his illegitimate daughter?*

*How will it affect the lives of those who now mourned his passing?*

I am at a loss to put it all into perspective, awash with a sensation of helplessness. As night follows day, more questions would be bound to surface.

More than likely, Lisa had not intended this conversation to be offensive or hurtful. Could be, she was just taking whatever steps she deemed necessary to ensure the future welfare of her daughter.

Mike had been living with this secret all those years we were married. He'd covered it up, had lied by omission, cheated on me in the worst possible way. Had he ever meant to tell the boys and me about their half-sister? I'll never know his side of the story now. More's the pity. Having to be told of this child's existence by an outsider was past bearing.

A host of feelings washed over me anew, like so many tidal waves. Relentlessly!

Then the tears fell. Hot and long. They blurred my vision. I did not even try to stem them—only thankful that Benjy and George were nowhere near to see my distress. Grief over the loss of their dad was something we shared. My distress on hearing about his illegitimate child, was a horse of another colour, as the saying goes.

Sooner or later, they would have to be told they had an older, half-sister. Laying this on them so soon after Mike's death would not be the easiest thing I had ever done. Anyhow, I doubt I would find the words…say them calmly and without rancour. Not today!

Oh, the irony! Benjy and George have always wanted a sister. Knowing my sons, they would have more questions than I could answer.

The rest of the family also needed to know; were entitled to be told about the additional branch on their family tree. When I was composed, I'd give some thought to putting Mike's parents, his sister, and Uncle Dave in the picture. Also Grace, her parents, and my mother. I certainly did not relish being the bearer of these tidings.

*T*he little room Mike used as his office was tiny and sparsely furnished. It contained a smallish desk, a chair, and a two-drawer filing cabinet. Despite its being tiny, the room was airy and light, even now, because the curtains on the window were never drawn.

His certificates for landscaping hung in a row above the desk. Just below them, Mike had attached a single shelf that housed his trophies for 'Best Gardener of the Year'. Except for a few other odds and ends, he kept a photo of the four of us on our most recent visit to Knysna on his desk. Also, a paperweight in the shape of a turtle which the boys had made for him many moons ago.

Small and Spartan is how he was wont to describe 'his space'.

I held Mike's office as sacrosanct. To the best of my knowledge, the contents were purely business-related, and I only crossed the threshold on cleaning days.

Today would be different…as different as night from day. One could say I was on a mission after Lisa's disclosure; hell-bent on finding anything and everything Mike had secreted over the years concerning Lisa and their daughter.

Making my way across the room, I made a beeline for his office, only to find the drawers locked with no key in sight. Mike had always carried his keys around with him. My brain had gone into top gear by now, and I remembered in a flash where they were.

They lay, inert, on Mike's chest of drawers in our bedroom. I had placed them there on my return from the hospital on the night we learned that his injuries were more than likely fatal.

My hands were damp with sweat as I took hold of the keys and tried to find the one which would unlock the filing cabinet. My first attempts failed dismally because I had started shaking like a leaf in a windstorm. I kept at it and tried key after key on the bunch until I found the one that fit.

I felt as though I had unlocked Pandora's box when I pulled open the first drawer. My heart was pounding hard. So hard, it felt as though it would split into little pieces and pop out of each orifice in my body!

Taking deep breaths to calm myself for the ordeal that lay before me, I scanned the neatly stored files until my eyes lit on the one labelled 'Canada'.

With trembling fingers, I removed it and found a single, sealed, sturdy brown envelope, which I hastily tore open. In my haste, its meagre contents spilled onto the desk. Before me lay a sheet of paper neatly folded in half. Also, a little package carefully wrapped in several layers of tissue paper that had been tied with a red ribbon. When unwrapped, the little package revealed a sand dollar. A perfect specimen. Perfectly preserved. I set it aside and picked up the folded sheet.

What would it reveal when unfolded? Did I *want* to know?

*No point now in being squeamish,* I berated myself.

The unfolded sheet revealed a copy of the birth certificate naming Michael James Moore the father of Michaela Moore. With my breath coming fast, I stared at the words confirming Lisa's unpalatable story.

Proof of the wild oats Mike had sowed during his brief stay in Canada. Proof, that Mike had violated my trust and kept me in the dark all these years…carried this secret to the grave.

All puns aside!

Dear Reader, I read this document through dry eyes while emotions flooded my brain like a raging torrent. Bowed down by the weight of it all, I felt like the world's oldest human being living.

Lisa's phone call had not lasted long, but, to me, it seemed as though an eon must have passed between the time I'd picked up the phone and this moment.

I can see how it must have happened. This stranger of the male species, charming, young, and handsome was let loose in a foreign land with attractive women thrown in his path at work and at play; flattering him, vying for his attention, out to get their hooks into him. I now know, without a shadow of a doubt, one such, at least, had succeeded. Those earlier feelings of betrayal and anger returned tenfold and left me fighting for breath like I'd been walking uphill against gale-force winds.

He'd caved! *How could you, Mike? How could you!*

The knowledge that Mike had slept with Lisa Shapiro, had known her body intimately, and had had the gall to whisper sweet nothings to me over the phone afterwards, sickened me! My stomach churned! How long had the affair lasted? How deeply had he cared for her?

*Did I really want to know?*

Picturing the two of them together was more than I could handle—more than I should be expected to bear at this juncture. Marshalling all my willpower, I tried to shut out these awful thoughts from my mind, closed the file, and hastily replaced it in the drawer. I locked the drawer and removed the key. God forbid the twins should stumble on this before I had a chance to break the news to them.

Like Scarlett O'Hara of *Gone with the Wind* fame was wont to say, "I can't think about that right now. If I do, I'll go crazy.

I'll think about that tomorrow."

Unlike Scarlett, however, I succumbed long before *my* to-morrow dawned. As I lay awake in the wee small hours, tossing and turning in what used to be our marriage bed, I pictured them together—my husband and another woman—could not stop the mental image blazing a debilitating trail across my brain. It trumped all thought of my exonerating Mike—try as I might!

More tears will come later. On this, you can bet your life!

To-morrow. That's when I'll think about the best approach to take because I cannot think about it anymore today.

Maybe, after to-morrow, I'll summon the will to reveal Mike's secret to his parents, his sister, and Uncle Dave.

I am persona non grata at Mike's parents' house, so for me to even think of telling them about their Canadian granddaughter is out of the question! His mother would almost certainly refuse to believe me. I could just hear her accusing me of being a troublemaker. Sullying Mike's memory. At some point, though, she would have to accept Michaela's existence as a fact.

Would, that I could be there, to see the look on her face...be a fly on the wall. My mother-in-law had made it abundantly clear her son had married beneath him. Well! This news will be a bitter pill for her to swallow! She would now have to deal with this development as well as the fact that Mike died while driving under the influence.

I decided to phone Iris, confide in her. Even though she and Mike had always been close, without fail, when her brother was in the wrong she had not sugar-coated his behaviour. She would be more likely to lend a sympathetic ear. I decided to let *her* field this time-bomb at home.

However, I was spared the onerous task of breaking the news to her. As it turned out, it was old news. When I phoned Iris, she told me Mike had needed to unburden himself when Michaela was born and had chosen her as his confidante.

Her face was a study in concern when I opened my front door to her an hour later. She embraced me right off the bat, and her tears fell on my neck as she said, "I can't imagine what went through your mind hearing about Michaela over the phone. Mike should have been the one to tell you. Believe me, I told him to. Many times over the years. I'm glad you decided to let me know about Lisa's call. I'll help in any way I can with the boys; tell them all I know about Michaela.

"Leave it all with me, Eve. I'll break the news to my parents and the rest of the family. Be sure to let me know when you've set up an appointment with your lawyer. I'll gladly go with you, so try not to worry about anything, hey! Okay?"

Her arms felt like a warm blanket around my shoulders.

"I'll phone our lawyer today. Iris, please, will you do me a favour? When you break the news to your family, ask them not to let on to the twins. I think I'll wait awhile before I tell them. They have more than enough to deal with at the moment, plus they have to start studying for the December exams. I'll tell them when the exams are over and, if you don't mind, I'd like you to be with me when I tell them.

"You know, it's no secret that Mike left us well provided for—I decided to take over the responsibility and continue to help with his daughter's schooling and day-to-day needs.

"In the meantime, let's see what the lawyer has to say. When this is settled, we can get in touch with Michaela's mother, let her know where she stands, financially. Another thing, if Lisa thinks it a good idea, I plan to take the boys to Canada to meet them when school closes in December…make a holiday out of it. How would you like to go with us?"

After having inhaled the fragrance of the flowers she had just picked in our garden, Iris said, "Everything you've to told me makes a lot of sense and I take my hat off to you, Eve. You are being extremely kind and generous. I'm sure Lisa will be grateful to you for helping out financially. I won't let you shoulder the burden alone, though. I'll make sure our family also chips in.

"As for the holiday to Canada, I'd love to go, and I'm glad you decided the twins should meet their sister. It's the right thing to do! When the time is right, we can sound the boys out together and, even if Lisa doesn't agree to meet with us, we could still take a holiday. It would be a welcome distraction for the guys, after all they have been through over the past months. In the meantime, I think we should get our ducks in a row—see to our passports and flights before things get hectic."

"Ja. The sooner the better. Iris, just know, I meant it when I said I want to assist Lisa—for Michaela's sake—in any way I can. I couldn't sleep easy, knowing Mike's flesh and blood is being short-changed because of his lack of foresight."

I said good-bye to my sister-in-law with a lighter heart, grateful for her willingness to step into the breach. Still, questions plagued me.

Would Mike's parents accept their granddaughter, though? Would they welcome her? Make room for her in their lives? After all, this definitely belongs in the category of 'dirty linen' to which my mother-in-law has such an aversion.

Knowing Iris, I was sure she would break the news as gently as she could, do her level best to help them over the shock, and smooth things over for all concerned. By all accounts, she was bound and determined to apprise her family of Michaela's existence. She would lose no time in wearing down whatever reluctance her parents might have had in accepting Mike's daughter. She could also be depended upon to leave no stone unturned until Michaela's future was secured. Both emotionally and financially.

As Iris later told it, "My mother was quite hurt because Mike had not seen fit to confide in her."

*I* had reluctantly made Grace privy to Mike's abhorrent, drunken behaviour in the months before he died. She had been my rock. Now, I needed my friend to see me through yet another ordeal; needed her support to cope with this deplorable, unwelcome, and unpalatable development!

Never, in my wildest dreams, did I imagine I would have another sorry tale to tell her. Having Mike's indiscretion known outside the family circle did not sit well with me, but I failed to see how I could possibly keep Michaela's existence a secret from those close to us.

Truth *will* out!

Mike had fathered an illegitimate child while he was in Canada. Unfortunately, there was just no way around the fact.

Grace had offered to help me sort through Mike's clothing today. I decided to simply show her Michaela's birth certificate. It bore all the pertinent information.

I was in my bedroom waiting for her to arrive, while putting aside the items of value which I thought our sons, Uncle Dave, and Mike's parents might want as keepsakes. Iris had asked, just yesterday, whether she could have one of his trophies.

The boys had already left for school, when she stopped by with two bottles of her homemade ginger beer. We set to sorting with a will but, from time to time, she or I would hold up a garment and take a moment to travel down memory lane. When everything had been bagged and boxed, we went to my backyard to enjoy the sunshine and a well-deserved cup of tea. The garden was a sight for sore eyes this time of year!

It's now or never, I thought and, wordlessly, handed her the birth certificate.

"What's this?" she asked, with a smile and put the cup down before taking it from me.

Tears glistened in her eyes after she had opened the folded page and taken it all in. She looked stunned. Dropping the paper on the table as though it were a hot potato, she bolted from her seat to hold me in a tight embrace.

"This can't be true! Oh, Evie...I truly don't know what to say...I'm shocked beyond words! Tell me, how on earth are you coping? What about the twins? My heart goes out to you...I can't believe Mike kept this huge secret locked away!" She said this between pauses of incredulity, and with tears streaming down her face.

"I'm over the worst now, but it was a nightmare in the beginning. I turned to Iris because I wanted her to know about this child, and I decided that she should be the one to tell her family. As it happens, she already knew. Mike had confided in her when the child was born. She was a rock and helped me straighten things out in my head." I said all this while still in her tight embrace and speaking between sobs.

"Iris has only told her closest family so far, and I will wait until after their exams before I tell the twins. So, please, Grace, when you tell Claud and your parents, also tell them I'd like this kept within our little circle of grown-ups for now. Stress that they shouldn't mention it to the twins until I've had a chance to let them know about their half-sister. Okay?"

In the end, we comforted each other. We both sorely needed comfort. Me, for having to endure this ordeal, and my dear friend, for feeling my pain.

*I*t was December. Three intolerable long months had come and gone since the day of Mike's funeral and the day of Lisa Shapiro's phone call. By this time, Iris and I had spoken to her several times on the phone, so we now knew more about Michaela. She sounded nice.

Lisa cried when we told her about the plans afoot. I could hear the emotion in her voice when she thanked me. She has an older brother who is disabled and lives with her parents in a nearby town. Other than those, she has no close family ties. They have little or no contact with aunts, uncles, and cousins who live in other provinces.

Having the support and involvement of Mike's family in her daughter's life meant the world to her and Michaela.

As agreed, Iris and I had waited until the year-end exams were over before we told the twins about their half-sibling. After the initial shock of learning about Michaela and the circumstances surrounding her birth had worn off, the twins were anxious to meet her, and their questions seemed never-ending.

Between the two of us, Iris and I appeared to lay their concerns to rest, and excitement ran high in our household after they learned we would be going overseas to meet her before long.

Our plane tickets, passports, and holiday arrangements to Vancouver were now well in hand. Sheldon Schwartz, Mike's erstwhile boss, phoned me soon after we'd given Lisa the details of our upcoming visit. I was pleasantly surprised, even overwhelmed, when he told me he would reserve a suite for us (as his guests) in one of his hotels where Mike had worked. He would brook no argument! Even offered to arrange transport from the airport to the hotel. How kind! How generous!

Our holiday could not come soon enough for my boys. Starting with the plane ride—since none of us had ever flown before—this would be quite an adventure. An interesting experience for all.

Capers in the snow? It was winter there, after all. Now, *that* would be something to write home about!

Before we left South Africa, Sheldon Schwartz phoned to wish us a safe flight and again expressed his condolences for our loss. Sheldon—he insisted we dispense with formalities—could not speak highly enough to Mike's professional work ethic and his likeability as a person. Apart from getting to know Lisa and Michaela, we now also looked forward to meeting Sheldon and his wife.

*L*isa and Michaela met us at the airport. Meeting them in the flesh proved less daunting than I had anticipated. Our many phone calls had paved the way. Having Iris beside me also went a long way to easing whatever tensions there might have been.

The twins were dead set on bonding with their sister and she seemed likeminded; after an understandably initial awkwardness, they just clicked. She loved the idea of having twin brothers as much as they loved having a sister.

We were settled in at the hotel, and our visit with Lisa and Michaela was off to a good start. They could not wait to show us around their city. Day after day they proved to be excellent tour guides. Between those two and the Schwarzes, we were having the time of our lives.

Sheldon's interest in Mike's sons was genuine. He took the three children on a helicopter ride and on an overnight trip to the Capilano Suspension Bridge. The children raved for days on end about those experiences. Iris and I had stayed behind with Lisa. We explored the possibility of having Michaela visit her family in South Africa. Lisa's relief and gratitude for our financial support were heartfelt. She was grateful to Iris for having opened the way for Michael's child to be made welcome in her grandparents' home.

*L*isa was abject in her apology for causing me unhappiness. In a private conversation, she opened up to me. Tears shone in her beautiful blue eyes and, as she reminisced, she dabbed at the ones trailing down her cheeks. She was a good-looking woman, and I could see why Mike had given in to his baser instincts.

"I thought Mike was really attractive and I figured, for sure, he must have a girlfriend back home. I'm really embarrassed to say I went after him anyway because I really liked him. He was always really polite when we would meet at work. He did not really talk much to me, even when we would all be together at Sheldon's place or at the beach. He would mostly hang out with the guys from work.

"Then, one evening when I was finishing my work in the office, he came in with some papers for Sheldon. It was a Friday when Sheldon was not in the office. On Friday evenings, people from work always got together for dinner at this really nice Italian place. I saw my chance to be with him, so I asked him if he would be going to meet up with the others. Then, when he said 'yes', I asked if I could catch a ride with him.

"He handed me the papers as he said, 'Sure. I'll wait for you in the truck'.

"I know I drank a little too much vino at the restaurant. Anyway, when everybody was leaving, I asked him for a ride back to my apartment. I guess he was too much of a gentleman to refuse. To cut a long story short, I invited him inside when he pulled up at my apartment. He first declined, but I offered him coffee so he came in. He asked if we could watch the end of the baseball game. When the game got really exciting, I offered a glass of wine, then one thing just led to another after the game.

"When I woke up in the morning, Mike was already gone, but he came by the next day to apologize. He said he had made a mistake and told me that he was going to get married when he went back home. When he came to the office on Monday, he was polite and just went about his business. I was really embarrassed, so I did not even try to make conversation and never asked him again for a ride.

"I got pregnant with Michaela that night. Mike was already in Ontario when I found out I was pregnant. He was really shocked when I told him on the phone, but he never questioned it, and, as you can see, there's a lot of Mike in Michaela. I don't regret having her. I'm just really sorry she never got to meet him. She would always say she was going to find her father when she would leave school. She was already saving her money for the plane ticket."

Lisa was proud of her daughter. It came over loud and clear in her voice as she said, "I have a feeling she will continue to save for her visit to South Africa to meet her father's family and really hang out with her twin brothers. She can't stop talking about Benjy and George when we're alone now. She will really miss them when you go back.

"For me, I did not know whether I would be doing the right thing to call you at the time, Eve, but I felt my back was to the wall. I really had nowhere else to turn to. I'm glad I did because you guys really came through for us! Michaela and I will always say a prayer of thanks for you."

Time to return to South Africa dawned, sure as God made little green apples, but not before we had made the rounds of a few Canadian stores. Souvenirs for friends and family was the order of the day as well as clothing for the four of us.

Our parting was sad, but all's well that ends well! We had achieved more than we had set out to do or dreamed. The twins and Mickey—as she had been dubbed by the boys—secure in the knowledge that there would be phone calls and letters to tide them over until their next meeting.

Thankfully, the emotional roller coaster we'd been riding seems to have come to a halt for us.

After hearing Lisa's side of their encounters, I could tell that Mike had not been womanising in the true sense of the word while he was overseas. Her forthrightness underlined this.

*Will* I ever come to terms with the heartbreak of his betrayal, though? This, *and* the reality of his and Lisa's daughter? True, he had broken my trust. Once. Just once. He had shown remorse, however, and had admitted my existence when he apologized to Lisa for his lapse. Surely, that counts for something! The pain of his one lapse lingers on, but I'm working to put it behind me now. Accepting Michaela is no hardship. She, after all, is blameless!

*A*s we approached the 'Mother City' on our return flight, from my window seat I marvelled anew at the majesty of Table Mountain. The 'smiling face' I'd seen etched there on the day of Mike's accident flashed before my eyes, and I remembered the significance I had attached to it then. That memory strengthens my belief that I *will* continue to find the courage to meet the challenges that must surely arise along the way.

I compare each sunrise to a beacon of hope—watch the swatch of silver lining on my horizon grow larger by the day!

*M*ike's memory lives on and so, too, the pain of life without him. I still look for him in the garden, still wait for him to come home from work, and still expect to hear his voice on the other end when I answer the phone. I've kept his aftershave in our bathroom where its fragrance still hangs in the air. Sadly, his head will never again rest on the pillow beside mine.

The sadness I naturally felt for the way my life had been derailed, and the regrets which had formerly walked side by side with self-doubt, were beginning to fade. The image of an angry Mike on that last night we spent together, and that of his mangled face and bruised body after the accident, appear less frequently in my mind's eye. I attributed all this to 'Time, the great healer'.

In time, one by one, the unwholesome, dark patches in my life will be replaced with fresh, sweet-smelling moments. Healing moments. All brought about by the constant nurturing of Grace, family members, and my friends from Al-Anon. Jonathan included.

I liken this to a bowl of dirty water into which a steady stream of clean water was being poured.

My sons and I can only thrive in this environment. With each new day, I help them move a step closer to accepting life without their dad. They are young, resilient. I pray they would have learned from this tragedy—how debilitating and dangerous it is when one becomes dependent on an addictive substance.

$\mathcal{H}$elping Hands, our project, had been partly conceived on that long-ago day when Grace had paid her first visit to the Al-Anon support group. Of the many ideas we floated, her idea to hold rummage and bake sales—practical, doable, with minimal financial output— won the day.

She and I had been involved from the outset. Unlike Grace, however, I had not openly participated. Unlike Grace—who had Claud's support from day one—I had played it safe and only worked on the project when Mike was not around. Knowing my husband, he would not have approved, and I'd had every reason to anticipate negative consequences whenever he was three sheets to the wind.

Hindsight proved me right; baring all to Mike had indeed been the catalyst that had had him falling off the wagon on the day of his accident.

Grace's efforts, behind the scenes, however, had been steadily ongoing. Due to her efforts, we'd been given permission to hold a bake and rummage sale once a month at her church. She had promised her rector we would donate forty percent of our takings to the church. The balance would be donated to organisations that provide counselling and a refuge for women and children in abusive relationships.

Unfortunately, all this had, of necessity, been shelved.

Shortly after Mike's funeral, she popped in for one of her daily visits and re-opened the subject; encouraged me to pick up where I'd left off, devote a little time each day to our project so that we could get it off the ground.

"The thing is, you need to get out of the house, Evie, and this will be just what the doctor ordered," she said, as she helped me set the table for our lunch. "You'll meet people and, for a little while each time, your focus will be on helping those less fortunate."

Jonathan had told something in the same vein earlier. Taking her words to heart, I set to it with a will the next day. Starting with people I knew, I requested donations of clothing and household items for our rummage sale and grocery contributions for our bake sale. Some good Samaritans even offered to bring home-baked goods to the church on the day of the sale. Others offered to sell raffle tickets.

Canvassing the neighbourhood on foot got me out of the house and my mind off past events. Chatting to people about mundane happenings of life, a boon in my time of loneliness and despair. Just knowing I was working towards a good cause gave me a sense of achievement at the end of my stint each day.

The community support for our project grew like weeds. If only Mike were here to see how well things were working out.

Benjy and George, with the help of Grace's son Christopher, were eager to pitch in. They were in the throes of organising a monthly car wash and had enlisted the help of some of the youth from the church as well as a couple of their school buddies.

They gathered their helpers in our backyard, making posters and leaflets to advertise their service and our rummage and bake sales. Christopher's principal authorised the loan of the school's bull horn if needed and Claud volunteered to oversee their on-site operations.

Georgina, my ex-boss, promised to contribute to our cause with regular sums of money. I did not doubt that her contributions would be no small cheese! Auntie Miriam would help with the baking and Uncle Jacob was always at the ready to pick up and deliver clothing and other donations. My mother joined the fray, willing to pitch in whenever there was a shortage of hands at the church.

Until now, Grace and I were the only ones involved in getting our project off the ground. Our discussions were informal, over the phone or over a cup of tea, as ideas occurred to us. Then came Jonathan. He offered to help with the bookkeeping and keeping track of our stock.

Both she and I respected and liked him, and we were happy to utilise his know-how. His, was a thoughtful, helpful, and kindly nature. The epitome of tact and sensitivity. His kindness stroked parts of my psyche that had long been laid low. It warmed me like the sun and made me feel good about myself.

Grace and I dispensed with the casual approach when Jonathan came on board. My home became the designated Center of Operations and the venue for our meetings. This worked out well. At the end of our planning sessions, Grace, Jonathan, and yours truly made time to socialise. Sometimes over a cuppa. On the odd occasion, such as a birthday and even Grace's wedding anniversary, we indulged in a glass of wine.

Jonathan kindly offered to float the details of our project to a few members at the next Al-Anon meeting and solicit their help.

Whenever Benjy and George happened to be home, Jonathan spoke to them, encouraging them, suggesting ways to help them adjust to our new lifestyle.

"Above all," he'd say, "keep on top of your marks, because a good education will definitely open doors for you!"

I'm happy to say, his advice sat well with both my sons. He also discussed various career options with them, and they debated the pros and cons of each path at length. After much sober deliberation, both Benjy and George decided teaching would be the most rewarding of all the choices.

*D*-day dawned. Our project was up and running, and we were gratified beyond belief. With so many helpers pitching in, our first rummage and bake sale was an unqualified success. The time flew by, and, before we knew it, the morning had come and was long gone. Barely a crumb, or garment, or bric-a-brac was left to tell the tale. The raffle tickets sold by the score and "Cleaner Cars" was also off to a promising start.

While the rest of us tackled the cleanup, Auntie Miriam and my mother had laid out sandwiches, *melktert*, and hot or cold drinks as a thank you to all our helpers. Grace's rector blessed the food and gave thanks to the Lord for the success of our endeavour.

We were on cloud nine when we handed over the promised donation to her rector. The young people, of their own volition, I'll have you know, decided to split their takings between the church and our project.

Grace and I were fairly bursting with pride at this show of goodwill on their part. We let them know this in no uncertain terms.

Claud, her amazing, helpful husband, toasted the success of our venture and wished us, and our helpers, a long and rewarding relationship. Jonathan took it upon himself to pay tribute to the twins and Christopher for their initiative. The young people who had worked so tirelessly alongside them came in for their fair share of the accolades and applause.

It stands to reason we were still brimming over with excitement at the meeting which followed our first rummage and bake sale. This time, the three of us toasted our success with champagne.

Little by little, at subsequent meetings, Grace and I were learning more about Jonathan. We already knew he was married *and* that his wife Jane had an alcohol addiction. In one of these meetings, he told us his job as Sales Manager for the Western Cape required frequent absences from home. Those absences, he said, were at the root of her addiction.

He has no siblings. Jane has two. They grew up in the same neighborhood— in Dorking, just outside of London, England. Both sets of parents and her two siblings still live there. Childless, something of an introvert, and with no family nearby, Jane had led a lonely life since they emigrated to South Africa. She became depressed and started drinking because she was lonely and felt neglected. Now, with a nervous disorder and hopelessly addicted, she lives in a nursing home under strict supervision, with the occasional weekend at home.

I felt moved to tears—saw moisture glisten in Grace's eyes as well—as he manfully bore the brunt of all their problems, Jane's illness, and their non-existent married life.

"Be kind to yourself, Jonathan. Life is not all white or all black," I said, reaching out to touch his hand, wanting instead to hold and console him the way he had held and consoled me on the day of Mike's funeral.

I'd read somewhere that pity is akin to love; experienced it then— unmistakable feelings of tenderness for this man. Feelings, borne of the sadness and loneliness I'd often espied in the depths of his eyes. I felt a fierce desire to replace his sadness and loneliness with laughter and companionship.

After our meetings, it was Grace's habit to give me a big hug when we parted. After some weeks had gone by, it seemed only natural for him to follow her lead. In the interim, he had become a strong shoulder on which I could lean. Our working relationship brought us closer and, even though we confined our meetings strictly to business issues, my initial attraction grew stronger. I sensed he found himself in the same boat.

Jonathan is a man with strong morals. I knew this from the outset. He has a sick wife for whom he had vowed to care—in sickness and in health! A marriage is still a marriage, especially to a man of honour. His actions, as always, befitting a gentleman. Like me, he is a stickler for propriety.

Recently widowed, I have two impressionable young sons and am only too aware of my good name and standing in the community. There is just no getting around those facts!

Because of my continued—now open—commitment to the Al-Anon group and our joint involvement with Helping Hands, our paths cross regularly. When we found ourselves alone, we shied away from the feelings which had sprung up between us. It was an inappropriate subject. Taboo! Better left!

Grundyism demands that those words remain unsaid. For now. However, each time my thoughts turned to him, I felt a river of excitement coursing through my being, damming up in anticipation of our next meeting.

Life stayed much the same over the next few months. Unbeknownst to us, however, Jonathan had been privately dealing with a situation of his own. Jane's health had been steadily declining, and she insisted on returning to England to be closer to her family. He supported her decision, sold their home, packed up, and was ready to leave in record time.

Loath, as he was, to part with his friends and his connection to Al-Anon, his wife's welfare must needs come first. Before their departure, Jonathan taught both Grace and me his bookkeeping method, promising to keep in touch with us once he and Jane had settled in their new home abroad.

He paid us a final visit on the day before their departure. Kneeling to give Boomer an affectionate rub behind the ears, he whispered in the dog's ear, "Do me a favour, you look after them, Boy." Boomer replied with an affectionate lick and an acquiescent bark.

"I can't believe Jane and I will be taking off for Merrie Olde England to-morrow. I *will* write and expect lots of news in return about everybody and your progress with Helping Hands, Ladies.

"Eve, you have every reason to be proud of your two wonderful boys. Be sure to tell your sons I said to keep up the good work with their studies. I expect nothing but good reports from them in December!"

"Thank you. I'll be sure to pass on your message. Godspeed, Jonathan!"

Grace handed him a cake tin. "These are some of my mother's shortbread biscuits. Enjoy! Remember, we'll be waiting for your letters, so be sure to write, hey…happy landings!"

"Thank you, Grace. Jane and I will share them with our family when we have our first cup of tea in England."

We walked together to the gate to see him off. Giving us each a hug in parting, he said, "I will never forget our special times together and I *will* write. I promise." With these last words, he climbed into his car and drove off while we waved him good-bye.

Jonathan was sorely missed in the weeks and months that followed. Even the twins asked for news about 'Uncle Jonathan'.

His absence hit me harder than I thought it would; I missed him like a piece of bread, and it took me a while before I stopped looking for him in the places where we used to bump into each other. I eventually stopped listening for his knock on the days Grace and I met to discuss our plans for Helping Hands. His presence lingered, though.

True to his word, he wrote to Grace and me. Separately. A few times. He kept us informed about his new life and surroundings. They had bought a flat quite close to his and Jane's parents, as well as to her siblings. She was overjoyed to be in the bosom of her family, but still needed medical attention and his constant supervision.

His parents owned and operated a Corner Store-cum-Post Office. They were relieved and happy to have him close by and, have him take some of the responsibility of running the shop. His days were full, going between the store to help his dad and his home to be with Jane.

"I miss my interaction with all the Al-Anon members and seeing their friendly faces. Yours too, Eve. I plan to keep in touch with a couple of people who were especially close to me, yourself and Grace included. Tell your sons I wish them well in their schooling."

He eventually stopped writing but his letters, the few I'd received, were a comfort and, in time, they were read and re-read. Already a trifle dog-eared, I might add.

*G*race and Claud have a wonderful, stable marriage. They were throwing a party at their home tonight to celebrate their fifteenth wedding anniversary. She and I had been planning this happy event for weeks. At first, I had declined their invitation to join them. They, however, had been adamant.

"The evening won't be the same without you and the twins. I will be miserable if you guys don't come. The thing is, when I'm miserable, Claud doesn't have much fun either.

"C'mon, Evie. It's been more than a year since you've accepted any invitation. It's not healthy for you to shut yourself away like this, you know. People from the old crowd will be asking after you…besides, you have to be here to drink a toast to our next fifteen years! Please, say you'll come," she implored, as she put the finishing touches to a colourful flower arrangement for the buffet table.

Genuine sadness lurked behind her cajoling tone. I knew she would be hurt if I stayed away, so I let myself be persuaded; found myself looking forward to celebrating with them, also to renewing some of the old friendships. Friendships going back to the days before Mike had come into the picture.

Until now, apart from going to church on Sundays and the odd Al-Anon meeting, I had tended to shy away from social gatherings. Tonight would certainly be different.

*Memorable* is how I would describe it after the event. Memorable, in more ways than one, because that night brought Gerald Kester into my life.

He was dancing the tango when I first laid eyes on him. From my vantage point, he appeared to be a past master on the dance floor. I admired his expertise. It put me in mind of the rare times I saw my father and mother dancing together. Gerald was on the short side, maybe an inch taller than me, but it did not take anything away from how he handled himself during the dance. I enjoyed watching him, as he steered his partner effortlessly around the room.

He circled the room several times and changed partners with each succeeding dance. When he came abreast of me, his eyes sought mine. Sometimes. One time, he even winked at me.

About my age, personable, with thick, black eyebrows coming together over his nose. His hair, too, was black. Thick, and wavy. As for his eyes, they were black as midnight. Flirty. He had a good sense of style. It sat well on him.

Later, there were the usual speeches and Uncle Jacob proposed a toast to the happy couple. The tantalizing aromas from the region of the buffet drew the guests soon after. I wandered over when the crowd had thinned. Gerald joined me—I do believe he had waited for me to make my move. We introduced ourselves as we stood side by side. He promptly struck up a conversation about the various dishes which Grace had set out to titillate our taste buds.

He was most attentive. He carried my plate and steered me to a seating arrangement in the backyard. Once settled, between each mouthful, we moved on to other topics of conversation. I felt quite comfortable making small talk with him.

Ours is a small community, so it came as no surprise when he mentioned Mike's death.

"I heard about your husband's accident and that he died. Please accept my heartfelt condolences. I hope it's not too late."

"It's been more than a year now, and, no, it's not too late! Thank you. How…how do you know about Mike's passing?"

"It's a small world, as they say. I know your late husband's uncle. Dave goes to my church; your husband's obituary was in our church bulletin."

By unspoken, mutual consent, we changed the subject. Then, after the usual banal exchanges, he went on to say he taught music in high school. Talking about music led to an invitation for me to partner him in the next dance.

"I have to warn you, Gerald, it's been a long time since I set foot on the dance floor."

"To my knowledge, Eve, it'll be like riding a bike. You never really lose the hang of it and I'm pretty sure you won't have any trouble at all following my lead."

Not one given to idle boasting, I do believe I acquitted myself well because I was invited to dance with him a few more times. In passing, between dances, he let slip a few snippets about himself and had me in stitches with his characterisation of some of his more challenging, obnoxious students.

Leading me expertly, one last time, through the steps of the foxtrot at the end of the evening, he said, "I'd like to spend some time with you, Eve. I'll give you my phone number so you can give me a bell when you have some free time. What say you?"

Dancing with Gerald had been the highlight of my evening, and, having found him quite entertaining, I thought, *Why not take him up on his suggestion?*

"Well, Grace and Claud sometimes come over on a Friday night to play cards. I'll let you know the next time they do. Okay? If you happen to be free, you'd be welcome to join us."

"I like the sound of that; I'll be waiting to hear from you. It's been a pleasure meeting you, Eve."

"Likewise. You excel on the dance floor; I really enjoyed the refresher course."

"Hey, think nothing of it! The pleasure was all mine. By the way, how are you getting home? I don't mind giving you a lift, pretty lady."

"Grace and Claud will see me home, but thanks all the same. I'll say Goodnight then. Drive safe!"

"Ta. Hope to see you soon...don't lose my number!" Then, with a jaunty wave, he went in search of his hosts.

My boys had come prepared to spend the night and had long since passed over into dreamland. I stayed to help with the cleanup; after everything had been tidied away, we relaxed with the obligatory end-of-the-evening cup of Rooibos tea.

While she and Claud were walking me home, Grace nudged me playfully. She, with her 'eagle eye', had not missed Gerald's interest in me.

"The thing is, I noticed you danced with him a couple of times, and you seemed to be enjoying yourself, Evie. Now, be honest...aren't you glad I twisted your arm?"

It was the perfect time to fill her in.

Gerald called a week later. "I hope you don't mind my calling. I looked you up in the phone book."

I was not at all surprised when he said he would make himself available for our next Friday night card evening.

Auntie Miriam would have said, "He's certainly not backward in coming forward."

I heartily agree with her sentiment!

Entertaining a man—a virtual stranger—in my home? *This* would take some getting used to! As it turned out, Grace and Claud had prior commitments for the next two Friday evenings, so it was a good three weeks after their anniversary when I finally invited Gerald. He accepted with alacrity! He came armed with chocolates for the ladies and other treats for our children. So thoughtful.

That first Friday evening would be a precursor to many others in the months to follow. Gerald proved to be well-versed in many of Claud's favourite subjects, so they got on like the proverbial house on fire. He was amusing, attentive to both Grace and me, and no slouch when it came to playing our choice of card games. He even taught us one of his favourites.

When it came to light that Gerald taught music, George immediately unearthed Mike's guitar which had been stowed away since goodness knows when. He won the boys over by giving them an impromptu lesson, while we boxed and stowed the cards. Over a nightcap, he entertained us grown-ups royally with our favourites. He certainly knew how to pay his dues. It earned him return visits on subsequent Friday evenings.

A couple of Fridays later, he offered to escort the twins and me to church on Sunday mornings. When asked what made him decide to attend Divine Services at my church, he said, "I want to be where you are."

An answer artfully designed to please. I ask you! How could I turn down his offer? In time, however, I would look back and attribute his motive to another, more self-serving one.

He was a likeable fellow. Liked, especially, by the ladies at church. He had an outstanding tenor voice and was soon invited to join our choir.

Here was a man who knew just how to put his best foot forward. He was charming, amiable, amusing, and highly entertaining, but not given to freely disclosing personal details. It was Grace, perspicacious Grace, who drew this fact to my attention. Still, in time, it was inevitable that I would learn a thing or two about the man and his past.

He'd been married before. The marriage had lasted fifteen years and ended in divorce some five years ago. His marriage bore a daughter and a son who lived with their mother in the family home. He shared a house with a young, married cousin and her husband. This much he had volunteered.

When asked why his first marriage failed, his answer was short and to the point.

"She went off with another man."

Of course, Grace had to be told. She wanted to know why the wife went off with another man. I hadn't asked, so I couldn't say. Probing for details was not my style. We were still just casual acquaintances, after all. I figured he would tell me if, and when, he wanted me to know. Besides, I was not all that curious and quite content with the status quo.

I still regarded him as no more than a casual friend. Someone with whom to while away the time. Inviting him to join the twins and me for the odd Sunday dinner when he took us home after church seemed the decent thing to do; followed as naturally as day follows night.

Quid pro quo!

"December exams are history! Hip, Hip, Hooray!" This was how the twins gleefully broadcast their news. They had done extremely well. Mike would have been proud of their high marks in all subjects.

Christmas was upon us almost before I knew it. Just one more week to go. Our shopping was done, and the presents wrapped. Thanks to my diligent sons.

My mother-in-law had invited the twins to spend a few days, so I drove them to their grandparents' home in Greenhaven. Even though Mike's mother's heated feelings for me had cooled off since she'd been told about Michaela, and the fact that I had assumed financial responsibility for her education, I still was not comfortable in her presence.

Never one to risk outstaying my welcome, I stopped in just long enough to be polite and for Iris to give me the latest news about Michaela and Lisa. On pretence of last-minute shopping, I made my exit and headed for home.

I let myself into the empty house. The silence was all around me. I welcomed it once I closed the door behind me. This was only the second Christmas since Mike's death, and I miss my husband—more than words can say. This solitude gave me a chance to connect with him in my mind.

Christmas was one of his favourite seasons. He had always managed to find an extra-special gift for the twins. He couldn't wait for them to unwrap their gifts, because he wanted to take a photo of the expression on each boy's face; just itching to catch the looks of surprise and delight.

Our wedding album was a fixture by my bedside. I found solace in paging through it and poring over photos of yesteryear. Back in the day, when our boys were infants, Mike loved changing their nappies and feeding them. He was the soul of patience when they were restless in the middle of the night. I can see him now, as he walked the twins, sometimes soothing and cuddling them both at the same time. He *had* been a doting father.

The boys and I still talk about him every day. Each of us with many stories to tell, elaborating on different incidents and places where Mike had been present. Benjy and George have started a journal in which they describe his various facial expressions which spelled out for them when he was pleased or amused or angry.

They put into words their dad's mannerisms, his favourite catch-phrases, the things that made him angry, and the jokes he had told and retold.

When they were younger, they held him in awe as he created shadow puppets on a wall for them with his hands. They recalled the countless jokes he had played on them. Like the times he decided to mismatch the socks in their drawers, or when he glued a few coins to our driveway. To this day, those coins are still stuck to the driveway. All-time favourite memories.

"Mom," George said, "Dad looked on, deadpan, when he pointed the coins out to us and, all the time, he was silently killing himself with laughter because we were struggling so hard to pick up those coins."

"Yep, Dad liked to tease, but he gave us some money to make up for it, later. Right? So, we kinda had the last laugh," said Ben.

Our Friday evening card games with Gerald had reached their three-month mark. He still escorted us to church, sang in our choir, and, of late, had taken the boys and me to the drive-in a couple of times.

Reading between the lines, Grace and I suspected that Gerald was beginning to hope for more.

"Somehow, I don't think he's the right person for you, my girl. I know he comes across like a nice person, but, the thing is, he's too cagey...too guarded! He talks a lot, always about the things he's read or the stuff he's heard on the radio or seen on TV, but he doesn't reveal his inner thoughts! I can't say I even begin to know what makes him tick, even though we've spent many Fridays together…" her voice trailed off in thoughtful silence.

I nodded my head in agreement as I said, "You're spot on…I noticed it too. It's as if he's covering up parts of himself that, maybe, even he doesn't like…putting his best foot forward all the time. It never bothered me, though. Probably because I can take him or leave him if you know what I mean. Granted, he *is* good company, but I don't see myself going the distance with him. On the whole, I have to say, I'm okay with the way things are going now. Uncomplicated."

Gerald joined us on the Friday before Christmas. This time, we met for cards at Grace and Claud's place. I planned to stay the night because the twins were with their grandparents. At the end of the evening, Gerald handed over the gifts he had brought for our children. Grace and I reciprocated with small gifts from her brood and mine.

The three gifts he handed me were beautifully wrapped. I was a teeny bit surprised to see my name on one of the gift tags. He read me like a book.

"You seem surprised at the gesture, Eve. I have to say, you've been more than kind to me. This seemed like the ideal time to show my appreciation, and, after all, it *is* Christmas! Rumour has it, *'tis the season for giving.*"

"Thank you, Gerald. It was sweet of you to think of me. I'll make sure the twins call to let you know how much they like your gifts. I hope you have a wonderful time with your family. If all goes well, we'll get together again for cards at my place on the first Friday in the new year. Let me know if you'll be around. Okay?"

His jaw dropped. I could tell he was disappointed on hearing we would not be spending any time together over the festive season.

Stepping closer, he reached for my hand and, speaking in a lowered voice, said, "If you have free time between now and the new year, I'd like to hear from you, Eve. We could get together, maybe spend some time at the beach. What say you?"

With my hand still firmly in his grasp, I said, "Sure. The boys always enjoy a day at the beach. Good idea…we'll play it by ear 'til then?"

"Yes Ma'am! Meantime, I wish you all a 'Happy Christmas!'"

To Grace, he said, "Please, give my best to your parents. See you in the new year."

"Thanks. I'll pass on your message to my folks. Have a Happy Christmas, Gerald!"

Claud, who had already said his good-byes, had gone to check on their children, so Grace and I led the way to the front door. Together, we watched as Gerald drove off.

"Did you see how sad he looked when he realized that he wouldn't be spending time with us over Christmas? I'm glad you did not leave me alone with him, Grace. It let me off the hook, in a big way."

*E*ver since I moved into the Solomon family home, celebrating Christmas with them was a given, and they graciously extended an invitation to my mother each year. Then I met Mike, and he was also welcomed into the fold. When Grace's babies and mine were old enough, we spread a rug on the floor, where they played contentedly amidst the wrappings. Uncle Jacob hovered. Of course!

Although the twins and I will again be spending Christmas Day with the Solomon family, sadly, this year, as in the last, Mike will be missing. My mother too. She had gone on an extended stay to take care of one of her sisters, who had suffered a stroke.

At Auntie Miriam's invitation, the twins and I would sleep over on Christmas Eve and the nights leading up to New Year's Day.

"Your old job of setting the dining room table will be waiting for you, Eve. Don't tell him I said this, but Uncle Jacob needs help with trimming the tree even more than before.

"We'll let the boys to bunk together…I'll make up a bed for our little Kathleen in her mother's old room—our Katie will love that. I'll put you in your old room…Grace and Claud will sleep on the fold-out couch in my little sewing room."

I had to admit, not being in our house, where everything was a reminder of Mike, would be a reprieve and would also make this a less stressful time for the boys and me. Our bags were packed and ready to go when we were duly picked up by Uncle Jacob on Christmas Eve. Boomer in tow.

When asked to water the garden and empty our letterbox in our absence, Uncle Dave was only too glad to oblige.

The fun for the children started as soon as everyone had come home from church on Christmas morning. With so many gifts to unwrap, excitement ran rife! Many words of appreciation—amidst much laughter and lighthearted chatter—accompanied the meal Auntie Miriam had so lovingly provided. Later, the piano music and sing-along added to the prevailing festive spirit.

It goes without saying, Mike was sorely missed. My mom too. Barring that, the celebration of Christmas—as in past years with this family—left nothing to be desired. Thanks in great part to Auntie Miriam and Uncle Jacob's kindness and concern for our well-being.

The Theunissens left on Boxing Day to visit with Claud's family. Knowing that their departure would be a sad time for Grace's parents had motivated me to accept Auntie Miriam's invitation for us to extend our visit until after Christmas.

To quote my late father, however, "All good things must come to an end."

Home beckoned. Uncle Jacob and Auntie Miriam drove us, and, when he had pulled into our driveway, she said, "It's been quite a while since we were here last, Eve. We'd love to see your garden. What say, Jacob? Do we have time?"

He leaned over and kissed her affectionately on the cheek. "Honey, I'm all for it. You know I always make time for the things you want to do!"

Still smiling, he turned to me and said, "Eve, you must have lots of flowers in bloom. I especially want to have a look at Mike's dahlias. The bulbs he gave me when you guys were courting are still doing well."

I did not hesitate to invite them in, because I loved any excuse to show off our garden—there were umpteen memories of Mike. They had nothing but praise for all my hard work in maintaining what Mike had so lovingly created and went home happily with a big bunch of delphinium and roses, *and* our heartfelt thanks for a wonderful visit.

Browsing through my mail, once they had driven off, my heart leapt at the sight of two envelopes, each with a British postmark—from Jonathan and Jane. The first one I opened was a Christmas card addressed to the twins and me, and the other, a birthday card for me. I was over the moon!

Just knowing he had remembered my birthday, warmed me like the sun and made me tingle all over. It'd been months since we'd last heard from him. Grace and I had been concerned and disappointed when he stopped writing.

I'd sent him a Christmas card from my little family some weeks before Christmas. Now, a thank you note would give me a good reason to contact him again; fill him in on our comings and goings. Hopefully, he'll write back with some news of his own.

School holidays were still in full swing, so there were activities to plan. Luckily, the Theunissens were also back home, which meant the boys and I could hang out with them. Claud, too, was still on holiday, so he took it on himself to keep the children occupied and entertained. He drove them to the bioscope, the library, and one or other sporting event.

Grace and I put our time to good use. We made lists and did other things that wives and mothers do. In my book, it's never too soon for 'back-to-school' planning and shopping for things our children had out-grown. Plus, the time to work on ideas for Helping Hands' next rummage and bake sale loomed.

Spending New Year's Day at the beach with Auntie Miriam and Uncle Jacob was a given. Grace and I would contribute the treats our children simply could not live without. Auntie Miriam would provide the scrumptious 'picnic food' as in years gone by.

After lunch, under my huge beach umbrella—a Christmas gift from Uncle Dave and Iris—I took a few moments to be by myself. Sitting apart from the others, I let my mind drift into the past. The happy, carefree past. I could clearly see Mike cavorting in the water with his sons. See him as he strolled to where I was lazing near the water's edge; see him shading his eyes against the glare of the sun; see the water glistening on his newly-tanned skin. A smile of pure bliss on his face.

*Oh! How I miss those days...I still miss you, Mike!*

Second New Year (*Tweede Nuwe Jaar*). Traditionally, on this day, families would gather by the hundreds all along Klipfontein Road in Athlone. They lined the road eight-to-ten deep while waiting patiently for the Cape Minstrels (*die Kaapse Klopse)* to make their way to Athlone Stadium.

The different troupes of men and boys—old and young, with painted faces—would sing and dance their way past the crowds in waves of costumes and umbrellas, flamboyantly coloured; the road coming alive with the music of tambourines, banjos and other instruments. The onlookers cheered them on, every step of their way.

Claud and the four children took off just before lunch to witness this colourful and noisy event. Between them, they carried enough eats in their knapsacks to feed an army. When they returned home hours later, we would be regaled with their account of the day. Tongues tripping over teeth in their excitement to tell it all.

*T*he festive season had come and gone. When the second week into the new year rolled by, it dawned on me that our Friday evening card games were due to resume shortly, and I had not yet phoned Gerald. I had given scant thought to him during the holidays. There just was no spark! It's no wonder he had been the last thing on my mind.

*Well, there's no time like the present,* I chided myself. So, after I'd confirmed the date with Grace, I phoned him.

"It's good to hear from you, Eve. Everybody well?"

"Yep! It's all good our end. How about you?"

"Can't complain! I've just come back from Sun City. A group of us went on a bus tour for seven days."

"Sounds like fun. Did you take in any shows?"

"Sure did! The big attraction was Cliff Richard. I'll tell you all about it when I see you, and I'll be glad to hear how your holidays went."

"Sounds like you had a nice time. If you can make it for cards on Friday, I'm sure everyone would love to hear about your trip and also share our happenings."

"Thanks, Eve. I'll be there, come hell or high water!"

"Good. See you around seven then."

As promised, when Friday evening rolled around, Gerald showed up and, during the evening, regaled us with his Sun City experiences.

"Sounds wonderful!" We three said, in chorus.

The twins had completed the jigsaw puzzles Gerald had given them at Christmas. I reminded my sons to show them to Gerald and to thank him for thinking of them. My gift had been a beautiful book on Japanese flowering shrubs and trees. It now sat in pride of place on my coffee table in the front room. I'll always treasure, it and told him so.

He rubbed his hands gleefully as he said, "Knowing how much you love your garden, I had a feeling it would be right up your alley."

I could tell, knowing his gift had hit the mark pleased him no end.

$W$e were halfway through February already. Schools had reopened in the middle of January. I could hardly believe the time had flown by so quickly. Things had returned to normal on the home front. Grace and I were hard at work recruiting helpers and asking for donations and what-have-you.

Our Friday night card games and Gerald's visits were up and running again. He drove the boys and me to church on Sundays, sang in the choir, and joined us for coffee at church afterwards. He still was reticent about his private life, but, after having known him a few months, it was inevitable that I would discern what I saw as other flaws in his character.

Nothing too bad on a scale of one to ten. Just traits that did not sit well with me.

For one, when we were in a group, he liked to be the center of attention. Especially with my lady friends at church. I'd also noticed he was not above giving one or two of my friends the 'glad eye'. Often, when I had something of interest to relate, he would jump in before I was halfway through my tale, talk right over me, adding his take on the subject. Stealing my thunder, so to speak. To me, this smacked of someone wanting to be in control, and always the one with the most to say on any given subject. *Always wanting the last word!*

Then again, when something he had done or said came to light, something that would reflect badly on him, his answer would invariably be, "I don't remember."

In time, I recognised this as his stock-in-trade response when he wanted to avoid owning his actions. To me, this did not bode well for honest communication in any relationship. I value honesty—need to be sure that everything's kosher. Even in my casual relationships.

Looking squarely at the big picture, I could see that these character traits would lead to confrontation, somewhere down the line. Make no mistake, this bloke had redeeming qualities. Still, for my peace of mind, I decided it was time to make a clean break—end on a friendly note.

People come into your life for a reason, a season, or a lifetime. I'd heard that somewhere. I figured Gerald had come into our lives for a season, and the season had run its course.

How to end this friendship, though?

Grace said, "Tell him you feel he is getting too attached to you, and that you don't feel the same about him. Then, say you don't want him to waste his time with you when he might be missing out on finding Ms. Right! Also, you feel that you should be driving yourself to church."

I dillied and dallied but eventually plucked up the courage to say my piece. When he drove us home from church on Good Friday, I invited him to join us for our traditional meal of pickled fish and hot cross buns. Later, over a cup of coffee, I broke the news to him in our backyard.

His face paled as he grasped my meaning. "Oh! Man! This is not good news. I thought I was making headway with you, Eve. This…this is certainly not what I expected to hear today. I appreciate your frankness, though, and have to respect your wishes. Now that I won't be sharing any more Sunday dinners with you, today somehow puts me in mind of the Last Supper."

He said this with a straight face, but we laughed together at his attempt to make light of things.

"Boy, you're funny to the end. Believe me, I'm sorry things did not work out the way you wanted, Gerald. My boys need me more than ever now. I hope you meet someone nice, real soon."

"Not as nice as you, though!"

"Flatterer! Of course, there are lots of nice women out there—some even nicer than me."

"Nah! No way! Well, as they say, 'Parting is such sweet sorrow'. For me, that's the truth, the whole truth, and nothing but the truth! So, on that sad note, I'll be on my bicycle and make tracks now. Being with you really was a happy time for me, Eve."

"You're good company and a good sport too, Gerald. I've enjoyed our time together, and our Friday evening card games simply won't be the same without you. This is also the truth, the whole truth, and nothing but the truth! I wish you all the best in the future."

He was the picture of dejection as he headed out the front door.

"Thanks! For everything, Eve. Say bye to those good-looking lads of yours, will you? So…I take it I needn't come by to drive you to church, right?"

"Right! Look after yourself and drive friendly!" His last visit to my home ended with a fizzle.

My shot at having a relationship with Gerald fell by the wayside. Other than Gerald, I've had the odd male try to woo me since Mike's death. No one had fit the bill. To me, the reason was as plain as the nose on my face. It's not that I'm averse to love and being loved again. Rather, it's because, deep down, I'm holding out for a special someone—someone else I'm longing to see.

Honest communication is key, so is trust, and respect. I want to be able to respect that special someone and be respected by him. He and I will share a deep connection. If I had my druthers, that is the kind of person with whom I would choose to spend the rest of my life.

I know of one who fits the bill to a T! Fate had brought us together on a far-off day at an Al-Anon meeting—on the day he looked into my eyes and asked whether the seat next to mine was taken. Pursuing a relationship had been out of the question then. The timing was off; still is, by all accounts.

*L*ife after Gerald is in full swing. The Theunissens and I are back on track with our three-handed card nights, and I was back in the driver's seat on Sunday mornings. There had been no sign of Gerald at church since the last time he had driven us there. He appeared to have fallen off the map.

There were countless enquiries to field at church, most of which came from the ladies, but I did not expand on the reason he and I had parted company. I did not want him to be embarrassed, were he to turn up sometime in the future. If he did not return, I figured people could draw their own conclusions. I confided in my minister, though.

The June school holidays would shortly be upon us. How time flies! The boys have big plans to go cycling to Ceres to stay with a school friend, and also to climb Table Mountain with their scouts group. Weather permitting!

It's already been eighteen months since Mike died. The twins turned sixteen earlier this year. Wonderful, caring, well-adjusted boys, forced to mature early. They miss their dad still; miss the father figure.

I told them at the outset that Gerald would not be visiting or driving us to church anymore. Of late, they've been teasing me. They want me to find a partner, one who would cherish me in ways they knew their father had sometimes fallen short. Someone with whom I would be happy. A soulmate.

The three of us were deep into a game of Scrabble after supper one Saturday evening when George said, "You know, Mum, you should find a nice bloke, so you won't be lonely when we're not around. Someone who can take you for moonlight drives, and to dances, and bring you chocolates, and rub your back when you're tired, and tickle you when you take things so seriously."

Ben added, "Just know, hey, we'll be asking him about his intentions and all that stuff!"

The mock-serious expression on both their faces had me smiling inwardly.

"From your lips to God's ears, guys!" This was my laughing response.

I admit, I have been lonely since Mike died. On occasion, I've envied my married friends and people from church. Once Gerald was no longer in the picture, it dawned on me just how much I missed having a mate. I prayed about finding the right partner.

*G*race and I were stunned when Jonathan sent us his word of wife's passing at the beginning of July, just a little more than a year after they had gone abroad.

The sympathy card we sent was signed by both Grace's little family and mine. I longed to give him the kind of support he had given me when Mike passed away—an ocean separates us now.

As it turned out, this would be the week for *sad* news. There was more to follow.

My sister-in-law sometimes stopped in, so it was no surprise to open my front door and see her standing there the next day. She had brought sad news as well. Her news concerned Lisa, Michaela's mum.

"Lisa died two days ago. According to her parents, she had been struggling with diabetes for many years. Her death was caused by complications from this condition."

"I'm truly sorry to hear this...so young! What's happening about Michaela? Poor girl...she's lost both her mother and her father. I know Lisa said the child never knew Mike...but still!"

"I spoke to Michaela on the phone. Needless to say, she is shattered! I'll be going over soon, but I won't make it in time for the funeral. While I'm there, I'll see what I can do to help them straighten out Lisa's affairs. Lisa's friend Trudy will stay with Michaela in the apartment for now.

"The child obviously can't stay there by herself, so she will be moving in with Lisa's parents before the next month's rent is due. Not an ideal situation for her or her grandparents. They, apparently also live in a small, rented place and already have a handicapped son living with them.

"My family and I think Michaela should make her home with us if Lisa's parents agree. Somehow, I don't think they will object to her coming to live with us. For one, they don't have room and secondly, from what Lisa told me, they are not too well-off either. Having to take on a teenager at their time of life might be more than they can manage.

"Timewise, it all works out perfectly because her school year has already ended. Hopefully, we will have her settled in with us before our school year begins."

"I pray all goes well, Iris. Michaela was quite excited when she told us about her plans to visit her family in South Africa, remember? This, however, will be a huge upheaval for her. I'd like to help. Let me know whether there's anything I can do. Okay?"

"*Ja!* There will be lots to do. Thanks for the offer. I've been thinking we should give Mike's old room a face-lift. Make it more suitable for a teenager. If you want, you can sew a nice duvet cover and pillow shams, with matching curtains. Together with new furniture, that should make her room pretty and welcoming. As soon as my travel plans are in place, you and I can go shopping together for the material and new furniture. What do you think?"

"I'm on board, and I'd love to tackle the sewing. We'll also get the boys involved. Wielding paint brushes has become quite their thing. I bet they would agree to paint her bedroom in a heartbeat. Meantime, how about you find out what her favourite colours are?"

The twins were sad that Michaela had lost her mum, but they were over the moon when they were told Iris would be arranging for their half-sister to make her home nearby.

*O* happy day! Jonathan replied to our sympathy card. He sent Grace a thank you note. I received a letter thanking me for reaching out and giving details of Jane's declining condition during the few months before she died. This letter would be the first of many, as it turned out, and phone calls too.

He gradually became more open and honest about his feelings for me—putting into words what I had long suspected. For obvious reasons, he had held these feelings in check while Jane was alive. Loneliness, his and mine, now caused the incipient feelings of mutual attraction, those which had started when I first attended the Al-Anon meetings, to snowball.

A marriage proposal was in the cards and not long in coming.

My answer, Dear Reader, I leave to your imagination. Then there were phone calls back and forth to express our joy and longing to be together as husband and wife.

"From your lips to God's ears…" I'd jokingly said this to my sons, not all that long ago. God *must* have been listening; He answered my prayer, and He *does* work in mysterious ways.

I know this full well.

In his next letter, he wrote, "…I miss you, Eve. I wish I could visit with you but for me to come to South Africa is out of the question now. You see, I've taken on most of the responsibilities which my dad used to handle in the shop; I'm reluctant to saddle him with the workload again.

"I think the next best thing would be if you came to England on a visit, Eve. We could then sort out our housing needs as well as schooling for the twins. Work together on our plans for the future. I'm hoping you can find a way to make it happen. Come soon, love!"

He never failed to ask after Benjy and George when he wrote, always showing a sincere interest in their well-being. When he telephoned, he invariably asked to speak to them.

In his last letter, he had made it abundantly clear he was looking forward to sharing all his worldly goods with us and having my sons permanently in his life—adopting them, if I agreed. He assured me he would love them as though they were his own; do everything within his power to be an influence for good. They would be the sons he never had but had always longed to have.

I was deeply touched by his concern and genuine affection for my sons.

The time has come for me to address my future. Choose my path, as it were. With this in mind, I turn to the ending of his most recent letter in which he says, "...the waiting is becoming unbearable. Come soon! All my love, Jonathan."

My reply was like an echo.

Grace, my confidante in all things. I'd been sharing my long-distance romance with her. She had commented on my shining eyes, noticed my changing demeanour, and knew my deepening relationship with Jonathan deserved most of the credit. She shared my joy and my waiting.

She was most emphatic!

"The thing is, Evie, you should take this as a gift from God. Between us, we'll figure out all the details. It'll be a piece of cake! *Believe me*! Benjy and George will bunk with us while you're gone. It's that simple!"

A few phone calls later, and after much soul-searching, I told Benjy and George what was afoot. They were in favour of my plans, so we put our heads together to make the necessary arrangements for them to stay with Grace until my return.

"See, Mum, we said you should find a nice bloke," said Ben.

George said, "Uncle Jonathan's a great bloke, but the timing's all wrong, man! We'll miss being with Mickey now. That's tough!"

"Sure, it will be tough, guys, but remember, we're not leaving just yet, not for quite a few months. It may even be as long as a year from now. Emigrating takes time. So, until then, you'll be spending as much time as you want with her.

"When we're in England, we'll arrange for you to come back for visits during the school holidays. Maybe, just maybe, she might even like to finish her schooling in England…who knows?"

The die was cast. I'm going to London to be with my new love!

*I*t had taken a few weeks to get a visa, but I'd booked my flight and I am set to leave for England in two weeks.

Jonathan's mum had kindly invited me to stay with them for the duration. He and I will visit prospective new schools for the twins, discuss our future and the wisdom of selling the only home the twins had ever known—we plan to settle these and other details of import during my visit. Not least of which would be house-hunting and making plans for our wedding. Grace was adamant! No matter where on earth I planned to get married, she and her little family would be there. With bells on!

She helped me pack all the winter clothes I could lay my hands on for my stay in England. We also made lists of all the things the twins might need while living at her house. My sons will be in the Theunissens' care during the weeks I'll be away. I *know* they will be in good hands. Grace would also keep an eye on our home and take care of a hundred and one other details. Should she need help, Iris promised to be on standby.

Uncle Dave gave me his blessing when I told him of my plans and kindly offered to see to the garden in our absence.

"From what I know, life has not always dealt you the best hand, Eve. You deserve to be happy. I wish you a good life with Jonathan in your new country. You'll write to us and let us know how things are going, won't you?"

"No two ways about it, Uncle. I *am* coming back in a few weeks, you know. You'll still be seeing a lot of me before we leave for good!"

Four months and one week after I received Jonathan's first letter saw me boarding a British Airways flight to London, England. I was on a roller coaster of emotions!

Meanwhile, Iris had returned from Canada with Michaela in tow. Much to the twins' delight, her maternal grandparents had agreed it was the best solution all round.

Michaela had taken to her move to South Africa like a duck to water. Iris and Uncle Dave were formalising custody and other legal issues.

*T*he Theunissen clan, Iris, Uncle Dave, Michaela, and my sons came to D. F. Malan Airport to wave me off. Benjy and George were somewhat sad when we said our good-byes but assured me, however, that I had their support. So mature. They wanted my happiness above all else.

Before we parted I said, "I'll miss you all, but I'll be back long before Christmas with lots to tell you. Presents too!"

My mother, sadly, could not be with us, because she had made her home with her ailing sister in Port Elizabeth. She phoned to wish me well, though.

Looking back at my mountain, I saw the tablecloth hanging low, as the (in)famous South-Easter held sway. Through the clouds, I imagined I saw the smiling face etched on the mountainside—the same as before. I took it as a harbinger…one that said, "Godspeed!"

Once I was on the plane and settled in my seat, I let my thoughts drift back.

Scenes from my past—thoughts of my unhappy childhood and the bleak periods in my marriage to Mike—flitted in and out of my consciousness. I did not wish to linger in those dark places. Rather, I gave my fantasies full rein and let them lead me along a new path; one with sunny vistas where Jonathan waited. My dependable, lovable, loyal, and altogether winsome Jonathan.

I saw myself clearly on this path, striding sure-footed toward him; felt the strength of his arms as if they were already enfolding me. Felt his lips as if ours were already touching; felt our hearts beating in sync; felt a wild surging in my blood.

Already, I saw the tenderness in his eyes as they gazed into mine; heard the huskiness in his voice and watched the shape of his mouth as it formed the words "I love you."

Words I need to hear. Words I *know* I soon *will* hear. Colour me rapturous! When we meet, my pent-up feelings will be released. My heart will sing a sweet melody, the lyrics to which will be easy to read in his eyes.

The plane soared ever higher above the clouds; taking me on a journey out of my past, into a future that I'll be sharing with a man who has been the embodiment of compassion and tenderness almost from the first day we met.

Metaphorically speaking, I was about to cross a threshold. Dreamy. This is how I felt when I replayed the recent, happy turn of events. Bad and sad feelings grew dim—those leftover from being rejected in my childhood, the anger I felt at Mike for not always playing by the rules, and the despair of a marriage gone wrong.

Parts of me had withered during the last few years of my marriage. Happily, they are alive and well now. I have been given a second chance to live my life. I feel young and vibrant again.

To coin Jonathan's favourite phrase, "While there's life, there's hope!"

Sleep had eluded me for most of the flight. Now, looking out the window of the airplane, I saw the dawn dancing brightly on the ocean below me, giving me a glimpse into a brand-new day.

Having my feet firmly planted on British soil, I was impatient to be with Jonathan. As a result, while I waited, slow and slower seemed to be the designated processing speed in Immigration and Customs. With my baggage securely stowed on a cart, I headed for the 'arrivals' lounge where I knew he would be waiting. Butterflies exhausted themselves inside my ribcage.

Breathless with the excitement of being so close to my journey's end, my eyes scanned the crowd. As if drawn by magnets, our eyes met, and, for a long moment, we just stood there, rooted, gazing at each other across that busy space. Almost afraid that this might be a dream from which I would soon wake, I closed the space between us in no time flat.

Now, locked in his arms, the realness of the moment could not be denied. A sweet, dizzying flame leapt between us. Then, as if to take in the whole of me, he held me at arm's length.

"You're here! Finally! Oh, Eve, this *is* a dream come true!"

"*Your* dream *and* mine, Jonathan. No words can express how happy I am to be here!"

"My parents are eager to meet you and hear all about your sons. I cannot wait to show you off! Let's head for my car…we will be on the road for less than an hour."

"Would you like to stop for some refreshments? A cup of tea, maybe? Be warned, my mum is preparing a proper 'Full English Fry-up'. She's hoping you'll have a good appetite."

"I think that is so sweet and thoughtful of your mother. So, let's not waste a minute. Anyway, I am much too excited to eat now, and I absolutely *do not* want to spoil my appetite! By the way, after reading your mum's letter, so warm and loving, it feels as if I already know her and your dad."

Then, with my hand tucked firmly in the crook of his arm, we made our way to his car.

We're off! Off to Dorking, with the windshield wipers going nineteen-to-the-dozen. There was so much to tell on both sides. He told me about the properties he had lined up for us to inspect and also the school he thought would best suit my sons.

"We should finalise our choices before you go back to South Africa, Eve. Mum said she would love to take you to the best shops for curtains and stuff to start the ball rolling."

"I'd like to go shopping with your mother. It sounds like a wonderful way to get close to her, and, just thinking about going house-hunting with you, Jamie…makes me all a-tingle!"

A good hour had elapsed and, before I knew it, we'd reached his parents' home. Jonathan stopped the car in front of a double-storey house at the end of a tree-lined road. Looking out the passenger window, I saw a garden planted mainly with shrubs. A vine crept along one side of the wall, while beautiful white snowdrops bloomed profusely in two containers near the front door.

"This is it, Eve! Let's get you inside, out of the rain. We'll see to your luggage later," he said, as he got out and came quickly to the passenger side to open the door for me.

As we walked hand in hand along a flagged pathway to the front door, I thought I saw a curtain being twitched in one of the front windows. Jonathan's mum, more than likely, on the lookout for our arrival.

He lost no time in leading me to the front door and, with his key, he let us in.

Ushering me inside, he called out, "We're home!" Mere seconds later, both his mum and dad appeared in the hallway. Broad, welcoming smiles on their faces, and tight hugs all round, made formal introductions seem almost unnecessary.

While his dad helped me off with my coat, his mum laid her hand gently on my arm and said, "Welcome, Eve! My, you look just as I pictured you from Jamie's description. We're so glad you had a safe flight. We want to know all about it and your first impressions of Merrie Olde England. Right, Dad?"

"Right, Mum!" Jonathan's dad was softly spoken. Listening to him, I was reminded of my own father. That fact and his warm words of welcome went a long way to setting me at ease. He steered me to the kitchen and guided me to where a table was already laid with a homely, checkered cloth, and where each steaming dish gave off a mouth-watering aroma. He pulled out a chair for me. So courteous. I can see who Jonathan takes after.

Mrs. du Preez put yet another steaming dish on the already laden table as she said, "First things first, though! Breakfast is waiting. I'm sure you must be hungry, my dear. Jamie too!"

The inviting smell of freshly cooked bacon and sausage permeated the room. My stomach rumbled. My mouth watered.

"Too right, Mrs. du Preez! I *am* famished. Jonathan told me you were preparing a 'Full English Fry-up'…so, as my boys would say, 'I cannot wait to sink my teeth into it'. Thank you for taking so much trouble."

His dad, who had seated himself at the head of the table, said, "His mum and I have been looking forward to this meeting since the first day that Jamie told us about you. We want you to make this your home for as long as you like."

"I appreciate your lovely warm welcome, Mr. and Mrs. du Preez. Your son has also told me lots about you both, and I've been longing to meet you. Believe me, now that I've met you in the flesh, I'm sure I *will* feel right at home."

Mrs. du Preez is an excellent cook. Jonathan sat beside me and handed me dish after dish—each one more appetising than the last—while I listened with avid interest to tidbits about his school years. I finished my meal with a second cuppa and a scone piled high with her homemade raspberry jam— raspberries, I was told, which were from her garden.

His mum is short, on the plump side, motherly, and as sweet as apple pie. I fell in love with her sunny nature. His dad, a little taller, but not quite as tall as his son, bushy-browed, with twinkling brown eyes and sporting a goatee which had turned a silvery-white. Just like his still full head of hair. Quite charming, and a wonderful host. In that moment, without a shadow of doubt, I knew they would be just the kind of grandparents my sons needed. I also knew my sons will adore them both.

Other than Auntie Miriam and Uncle Jacob, no other strangers had ever accepted me so readily into their home or made me as welcome as did Jonathan's parents.

His dad had to leave shortly after breakfast. When he had taken his leave, a dozen or so photo albums were brought out for my benefit. I, in turn, proudly showed off those of my sons at first, then those of other family members and close friends.

"Jamie speaks very highly of your boys, Eve. As you may know, we've not been blessed with grandchildren. Believe me, it will be a real joy for us to have a couple of youngsters in the family. Youngsters we can spoil to our heart's content." His mum had a trace of tears in her lovely gray eyes as she said this.

I put my arm around her and held her close. "George and Benjy are lovely boys. Helpful, too. We three will consider ourselves blest to be part of such an open-hearted family. I wouldn't be surprised if they end up helping out in your shop on a regular basis, only if you *would* like them to, of course!"

"My dear, that's wonderful!" Turning to Jonathan, she said, "Your dad was hoping to have some young blood in the shop, wasn't he, love?"

"Yes, he was, Mum. It does sound like a good idea all round. Now, if you ladies will excuse me, I have some luggage that needs to be brought inside." He hugged me before he headed out the door.

Mrs. du Preez said, "You know, our Jamie's been so happy in the last few months. It does my heart good to see the change in him." She hesitated before she continued, "I've been thinking...you'll soon be part of our family, Eve. We would dearly love to be yours. Do you think your sons would want to call us 'Nan' and 'Grandad'? When Jamie adopts them, they will be as good as our own, and they will be the *only* grandchildren we'll ever have. You could also call us by those names if 'Mum' and 'Dad' don't suit."

"'Mum' and 'Dad' sound just fine to me. I would be honoured, Mum," I said with a big smile.

She and I embraced and kissed each other on both cheeks. I felt warm, cherished, and tears of happiness welled up in my eyes. Jonathan witnessed this loving scene as returned with my luggage. He dropped the cases and joined us in a group hug.

"This is a good sign," he said, when we drew apart after several moments. "I could not have hoped for better!"

Mum smiled her by now already familiar, beautiful, warm smile as she shooed us out of the room. "You two, go along now. Show Eve around and take those suitcases to her room, Jamie. I'll be here when you're done."

We left her gazing fondly after us, while we headed down the passage and up the stairs to Jonathan's spacious bedroom which I would be using for the duration. He had opted to sleep in the room which had been converted into his mother's sewing room on the ground floor. The flat he had lived in with Jane was up for sale because he wanted us to have a fresh start.

Once on the landing, he looked deep into my eyes, and I was drawn into his embrace as though by a magnet.

"This, Eve, *is* by far, the happiest day of my life!"

Locked in his strong embrace, I could only nod in silent agreement. I felt loved and protected, and my heart was full-to-bursting!

*"I may not have gone where I intended to go,
but I think I have ended up where I needed to be."*

—Douglas Adams, *The Long Dark Tea-Time of the Soul.*

# Glossary

| | |
|---|---|
| *Bobotie:* | Curried, minced beef, baked with an egg and milk topping. |
| *Breyani:* | A dish made with rice, lentils, meat or chicken, hard-boiled eggs, potato, and Indian spices. Of Muslim/ Indian origin. |
| *Boerewors:* | Spicy South African sausage. Literally 'farmer's sausage'. |
| *Braai:* | Barbecue. |
| *Broekie lace:* | Ornate ironwork trim, found on Victorian buildings. |
| *Fynbos:* | Fine Bush (literally meaning fine-leaved plants), refers to many species/groups of plants that grow wild in parts of the Western Cape. |
| *Gemmerbier:* | South African Ginger beer. *Gramma's Recipe follows. |
| *Gemmerkoekies:* | Ginger biscuits. |
| *Hertzoggies:* | Coconut and jam tartlets. |
| *Ja:* | Yes. Affirmative. |
| *Kaapse Klopse:* | Cape Minstrels. |
| *Koeksisters:* | Oblong-shaped fried dough, dipped in syrup and rolled in desiccated coconut. |

| | |
|---|---|
| *Konfyt:* | Preserved fruit. |
| *Lekker:* | Good. Nice. Great. Cool. |
| *Melktert:* | Milk tart—traditional custard tart of Dutch origin with a dash of cinnamon sprinkled on top. |
| *Roti:* | A round, flat unleavened Indian bread. |
| *Samoosas:* | Fried or baked pastry with a savoury meat and potato or vegetable filling. An Indian snack made with a mixture of spicy, dried ingredients, such as puffed rice, fried lentils, peanuts, chickpea flour, and vegetable oil, etc. |
| *Soetkoekies:* | Sugar biscuits infused with a combination of spices. |
| *Sosaties:* | South African kebabs—usually lamb or mutton. |
| *Stoep:* | Porch/veranda. |
| *Ta-ta:* | Informal good-bye. |
| *Totsiens:* | Good-bye/Until we meet again. |
| *Tweede Nuwe Jaar:* | Second New Year *aka* January 2nd. |

**Gramma's Gemmerbier**　　　　　(Yield: Approx. 22 (750ml) bottles)

Ingredients:

17 liters lukewarm water (divided)

2,5 kg sugar

3 tablespoons crushed ginger root

1 tablespoon dried yeast

1 cup of raisins (with seeds)

Method:

Dissolve the sugar in three liters of water.

Sprinkle the dried yeast over the surface. Leave until frothy—about ten minutes.

Pour the yeast mixture and sugar water into a twenty-liter enamel bucket.

Add the ginger root and the rest of the water. Stir and cover securely.

Add the raisins and leave the mixture to mature for at least twenty-four hours at room temperature, away from sunlight.

The ginger beer is ready to drink when the raisins rise to the surface.

Strain through a cheesecloth.

Use a funnel to pour into sterilised bottles. Add a couple of raisins to each bottle.

Seal the bottles. Not too tight.

Store in the refrigerator or a cool place.

When ready to serve, open slowly…carefully. Enjoy!

# Acknowledgements

My sincerest thanks to my children. Loyal, and generous to a fault, you have each supported me, and continue to do so in numerous ways—I am proud of you all.

Wayne, our trailblazer, you made it possible for our entire family to emigrate from South Africa to a better life in Canada. We'll always be indebted to you!

Lynndee…the joy of giving birth to you on my birthday is truly 'the gift that keeps on giving'. You never fail to amaze me with your thoughtfulness, and, in my eyes, your cooking skills for family dinners equal Martha Stewart's. To quote Martha, 'It's a 'good thing'!

Clive, as a youngster, you were the joker of the family. You made us smile with your antics and funny sayings. 'I can't wait to sink my teeth into it', comes most often to mind, and invariably sparks a smile!

Kudos to Annaliese and my late son-in-law Tedd. You were my first fans, and I am indebted to you for your help in getting my novel off the ground—from cover to cover and to its unveiling. Annaliese, your astute and painstaking reading, constructive criticism, and discerning eye have enriched my work. Tedd, my appreciation for your expertise and involvement—including the creative direction in developing my JK Beukes brand—knows no bounds. I am in awe of your know-how!

My first acceptance letter came from *Today's Bride*, a Canadian Magazine, which published my article entitled "For The Love Of Flowers." Your excitement rivalled mine at the time, Andrea, and your appreciation of my other crafts has always been unstinting. It's meant a lot to me.

I include my son-in-law Carl and my grandson Pierre in this list. You guys were my computer maintenance gurus over the years. I would have floundered without your help.

A long round of applause to my husband Harry. Staunch supporter in all my undertakings (be it my various crafts—including those I submitted to the Norwood Fall Fair—or my culinary efforts) and an ever-willing chauffeur when I needed to track down the materials for my many projects.

*The End*